NAME OF THE GAME IS LIFE

DATE DUE

JE 17 '91			
NO 25 '96			

DEMCO 38-296

THE NAME OF THE GAME IS LIFE

THE NAME OF THE GAME IS LIFE

ROBERT L. SHOOK and RAMON GREENWOOD

CB

CONTEMPORARY
BOOKS

CHICAGO

Shook, Robert L., 1938–
    The name of the game is life : thirteen of life's winners reflect
on the lessons of athletics that helped make them successful /
Robert L. Shook and Ramon Greenwood : foreword by Richard
D. Schultz.
        p.   cm.
    Includes index.
    ISBN 0-8092-3910-8
    1. Athletes—United States—Biography.   2. Success—
United States.   I. Greenwood, Ramon.   II. Title.
GV697.A1S4795   1992
796'.092'2—dc20
[B]   91-38516
                                                    CIP

Published by Contemporary Books, Inc.
180 North Michigan Avenue, Chicago, Illinois 60601
Manufactured in the United States of America
International Standard Book Number: 0-8092-3910-8

This book is dedicated to
Elinor Shook and Martha Greenwood,
winners in their own right.

■ CONTENTS ■

▪ FOREWORD ▪

Unquestionably athletics plays several significant roles in America. It provides entertainment and satisfies the desire for competition. Sports offer a forum for large numbers of people to come together for one event—which in turn transcends to a sequence of still more events.

The real purpose of intercollegiate sports, however, is educating young people. This is our mission at the National Collegiate Athletic Association. Men and women are not recruited to our campuses for the purpose of pursuing careers as professional athletes. They are there to receive a meaningful degree so that when they leave our institutions they are well prepared to be contributors in our society. Now, if an individual has outstanding athletic talent, we want a program to be available that will develop his or her talent and enhance the chances for success in the same manner we prepare other professional people to be doctors, dentists, attorneys, and so forth.

We realize that the percentage of college athletes who will play at a professional level is so small that it does not justify being a part of our major mission. Then too, with the average professional sports career lasting less than five years, the need for an education to prepare for life after sports always prevails.

Throughout my career as a coach, athletic director, and NCAA executive director, I have met with many former athletes who have succeeded in high-profile careers—people such as Fortune 500 CEOs—whom I have asked, "What did participation in athletics do for you, and what part did it play in your life?" The answer I keep hearing again and again is *"It really teaches about life."*

Careers do not start at one point and skyrocket to the top. There are many peaks and valleys along the way. While intercollegiate athletics teach how to win, equally important are the lessons on *how to lose*. When you lose, you've got to pick yourself up off the floor, mentally and emotionally, and deal with disappointment and conflict. Then you must get yourself remotivated and continue to go on to bigger and better things. This is what life is all about. It is a series of disappointments, and those people who succeed understand about dealing with the challenges of life. How appropriately authors Ramon Greenwood and Robert Shook have selected the title *The Name of the Game Is Life* for this book!

A series of challenges is taught in athletics, ranging from making the team to competing with the opposition to taking yourself to levels that you have never before experienced. As coach for twenty-five years I witnessed players push themselves beyond a limit they previously thought unattainable. This is part of the challenge of coaching—getting them to take that next step, to go just a little further tomorrow than today and suddenly find new experiences. You discover that you have more talent and ability than you thought you had. The adrenaline starts flowing, and you drive yourself to meet the competition.

The thirteen men and women profiled in this book are outstanding role models who, I believe, represent thousands of other athletes once active in intercollegiate sports and subsequently winners in the game of life. It is true that, on occasion, the media reports the sensational news about college athletes who have gone astray. Similarly, stories are told about a robbery on Main Street, but the story about a woman on Elm Street who takes time to bake an apple pie for a sick neighbor goes unreported.

Today more than 275,000 men and women are participating in intercollegiate athletics, and a vast majority of these fine young people are just what you would want them to be. They are good students who are graduating at a higher rate than the nonathlete student body; they are involved in activities such as Big Brother and Big Sister programs; they are visiting nursing homes; they are leaders on their respective campuses; and it is anticipated that upon graduation they will be good citizens in the community.

The intercollegiate athletic program in America is working. *The Name of the Game Is Life* demonstrates it is working exceedingly well.

Richard D. Schultz
Executive Director,
National Collegiate Athletic Association

▪ ACKNOWLEDGMENTS ▪

Not unlike the teamwork talked about in *The Name of the Game Is Life*, many people made significant contributions in the writing of this book. It is with this thought in mind that we thank the members of our team.

Our special thanks to Milton Fenster, our valued friend and mentor. From the very beginning, he was a strong supporter, and he served as an inspiration throughout the entire writing of the manuscript. We were very fortunate that he opened doors for us in high places, which enabled us to secure otherwise difficult-to-get interviews. We both owe you one, Milt.

Another ally who put us together with several key people to interview for this book is Harold Burson, the talented and internationally renowned public relations expert.

We deeply appreciate our good friends at the NCAA. These include Dick Schultz, executive director; Robert C. Khayat, NCAA Foundation president; and especially Emmy Morrissey, who served diligently and patiently as our liaison person during the entire preparation and writing of our manuscript. Without these invaluable people, *The Name of the Game Is Life* would not have been written.

Then, too, another important team player was Jim Host, a

highly respected marketing expert. Like Milt, Harold, and the NCAA staff, Jim ranks at the top in his field.

We also made many friends along the way who contributed to this book. These people include: Penny Circle, Roz Cole, Patrick Escobar, Janice Fair, Kathy Goldberg, Michael Jones, Judi Risk, Bruce Ruhl, Kathy Watson, and Ray Wilson.

As usual, Mary Liff did a superb job of transcribing interviews, a hard and time-consuming task. Mary also spent many hours at both typing and retyping chapters.

Our gratitude to Al Zuckerman, our agent, who put us together with Contemporary Books. And, of course, Harvey Plotnick, who, in addition to performing his role as our publisher, personally edited the manuscript. We also appreciate Linda Gray and Kathy Willhoite, two fine editors at Contemporary.

Yes, this book is a result of a team effort, and it took such attributes as tenacity, discipline, and goal setting to complete it. Interestingly, these are many of the attributes of the fine men and women profiled in this book. We are indebted to these inspiring people who graciously shared their valuable time with us so that we could write their stories. This book would not have become a reality without *their* contributions.

THE NAME OF THE GAME IS LIFE

▪ INTRODUCTION ▪

Competitive sports are treasured in the American way of life. While the Greeks and other peoples made religious ceremonies of their games and elevated their athletic heros to the status of gods, no society has ever focused as much attention on sports, nor have as many citizens ever participated in sports with such vigor and enthusiasm as those who live in the United States.

Virtually everyone perceives something of value in sports. Untold numbers play games for the pure and simple pleasures of the moment and as a means of recreation for their minds and bodies. For millions, athletics is a vicarious pursuit, seen in terms of television's sound and sight bites; roars of the crowds; the effortless, fluid movements of Herculean actions captured on slow-motion film; the spectacular last-second basket; the Hail-Mary pass that finds its mark; and the ninth inning, bases-loaded home run. With a flick of the dial, sports become an escape from an ordinary world into the realm of superstars, out-of-sight paychecks, and glamorous people in exotic settings.

Some young people dream impossible dreams of playing professional sports as their one-way ticket out of the ghettos of financial suppression and bigotry. Sports appear so easy and enticing. But these hopes ignore the astronomical odds against success. Realistically speaking, only a few thousand individuals out of 250 million Americans earn a living as professional athletes. Defeat is waiting to ambush those youngsters whose approach to sports is based primarily on dreams, even if they are physically talented.

Others, like the thirteen men and women profiled in *The Name of the Game Is Life*, know that being a true winner means keeping sports in perspective; it is one plank in the platform of a whole life. Therefore, for these athletes sports became one vital tool in their preparation for living productively. They put into practice the knowledge and skills gained from competition to be winners in other avenues of life after the stadium lights went out. They know that winning is more than a higher number flashing on the scoreboard at the final whistle and understand that real success in sports lasts more than a game, a season, or an entire athletic career.

Take, for example, Alex Kroll, chairman of the board of Young & Rubicam, one of the world's largest advertising agencies. Kroll recalls that even as a scrawny teenaged son of a laborer in a Pennsylvania steel-mill town he was determined to be a great football player. "I always knew that somehow, no matter how inadequate a physical start I endured, I'd be a star," Kroll remembers. "I'd go to sleep every night and dream about exactly what I was going to accomplish as a football player. I was going to be great, and while I didn't know how I'd accomplish it, I truly believed it was my destiny."

Determined to fulfill his dream, he concocted a set of barbells from junk and pumped iron day and night. In his spare time he studied the Harvard classics. Kroll went on to become an All-American football player at Rutgers University, a standout in the professional ranks, and a successful business executive.

Willye B. White came out of the cotton fields of Mississippi, the granddaughter of illiterate farmers. Beginning at age sixteen she appeared in five consecutive Olympic Games, but she never achieved her life's goal of winning a gold medal. Reviewing her life, White declares that she "lost by inches, but won by a mile."

"Athletics were my flight to freedom from ignorance and prejudice. Athletics have meant everything to me—socially, spiritually, morally, and academically. Had I not been in athletics my life would have been totally different in a negative way. I found my self-worth through athletics."

Roy Kramer, commissioner of the Southeast Athletic Conference, describes sports as laboratories in learning and self-discipline. "I believe," he says, "that intercollegiate athletics offer one of the best laboratories for all types of things, including social values, the ability to work together with people of different backgrounds and different traditions . . . the bringing together of ethnic groups of all types and heritages to work toward a common goal."

EXCESSES AND REFORM

The views of Kroll, White, and Kramer are representative of the attitudes and habits of a vast army of men and women who pursue the best values of sports and use them as the foundation for their lives off the playing fields. But this world is under constant challenge because competition and the desire to win, which are the life and breath of sports, carry with them the ever-present temptation to indulge in excesses.

The news media report almost daily the stories of academic standards being lowered to accommodate young people who excel in athletics but fail in the classroom; of money being paid under the table to attract potential superstars; of athletes who drop out of school before earning degrees; and of the

tragedies of drug abusers. The mood in America today suggests that these well-publicized excesses are reaching a level
that threatens the health, if not the very being, of amateur
sports as they have been known.

As a result, the world of intercollegiate athletics is con-
fronted with the need to make some basic changes in order to
defuse this danger. These changes are likely to extend to all
levels of amateur sports.

Those at the forefront of these changes do not envision new
games, nor do they see new standards to govern the ways
traditional games are played. Instead they have their sights set
on rebalancing the equation to put greater emphasis on and
restore honor to the basic lessons and values that man has
always found in sports. The results will be a stronger society
for participants and spectators alike.

"The time for reforming intercollegiate sports is at hand,"
declares Richard D. Schultz, executive director of the National
Collegiate Athletic Association. "The objective is to create a
'new model' for intercollegiate athletics."

According to Schultz and other leaders of the reformation,
the new model will be built on the fundamental belief that
intercollegiate sports are but one integral part of the total
process of education. In essence sports provide great tools
young men and women can use to prepare themselves for life.

"Games and sports are educational in the best sense of the
word because they teach the participant and the observer new
truths about testing oneself and others, about the enduring
values of challenge and response, about teamwork, discipline
and perseverance," proclaims a 1991 report from the Knight
Commission, titled *Keeping Faith with the Student-Athlete.*
"Above all, intercollegiate contests—at any level of skill—
drive home a fundamental lesson: Goals worth achieving will
be attained only through effort, hard work and sacrifice, and
sometimes even these will not be enough to overcome the
obstacles life places in our path."

AT THE HEART OF HUMAN EXISTENCE

The basic elements of what we know today as sports were engrained in early man's preparation for life and his struggle to survive. Skills like running, jumping, and throwing objects at targets were essential to hunt wild animals for food and defend against enemies—both man and beast. These skills improved considerably when several people worked together as a team. Individuals and tribes who were best at these skills were the winners; they survived. The less able lost their territories, if not their lives.

Sports were also essential for recreation that would distract and refresh man from the grim realities of life. Athletic skills were inculcated in his religious rites.

Greeks in the mid-1400s B.C. glorified their athletes, the best of whom were treated as gods. They also saw sports as a social force for peace and harmony. Greece was a society torn by internal conflict, one city fighting another city for power and supremacy. At the suggestion of a diplomat named Heracles, warring cities agreed to engage in games rather than war as a means of competition.

A neutral site known as Mount Olympus on the Greek-Macedonian border, was chosen as the location of the first games. The contests took on the aura of religious ceremonies partly because Mount Olympus was revered as an abode of the gods. The competition was held every four years and became a great success, helping to unite the Greek nation. Some seven hundred years later the contests were named the Olympian Games.

It is not surprising that the competition got out of hand with so much at stake in the rivalry between cities and superstars. In the year A.D. 392, eleven centuries after the founding of the games, the Roman emperor Theodosius banned the Olympics as a public nuisance. The ban lasted for 1,500 years, proving that the need to find the ideal balance in sports is not a new challenge.

Football began about A.D. 1050 when a group of idle English lads discovered it was fun and an outlet for their energies to kick an inflated cow bladder about on an open field. But soon "futballe", as the sport was known, became a violent contest between whole villages.

Small armies of men would meet on neutral ground between two communities. Each team fought to kick the bladder through the streets of the opposing town. The unrestrained competition, often fueled by a warmup at the local pub, resulted in violence and injuries. King Henry II of England (1154-89) finally declared futballe a "vile game" on which grown men should not be wasting their time. He instituted a ban that lasted some 400 years.

Those in positions of authority often opposed sports on moralistic grounds, deeming such activities a frivolous waste of God's time. Others, like King James II of England and his immediate successors, saw sports as a temptation to forego duty to the crown. James II petitioned the Scottish Parliament to ban "futballe and golfe," declaring that the sports should be "cryed downe and not be used."

When the Puritans fled to America in search of religious freedom, they brought their overbearing moralizing attitudes with them. But man's love of sports could not be suppressed. People continued to play games in spite of their neighbors' scorn and punishment at the hands of the authorities. The records show that citizens were fined and placed in the stocks for "playing ball on the Sabbath after being warned against such an abomination."

QUESTIONING THE VERY SURVIVAL OF SPORTS

The criticism of sports reached a new degree of intensity by the 1880s and 1890s, when serious public concerns, even outrage, erupted about intercollegiate football. So intense was the outcry from would-be reformers that questions were raised in the media and by politicians about the survival of organized sports at the college level in America.

The epitome of these concerns was the "flying wedge," a formation in which ten men in a V-shape served as a battering ram in the center of which a runner carried the ball. The flying wedge, which originated at Princeton University in 1884, ran over defenders like a herd of wild buffalo and often left seriously injured players in its wake. Gang tackling was the preferred defensive tactic.

A dozen deaths were attributed to football injuries in 1902. Four years later the *Chicago Tribune* cited an unconfirmed report that the game had resulted in eighteen deaths among college players, forty-six among high schoolers, and nine among semi-professionals.

Shailer Mathews, dean of the Chicago Divinity School, called football a "social obsession . . . a boy-killer, education-prostituting, gladiatorial sport. It teaches virility and courage, but so does war. I do not know what should take its place, but the new game should not require the services of a physician, the maintenance of a hospital, and the celebration of funerals."

There was even talk that football might be outlawed by Congress.

Meanwhile, there were others who spoke and acted in more measured and reasonable terms about the benefits of the sport. They called for reform rather than abolition. A shining example among them was Walter Camp, whom many consider to be the architect of the game of football and who exemplified the model student-athlete. Camp was born in 1859 in New Haven, Connecticut. The son of well-to-do parents, he was a young man who "studied hard, made good grades, played baseball, swam, ran track and experimented with the newly imported game of tennis," according to Wells Twombly in his book *200 Years of Sport in America.* "He was the finest swimmer of his time, winning everything from sprints to five-mile races. He rowed with his class crew."

Camp stood six feet tall and weighed almost 200 pounds. He was the first man to sign up for Yale University's first football squad and he felt early on that football built character. As a coach, he admonished: "When it comes to the football field, mind will always win over muscle and brute force. What a gentleman wants is fair play and for the best man to win. If he accepts these principles, he will find his own character greatly enriched. If your opponent takes trifling liberties with you, such as slapping your face, let all such action merely determine you to keep a close watch on the ball.

"There is no substitute for hard work and effort beyond the call of mere duty. That is what strengthens the soul and ennobles one's character."

He spoke of the qualities of "knowledge, skill, strength, speed, obedience, initiative, aggressiveness, courage, honor and morale."

ENTER THE NCAA

The defenders of football had a powerful ally in the twenty-sixth President of the United States, Theodore Roosevelt, living proof of the value of sports. Teddy Roosevelt had been a sickly child, suffering from a heart murmur complicated by asthma and other ailments. Through his zestful embracing of vigorous exercise and participation in sports—especially boxing, running, horseback riding, swimming, hunting, and fishing—he grew to be a robust man, a model for his fellow countrymen.

When he became President in 1901 at the age of forty-two, Roosevelt installed a boxing ring in the basement of the White House. He was the first President to be an all-out evangelist for physical fitness.

Many people wanted Roosevelt to exercise the power of the presidency to abolish football. He refused. Instead at the end of the season of 1905 he summoned representatives of Harvard, Yale, and Princeton to the Oval Office and told them they must act to reform the game of football. "Do not report back to me until you have a game that is acceptable to the entire nation," he declared. "You must act in the public interest. This glorious sport must be freed from brutality and foul play. The future of the republic is dependent upon what you do. The character of future generations is in your hands."

A few weeks later Chancellor Henry M. MacCracken of New York University convened a meeting of thirteen institutions to initiate changes in the playing rules for football. Sixty-two institutions of higher education subsequently formed the Intercollegiate Athletic Association of the United States. The organization adopted its present name, the National Collegiate Athletic Association (NCAA), in 1910.

For many years the NCAA was so small that it did not have a professional staff. It operated on a part-time basis as part of the Big 10 Conference headquartered in Chicago. As collegiate sports flourished in America the NCAA grew, and it became a free-standing entity in 1951 when Walter Byers became its first executive director.

Today, headquartered in Kansas City in its own building with over two hundred staff members, the NCAA is made of 1,020 entities—individual colleges and universities, conferences, and affiliated members. These members make and enforce rules that govern competition in athletics at NCAA institutions. This competition currently includes more than 275,000 young men and women and encompasses seventy-seven championships in twenty-one sports.

The organization sponsors numerous programs for the benefit of student-athletes, including honors and scholarships, grants to undergraduates who have exhausted their opportunities for institutional financial aid, and women's and minority enhancements.

"Our mission within the NCAA—members, officers and staff—is not football, not basketball, nor national championships; our mission is education of young people," Schultz explains. "Our real purpose is to prepare student-athletes to be major contributors to and successful people in society while also providing meaningful opportunities for intercollegiate competition on a level playing field."

This mission is being executed at a time when the public's interest in and concern for intercollegiate athletics are at an all-time high. The NCAA focuses its attention on several issues, including:

• the perception that an undue amount of pressure is often put on young people to win, sometimes at any cost
• the methods used to recruit athletes
• the educational standards applied to athletes and the quality of their work in the classroom
• the percentage of athletes who eventually earn college diplomas
• the preparation athletes receive for coping successfully with life after their playing days are over
• the health and welfare of student-athletes and the integrity of educational institutions
• the increased commercialization of sports in general

"It is time for us to take stock of what we have created— save the positives but immediately rid ourselves of the negatives and develop a new, innovative approach for athletics that places in perspective and allows athletics to be a vital, honorable part of higher education," declares NCAA's chief executive.

The NCAA took a major step forward in 1988 when it formed the NCAA Foundation to support the academic mission of intercollegiate athletics. The foundation promotes personal growth and development opportunities for young men and women.

The organization is governed by a board of directors composed of nationally prominent leaders in education, business, sports, and entertainment. Dr. Robert C. Khayat, a former college and professional football player and legal academician, is president of the NCAA Foundation. "Our programs mean to encourage every student-athlete to complete a meaningful academic degree program, participate fully in the college community, and prepare for life after college athletics," he explains.

Schultz, Khayat, and their staffs at the NCAA represent the thinking of reform-minded academicians across the country. They aggressively support basic changes that they believe will move intercollegiate athletics back to the original values of sports. These leaders foresee a future in which the NCAA's goal of having educators play the dominant role in setting the standards and controlling intercollegiate sports will be realized.

John A. DiBiaggio, president of Michigan State University, advocates making the educational standards for admission into school and participation in extracurricular activities uniform for all students at all universities. "I am constantly told by coaches that we must maintain a level playing field. Well, a play field can be leveled as easily by raising it as it can be by lowering it. I contend that if we were all to raise our standards together, our games would be equally interesting and competitive."

Dr. DiBiaggio addresses the coaches and athletes several times each year. His message is essentially the same, he says. "I tell them that while we perceive athletics to be very important, they should appreciate that winning athletic contests is not what a university is all about. Being winners is what we are about. To me that means student-athletes are at a university to get an education and to have a real-life experience in which winning or losing a game will not be the measure by which they are assessed.

"I remind the athletes," he continues, "that very, very few of them will make it to the professional ranks; even fewer will stay. Therefore their primary goal should be to get an education so they can succeed in life.

"They have the good fortune of being gifted as athletes. Therefore they have a special responsibility to themselves, the university, and society as a whole to serve as positive role models for younger people."

Reverend Edward A. Malloy, the youthful president of Notre Dame, cites his institution's policy on intercollegiate athletics as the sort of position he believes more and more universities are adapting. "We consider our coaches as part of the teaching faculty," declares Malloy. "If you are a teacher, one of your primary goals is to work for the common good, to bring out the best in each individual, to confront people with their own inadequacies and to show them how to make corrections.

"Our policy holds that the student-athletes are first of all students. Our goal is to see them completely integrated into the student body."

The graduation rate for all student-athletes at Notre Dame since 1987-88 is 91.57 percent, slightly higher than the rate for the university's student body as a whole.

Leaders such as Schultz, Kramer, Khayat, DiBiaggio, and Malloy espouse the belief that competitive sports provide powerful values even for those who lose.

"I played on a high-school team which won fifty-five consecutive games," relates Reverend Malloy, a former scholarship basketball player at Notre Dame. "There is no doubt there is a certain amount of exhilaration and satisfaction that comes from winning. But I think I learned as much if not more as far as lessons of life are concerned from losing as defined by the scoreboard."

"There is nothing wrong with failing as long as you learn from it," says Coach Mike Krzyzewski, who led Duke University to compete in five Final Four tournaments in six years and to win the title in 1991.

MORE WINNERS THAN LOSERS

Intercollegiate sports have produced far more winners than losers. The triumphant ones are the men and women—superstars and also-rans—who have won and lost games, worked, persisted when others quit, and competed against the standards of excellence. They have learned their lessons well and found success in business and public service as well as their personal lives after the grandstands have emptied.

Thirteen of these superstars are profiled in *The Name of the Game Is Life*. They represent literally tens of thousands of athletes who epitomize the best all-around values in sports. The authors selected those featured in this book after considering scores of candidates. The criteria for selection recognized the achieving of distinction in competitive sports and a well-rounded richness in their professional and personal lives.

Each chapter was written following lengthy one-on-one interviews between the authors and the subject. Each story is worthy of a full-length book itself.

1

▪ DAVE BING ▪

Basketball Star, Owner of Bing Steel, Civic Leader

It's a wonder Dave Bing isn't called Superman. As the founder and chairman of the board of Bing Steel, he's indeed a man of steel. During his twelve-year NBA career, Bing was able to leap over tall buildings—there were occasions when he actually leaped high enough to slam-dunk the ball over Kareem Abdul-Jabbar, who, at 7'2", towered over the 6'3" guard.

At 180 pounds, the slender all-time highest scoring guard for the Pistons doesn't have the appearance of a superstar. Yet during his nine years with Detroit, a two-year stint with the Washington Bullets, and a single season with the Boston Celtics, Bing amassed 18,327 points, averaging 20 points per game by the time he retired from basketball in 1978. One of only four players in NBA history included in the all-time top twenty in both scoring and assists, Bing played on seven All-Star teams and in 1990 was elected to the Basketball Hall of Fame. His number, 21, is the only number ever to be retired by the Pistons.

Like many other black basketball players, Washington, D.C. native Dave Bing began hitting the boards at the playgrounds in the inner city. A natural athlete, he had dreams during his youth of someday playing major league baseball. His father, a

15

construction worker, first saw him play organized sports in a Little League playoff game. "It was the first time our team ever played in a real ballpark," Bing recalls. "We had a dugout, a real infield, and a fence around the outfield. I hit three home runs out of the park that day, and it was a real high to see my father get so excited. He was swelled with pride, and that made me proud. It was a wonderful father-son experience, and from that point on, my participation in athletics was something we shared. During my professional career he'd meet me at games around the country, and I'd introduce him to all the players he had read about. It was quite a thrill for him. You see, my father was a good athlete himself, who played sandlot baseball as a kid growing up in South Carolina. With the same opportunities I had, he could have been a professional ball player too."

Basketball was the most popular sport in the nation's capital, so even though Bing continued to play baseball, basketball became his primary sport. This decision was undoubtedly influenced by the fact that Spingarm High School, which he attended, was rich in basketball tradition; only a few years earlier, Elgin Baylor, one of the sport's greats, had starred there. Bing credits his high school coach, William Roundtree, with playing a significant role in his development as a basketball player and as a person. "Roundtree taught us to be team players. He never pushed anyone to be a star. We had seven players who averaged in double figures," Bing tells.

During his senior year Bing was the team's high scorer; he was also the number-one assist player and one of the team's top rebounders. While there were big shooters who had more impressive scoring statistics, Bing's all-around play made him one of the most sought-after high school players in the nation in 1962.

In addition to being a standout athlete, Bing was a fine student, graduating with a 3.1 grade-point average. And his parents gave him a strong religious background; he faithfully attended church on Sunday mornings. "I had some wonderful role models to follow, namely my father, my basketball coach, and my minister. It's true that they weren't the most celebrated people, but to me they were heroes. I owe a lot to them for what they taught me. Looking back, I was very fortunate to have these folks guiding me," Bing continues. "They'd point out certain pitfalls, and I'd *listen*. I took what they said to heart when they'd say, 'You're a hell of an athlete, but you have to be a good student too.' I think many young people get good advice but they just don't listen to it.

"Sure, there were guys in my peer group who said, 'Why in hell are you going to church? What's with you, Dave?' and 'Why are you wasting your time with schoolwork? You don't have to do that—you're a basketball player.' Luckily, I was raised in a way that gave me the strength to resist peer pressure that could hurt me. Sure, I did a lot of the mischievous things that most kids do, but I was fortunate to be raised in an environment that taught me right from wrong. As a result, I never got into serious trouble while I was growing up. Over the years, I witnessed a lot of young people with a great deal of potential who weren't so fortunate, and as a consequence they never amounted to anything."

An honor student and outstanding athlete, Bing could pick practically any college in the country to attend, but ironically his first choice, Princeton, turned him down. "For an Ivy League school, they had a fine basketball program, but they didn't give athletic scholarships," Bing explains. "However, they did offer academic scholarships on a need basis. And while I qualified from a need standpoint, they didn't think my grades were at a level that would allow me to compete academically. For the first time in my life, I was rejected because somebody told me that I wasn't good enough. I was devastated! I decided to enter my second choice, Syracuse University, and I made up my mind that I would never again put myself in a position where I would have to face rejection. In retrospect, it was an invaluable lesson because I became determined to do whatever it would take to be a good college student." When Bing entered Syracuse University, he became the first member of his family ever to attend college.

While Syracuse was one of the nation's leading football powers in the 1950s and 1960s, it had never been known for its prowess on the basketball court. In fact, during the 1961–62 season, its basketball team had lost twenty-nine consecutive games, a dubious record for a major college. So what influenced Bing to attend this upper New York state university, a haven for skiers and skaters, known for its winterland beauty? "How can you choose Syracuse? They're terrible," he heard again and again. "And, besides, their basketball team has no black players."

Two individuals made a strong impression on him during the weekend he visited Syracuse University. One was Ernie Davis, the 1962 Heisman Trophy winner and the biggest name in college sports; the other was John Mackey, also a Syracuse All-American, who went on to play for the Baltimore Colts and become the decade's top tight end in pro football. The university assigned Davis and Mackey to recruit Bing. "I was a very impressionable young kid," Bing admits, "and having these guys take me around and tell me why I should come to Syracuse obviously had a strong impact. Both of them were B students, and, rather than emphasizing sports at the school, they talked a great deal about the good education I'd receive."

Although Syracuse had never been known for its basketball program, in 1962 changes occurred that marked the beginning of a new era. That year Bing was one of seven players recruited by the school, five of whom were ranked among the top twenty-five high-school players on the eastern seaboard. It was a time when college freshmen weren't eligible to play on the varsity team, but during practice games played before a packed field house Bing and his young teammates trounced the varsity team. When Bing and his fellow classmen entered their sophomore year, Syracuse became a basketball power-house. For the next three years the school went to a postsea-son tournament. By Bing's senior year, Syracuse was ranked seventh in the nation, finishing the season with 23 wins and only 5 losses. The team was beaten by Duke in the Eastern Regional Finals in its attempt to become one of the final four.

In the beginning, Bing had a difficult time with the transi-tion from an all-black, inner-city environment to what he found at Syracuse. "The school's population was more than 95 percent white, and it was predominantly made up of students from affluent backgrounds who had attended prep schools and competitive all-white suburban schools," Bing remembers. "I had to adjust to being a minority. Growing up in the District of Columbia I was always surrounded by other blacks. Yet out of the roughly twelve thousand students on campus, I don't think there were ever any more than one hundred black stu-dents during my four years at Syracuse.

"Interestingly, perhaps as many as fifty out of the seventy black males were there on athletic scholarships. So not only did I have to compete on the basketball court, but also in the classroom where people were telling me that I wouldn't do well because my inner-city academic foundation was too weak. I accepted it as a challenge and applied the same competitive attitude I had on the basketball court to the classroom. I wanted to prove that I could compete with people from all over the country—I refused to accept that they were better or smarter than I."

As a freshman Bing shared a room with Frank Nicoletti, a highly publicized high school All-American from Weehawken, New Jersey, who was considered one of the five best graduates in the country. Nicoletti, today a successful attorney in New York, had attended St. Peter's Prep School and was an excel-lent student. "I mimicked Frank's study habits," Bing tells, "and I'm sure some of him rubbed off on me." The two men remain close friends.

While his prime objective at Syracuse was to obtain a good education, Bing continued to improve as a basketball player and during his junior and senior years was voted an All-American. "Although I loved basketball," he states, "I knew I had to prepare myself for life after sports. I witnessed too many guys who were better than I in high school who, for whatever reason, stopped improving and, because they didn't look past the game, stopped growing as human beings. Perhaps they got hurt, or they stayed the same height or simply peaked and their game never got better. Whatever the reason—and it happens to a lot of guys in college and even in the pros—once out of basketball, for the rest of their lives they live in yesterday's world because they fail to plan for the future.

"It's a devastating experience for a kid who's the best in his school, in his division, or in his state to learn that when he's competing against people from all over the country he's not as good as he thought he was. The guy goes to college thinking he's NBA material and then has a rude awakening when he discovers at best he's just another player at the level of big-time college basketball. Even the guy who stars at a top-ranked school has a slim chance to make the NBA. Only a small fraction of one percent of those who aspire to play pro ball actually will. If somebody has only one thing in mind—to make a living out of professional sports—and that's the basis on which he plans his whole life, he's dealing with percentages that are stacked enormously against him. Then too, even if you make the pros, considering the short span of a career as a professional, an athlete has to prepare himself for the day when he's out of sports. Sure, nobody likes to think about the negatives, but one has to be realistic.

"I've gone back to the old neighborhood where I grew up," he goes on, "and I've seen what's happened to those guys who had nothing in mind but sports, and now they have nothing to show for it but memories. As a consequence, they've never left the inner-city environment. Many of them dwell on the past, and some say they're victims. Perhaps some are. It's not always their fault. Perhaps they didn't have the folks in the home, in the school, in the community, telling them, 'You've got to get prepared for something else.' It's sad to see a grown man who as a youngster was a highly touted athlete, with his name in the newspapers and magazines, who appeared on radio and television, and now, for the rest of his life, will never be in the limelight again. Not only is it devastating, in some cases it's humiliating. I'm not just referring to the high school stand-out, but even the guy playing in the NBA who's considered one of the best in his profession, and when his athletic career comes to a sudden end, he's not prepared to do anything else."

Dave Bing was aware that his future would not always be in basketball, so he was determined to get a diploma. In 1966 he graduated with a 2.7 grade-point average, majoring in economics. Although he was prepared to seek a job in the business world, Bing was one of the fortunate players who did get to play in the NBA. The year he graduated from Syracuse, he was the number-two draft choice behind the University of Michigan's Cazzie Russell. Russell was a natural choice to play for the Pistons, for he had thrilled Detroit fans during his college days. By the same token, Bing had played perhaps as many as twenty games in Madison Square Garden during his college career and was adored by New York fans. But a strange twist of fate occurred—the toss of a coin determined that Russell would go to the New York Knicks and Bing to the Pistons. Of course it didn't take long for either to make his mark, but while both went on to be stars, it was Bing who received NBA Rookie of the Year honors.

Unlike today's top draft choices, Bing did not become an instant multimillionaire in 1966. As the number-two college player, he received a starting salary of $15,000—without a bonus. In comparison, in 1990 Bing negotiated the contract for the nation's number-one college player, Derrick Coleman, a Syracuse graduate, who Bing says is "like a little brother of mine." Coleman received a guaranteed five-year contract in the neighborhood of $14 million. Bing served as Coleman's agent. Bing also served as his own agent. "Back in those days, we didn't make enough money to have agents," he smiles. "Besides, being in college with a wife and two children, I surely didn't need to share my salary with an agent who would have taken 10 percent of what I received." Throughout his professional career Bing never employed an agent. "I felt very strongly that I went to college to get an education in business, so I always represented myself," he tells. "It had to do with pride, but I'm aware that it might have also had to do with stupidity. Nonetheless, I felt I could speak for myself and do my own negotiating. Besides, I looked at it as part of the learning process."

Although Bing was one of the great NBA players of his day, he finished his career earning $250,000 a year, which by today's standards is a drop in the bucket. He never made enough during his NBA career to be able to sit back and feel his financial future had been secured. It was common then, as it is now, for well-known athletes to be seduced by large endorsement contracts. Bing had offers to endorse products and opportunities to collect sizable fees as an after-dinner speaker—after all, he was the league's leading scorer in his second season. But he chose not to take advantage of these offers because he didn't want to prostitute his name. Instead Bing accepted a job with the National Bank of Detroit in the off-seasons, beginning in 1966 as a management trainee working first as a teller and then becoming a branch manager. He also worked in various specialty departments at the bank. He chose banking because "everything revolves around finance in business."

His off-season work was, in part, motivated by the need to earn additional money, but it also provided him with an opportunity to venture out into the real world—one that didn't revolve around being a professional ballplayer. "I think many athletes make the common mistake of associating only with a small group of people," stresses Bing, "people like them who are involved in sports. This causes them to stop growing as a person. By wearing blinders, they don't see what's happening in the real world. Working at a normal job during the off-season, I had to get up every morning and be at work at a specific time like everyone else. I also had an hour for lunch, and there was no bending the rules. I had to adhere to everything other people must deal with in their daily routines. And I had to face the same problems everyone else has."

By his third year in the NBA Bing was making enough money to stop working off-season, yet he continued to work at the bank for seven years. During this period, he completed the bank's management training program, each summer having a different position. Then, for two years, he worked in the Chrysler dealer training program, thinking that he might own a car dealership when his basketball career was over. "I knew my days in the NBA were soon to end," he tells, "and I needed to decide what I would do for a second career. I knew there was an opportunity for me to coach or possibly get into some other area of management in basketball. But I wanted to find out if there was something for me to do outside of sports, away from basketball. I just wasn't sure. I knew I didn't want to be a career banker, and I didn't want to be a car dealer either. So I began thinking about what would be available when I retired, and I started to look around."

When the 1978 season came to an end, Bing hung up his basketball shoes and took a job with Paragon Steel, a now-defunct company that was then owned by two owners of the Pistons. They offered him a public relations job, but Bing refused. Instead he started working in the warehouse, the shipping department, accounting, international sales, marketing, and purchasing. Here too he had to negotiate a contract. This time, after a series of interviews, he met with a group of five Paragon managers to work out an agreement for a starting salary of $35,000. It was quite a drop from the NBA annual paycheck of $250,000 that he had earned that same year.

"Considering my NBA pay," Bing tells, "it struck me as kind of funny to be talking about a $35,000 job, but to them it was a lot of money for a low-entry person. Actually, while the money was important to them, it didn't matter to me how much I made. What I needed was the experience. I didn't want to be some ex-athlete who, because of his high visibility and popularity in the area, would live off his name. I had too much pride to allow myself to be put in front of the public to peddle some product and not know what I was talking about. There was no way I was going to knowingly make an ass of myself. I was determined to start at the bottom and learn the fundamentals. That's the way I did it when I first played basketball, and I was willing to do the same thing in the business world."

After working at Paragon for two years, Bing decided in 1980 to start his own business, Bing Steel. It was the fulfillment of a lifetime dream. In hindsight, it was predictable that Bing would someday run his own company. Anyone who carefully observed him on the basketball court understood he was a natural leader—the team captain and the team leader, the kind of guy who teammates looked to when it was time to make the big play. He was the one they passed the ball to when there was one final shot. Dave Bing was then, and is today, a man who needs to call his own shots.

Bing Steel is a steel service company that acts as a middleman between mills and user firms. Called a processor, the firm cuts, shapes, and bends raw steel to the different specifications of its customers, such as automotive, appliance, and farm equipment plants, and then ships the finished product to them. In 1980, as well as today, Bing Steel's prime customers were automotive companies, and the year the company was formed, both the steel and the automotive industries were suffering from their worst-ever depression. "Back then, people

were calling me a dummy and a masochist," Bing reminisces.
" 'Why in the world would you pick such a difficult business to
start and at the worst possible time?' they'd ask. I recognized
the risk, but I thought there was an opportunity because mine
would be the first black-owned company in the business. And
with the auto industry being in such bad shape, I figured that
would afford me the opportunity to talk to people I normally
couldn't reach, because they didn't have much to do.

"Looking back, my biggest frustration, however, was coming from sports and having to overcome the stigma that a lot
of people have about the jock mentality," he concludes. "There
was a stereotype that all jocks are dumb and lazy. When I
walked into somebody's office, the guy would immediately
identify me as the Piston player and be thinking, 'What the
hell does a basketball player know about the steel business?'
On top of that, there weren't many black folks in the automobile manufacturing industry. So I was up against a double
prejudice. Ten years ago, I was viewed as an outsider. The
good ol' boys' club consisted of a relatively small nucleus of
people, and it wasn't soliciting me to be one of its members. So
for good reason, my well-meaning friends were telling me, 'You
can't just "go into" that business, Bing. Why would you want
to do it?' But the more they said things like that, the more I
was challenged to be a success with my company."

Today each of the Big Three has established programs that
seek out minority suppliers. By doing so, General Motors,
Ford, and Chrysler are making up for what many consider past
injustices. Interestingly, because Bing Steel was one of the
first minority suppliers to be awarded contracts with the
Detroit automakers, some people questioned who its real owners were. "It hurt me when someone would suggest that I was
fronting for the company in order to get minority contracts,"
Bing comments. "I resented having people question my integrity. Anyone who knows me knows I'd never do anything like
that. Even to this day, people call me at work at seven o'clock

in the morning and then again at seven o'clock that same night. They act surprised to get me on the telephone. They weren't expecting me, but I'm conditioned to work sixty to seventy hours a week. I love what I'm doing, and I'm building something. It won't happen by itself."

During its first year in operation, Bing Steel employed only four people and its sales volume was $1.7 million—a meager beginning for a steel company. It took only six months for $90,000 of Bing's initial $150,000 investment to get eaten up by losses. As he recalls, "It was a very frightening experience to lose 60 percent of my equity in such a short period—this was hard-earned money that took me twelve years to accumulate during my professional basketball career. I felt as though I got hit with a double whammy. Not only did I lose money, but during the first year I didn't draw a salary from the business. So I suffered a loss of income to boot."

There were plenty of doomsayers on hand to advise the fledgling entrepreneur to bail out while he could still salvage some of his investment. They were quick to point out other past superstars who accumulated large sums of money and were later wiped out by poor money management following their athletic careers. Bing confesses that such worries were indeed the source of many sleepless nights, yet, rather than give up, he took such comments as a challenge.

He had heard the same kind of negative remarks back in 1966 when people said he was, at 6'3" and 180 pounds, too small to make it in the NBA. "I knew how to deal with defeat," he shrugs. "I learned that lesson well as an athlete. When you don't succeed, you don't see it as a failure because you know you'll always come back the next game. You take on the challenge, and it's something you love every time it happens. Even when I didn't make the last shot in a big game and we'd lose, I understood that one missed basket didn't make me a failure. Coming from this background, I wasn't about to accept a setback simply because my company lost money during its first year. Hell, I'm in this business for the long run. My success isn't measured by the result of a single year.

"I anticipated losing money the first year," he admits. "Just like in athletics, I went in with a game plan, knowing our revenues wouldn't cover our start-up costs and expenses. Yet, even though I had expected to go into the hole, I lost more than I had projected. Needless to say, that made me very nervous. But instead of dwelling on the negative, that the business didn't grow as fast as I would have liked it to, I focused on the positives. I analyzed why we had losses and observed that they occurred during the first six months. And while the second six months were flat, our losses were reduced to about $50,000. So, even though the business was still operating in the red, the fact that it didn't lose as much money represented progress.

"I felt it was progress because I was beginning to build a stable customer base," Bing reasons. "I had some decent contracts that would eventually bring profits down to the bottom line. There was light at the end of the tunnel. It was a matter of being able to hold on, from both a financial and a psychological standpoint. I knew that by the time the business got into its second year, we'd turn the corner. Well, we did. Our sales jumped to $4.2 million that second year, and we made money. We continued to generate profits for six consecutive years after that, although for the past two years we have lost money. I understand the reasons, and I'm now in the process of developing another game plan. If success was predicated on year-to-year success, there'd be a lot more businesses and people who would be deemed failures in this world."

After several profitable years during the mid-1980s, U.S. domestic automobile sales took a nosedive in the last half of 1989. The beginning of the 1990s offered little relief as the nation braced itself for a recession. After several prosperous years, Bing's enterprises suffered with the rest of the economy. This time, however, the red ink ran much thicker than when the company was in its infancy. "As a big company," Bing points out, "instead of losing $150,000 in one year, we faced losses of $150,000 on a monthly basis. Even though our business had enjoyed its share of prosperity, success can be short-lived. In a matter of months, losses wiped out gains that took us several years to accumulate. We're now in the process of reorganizing, so we're putting together a new game plan."

Bing pauses and continues, "There's a transition a small business must endure in order to operate as a big business—and that's where we are now. I think it took a different set of skills to start our business than what's needed today. In part, this will mean bringing in additional management who possess certain talents our business requires to grow. Fortunately, our lending institutions are sensitive to our problems and our customers are very loyal. With their support, we are confident we'll solve our present problems."

Knowing how to set attainable goals is a lesson Bing learned during his basketball days. "I've always strived to achieve the maximum of my ability," the industrious man explains. "Whenever I'd reach a certain plateau as a player, say averaging 15 points a game, I wouldn't be satisfied. I'd set my objective for the next season to improve my game point average to 18 points. Even after I'd have a great game and be surrounded by admiring reporters, I'd be thinking about the things I did wrong. 'I didn't play a perfect game,' I'd say to myself, and until I did I wasn't willing to accept the status quo. I always believed I could do better. Naturally I know the perfect game is never attainable, so there's always room for improvement—and with it, humility. It's the same in business. When I reach a certain level of success, I reestablish my goals. Of course it's important to recognize one's limitations and then to strive to maximize one's potential. I am never willing to accept mediocrity. I've seen too many people who repeat that old cliché, 'If I can be average I'm OK, I'm getting by.' I don't buy that."

Dave Bing is not content to be an average businessman. Bing Steel continued to grow in the 1980s, and during that decade he formed two additional companies—one is Superb Manufacturing, which produces pressed steel for each of the Big Three and Mazda, and the other is Heritage 21, a successful construction management company. These three enterprises now employ two hundred people and have gross sales approaching the $100 million mark. Bing's enterprises now rank among the top fifteen black-owned businesses in the nation.

Like his triumphs in sports, Bing's successes in the business world have not gone unnoticed. In 1984 President Reagan honored him at the White House as the Nation's Outstanding Minority Small-Business Entrepreneur as well as the National Minority Supplier of the year. Other recognitions include being named the Minority Supplier of the Year by General Motors and Michigan's Outstanding Minority Businessperson. In 1990 he became the first recipient of the Schick Achievement Award, an honor accorded to a former NBA coach or player who has achieved prominence following his basketball career.

Perhaps the plaque that holds the most significance for Dave Bing is the one on the wall of his office, engraved with a statement declaring his company's commitment to quality in manufacturing, to quality in product, and to excellence. Pointing at it with a sense of accomplishment, he comments, "This commitment is a carryover from athletics. It's a matter of pride to set the highest standards. In sports, a team starts off every season with the desire to go all the way—to win the championship. No self-respecting team starts off its year with a goal to win only half of its games. Now, realistically speaking, only one team will win the championship, but just the same you want it to be your team. You strive to be the best . . . in sports, business, everything."

In spite of enjoying one of the most successful careers in

college basketball and NBA history, after high school Bing
never played on a championship team. "I can remember my
coach telling us, 'Cherish the moment because you may never
have this opportunity again.' He was right. While I've had a
lot of good moments—I've been in several playoff games—
during my college and NBA days, I've never been on a team
that played in the finals. Sure it's a disappointment, but you
have to remember that only twelve guys are on the championship team in the NBA during any given year. That's out of
twenty-seven teams, so the mere fact that you don't go home
with all the marbles doesn't mean you aren't a winner. And no
matter how badly you feel when your team loses," Bing continues, "you must always remember there's always going to be
a tomorrow. You can't dwell on your defeats. You've got to pick
yourself up and concentrate on the positive."

In sports and business, Dave Bing has always had a commitment to helping the members of his team. Bing believes in
sharing his success, and he does so by being an outstanding
citizen and community leader. He's active on a dozen or so
boards in the Detroit area. He is determined to make a difference in a city where the school system is a near disaster, hard
drugs are rampant, and thousands of youngsters see little hope
in the future. Bing refuses to lend his name as an ex-NBA star
to make deals in business, but he will use it for such causes as
the YMCA, the Boy Scouts, and the Big Brothers Association.
In fact, he served as a Big Brother for four youngsters while he
played for the Pistons. Two of the boys are now college graduates, and he keeps close tabs on all of them. "We are truly
like brothers," he tells. "When they were small, I took them to
the games, summer camps, and my home, always trying to be
a positive role model for them. Each of them is now a Big
Brother himself because I said to them, 'If you think I helped
you when you were a kid, then don't you think you should do
the same thing for somebody else?' By getting them involved,
there's a domino effect."

In 1989 the Detroit school system was in jeopardy of losing its extracurricular activities. The city's education program was due to get a $50 million budget cut as a result of a $160 million deficit. As a consequence, sports, music, and arts programs would be dropped. Six hundred thousand dollars was needed to save these activities for the fall term. That September it was up to voters to decide on a bond issue which, if passed, would increase school taxes and restore these programs. But the vote would come too late to save the fall programs. In July Bing was asked to lead the campaign to save the fall programs, and he accepted the challenge. Along with Isiah Thomas and other high-profile people in the community, he solicited companies to contribute to the cause. The campaign was successful, and in late August he presented the Board of Education a check in the amount of $600,000, which served as a stopgap measure. After that, Bing remained vocal and warned voters: "We only bought time. We need your vote on September 12th. The easiest thing to do is quit on Detroit. We're not trying to hold a gun to the people's heads. We're dealing with reality." The levy was passed.

Not everybody in Detroit was pleased with a campaign aimed at saving sports. Bing received some mild criticism that his efforts to raise money for athletics in a troubled school system confirmed allegations that there was an overemphasis on sports in America's educational systems. Some of his critics questioned whether school sports was a luxury Detroit could afford. Bing retorted that his effort should not discourage others from solving other economic ills confronting the public schools. He adds: "There are a lot of lessons that can be learned in school sports. Everything is not academics. You look at the 4,500 kids who are involved with sports at school in Detroit, and that's a significant number. Many of them would become dropouts if these things were taken away." While the former backcourt star believes athletics are not a luxury and play an important role in the schools, he emphasizes that receiving a good education is essential. He puts his money where his mouth is. In 1987 he made a six-figure contribution to the United Negro College Fund.

Bing's high visibility in the community demands that he make frequent appearances at civic and political affairs. At these functions he repeats his commitment to the city of Detroit: "The drug abuse, rape, and other crimes committed in a lot of cities result from people being uneducated, causing them to be unemployed and have a lot of time on their hands. We've got to get people doing productive things and receiving decent pay. When we do, a lot of our inner-city problems will be solved." Speeches like this cause his name to be mentioned as a future mayoral candidate. However, he claims not to have a current interest in running for public office.

Why does Dave Bing put so much time into the inner-city community? It would be much easier for him to head for the suburbs and not concern himself with the problems facing the city. From a business standpoint, he would simply be following the lead of scores of other Detroit corporations that have moved to industrial parks in the outlying areas, many of which offer a lower tax base. The labor force in the suburbs is better educated, and interest rates paid by Detroit-based companies are higher because more risks are incurred in areas where crime and the use of drugs prevail.

"Sure, I could abandon the city," Bing shrugs, "but running away from a problem never solved a problem. The way I was taught and raised is that you can never forget where you came from. You've always got to go back and help. I'm fortunate because I'm in a position where I can make a difference. I can make an impact. It's easy to think the problems of the inner city are so insurmountable that you ask, 'Where is it going to end?' I'm convinced that it is not going to end during my lifetime. But if some of us don't make the commitment right now to try to change things, then there's not going to be any change during the next generation. This is why I'm committed to stay and deal with the problems. I want to do what I can to give a better start to others than I had.

"You've always got to go back and help," Bing insists. "My motivation in life is not to see how much money I can make. I want to be the right kind of role model to young people. I get a high when little kids approach me with their parents, and the kids don't know me from Adam as a former ball player. To them I'm a businessperson and a community leader, and still they ask for my autograph. Only after their parents say something do the kids say, 'Is it true that you were the Isiah Thomas of your day?'

"I want to encourage black kids to get a good education and prepare themselves for the future," Bing continues. "I have a responsibility to them. And I want to build my business so it can provide jobs for blacks. Eighty percent of my staff is black, and that's part of my plan. The minority development programs of Ford, General Motors, and Chrysler that help support my company are not about making Dave Bing, as an individual, a rich person. These programs exist to provide opportunity and employment to minority people. By having decent jobs, they can, in fact, buy into the American dream. They become consumers and they help to build the tax base. What's more, they become concerned citizens—and good citizens. I advocate paying them decent wages—I don't think you're helping people by paying them minimum wage; in fact, you do them a disservice.

"It's important to me to have success," Bing adds, "but I'm not so driven to make money that I forget what my community is going through right now. I want to succeed so I can be a good role model and have a positive impact on my community. I want to help people and let them know that somebody cares about them. In my organization I let them know that, with proper education, preparation, and effort, they can upgrade themselves to become an important part of this company. I enjoy seeking out and identifying ambitious people who want to do something with their lives but never had the opportunity."

Today Dave Bing, the former basketball star, is building a team by providing jobs and opportunities for success to people who join his enterprises. In the process, he has surrounded himself with good people. He also knows that it takes a lot of specialists to succeed. "One guy may be the shooter, another the rebounder, somebody else the good ball handler, and others are good at defense," he explains in sports jargon. "The same thing is applicable in business. I have some good general knowledge, but I'm not a specialist in any particular area. I do think I'm a good leader. So my goal is to attract people and allow them to grow—men and women who are capable of making good decisions. I want them to make me think about things that I would never otherwise think about."

Bing may be out of sports but he's still part of a team. And it's a *winning* team.

2

▪ BILL BRADLEY ▪

Basketball Player, U.S. Senator

Anyone who reads the résumé of the senior U.S. Senator from New Jersey is certain to come to the obvious conclusion: *Bill Bradley is an overachiever.*

A three-time All-American basketball player at Princeton where he graduated with honors, Bradley was a member of the 1964 gold-medal-winning Olympic basketball team. Then he was a Rhodes Scholar at Oxford University; upon returning to the States, he starred in the NBA with the New York Knickerbockers for ten years, during which period the team won two world championships. At present he is serving his third term in the U.S. Senate. With Bradley's credentials, it should come as no surprise that his name is constantly mentioned as a future Democratic presidential candidate. When asked about his plans to run for the nation's highest office in 1992 or 1996, his standard comment is: "I'll say no until I say yes." This reply tells you two things about the man: nobody pushes Bill Bradley, and his low-key appearance and mannerisms are deceptive—he is an astute senator and a fine politician.

He hails from Crystal City, Missouri, a small river town on the Mississippi about thirty miles south of St. Louis. Local townspeople claim it's a Bill Bradley trait to excel at all undertakings. They also think of him as Big Bill Bradley. For most people, it's hard to recall when he was little. In the eighth grade he stood 6'1", by the ninth grade he was 6'3", and in the tenth grade he reached his present height of 6'5". The high-school football coach had visions of Bradley playing on the gridiron but the young boy opted for the hoops. As a freshman he was tall enough for the game but a perfectionist even back then, he wasn't satisfied that his legs were strong enough. To strengthen them, young Bill religiously wore lead weights in his sneakers during daily practice sessions in his backyard. His self-imposed training also included an obstacle course of chairs set up in the family driveway, and with self-made blinders he dribbled basketballs for hours, day after day after day.

Interestingly, it was not Warren Bradley, the boy's father, but Susan Bradley, his mother, who was the driving force behind his athletic endeavors. When Bill Bradley was born on July 28, 1943, his forty-two-year-old father was already stricken with debilitating calcified arthritis in his spine. It was so severe that the tall, distinguished banker was unable to bend from the waist. By then he had worked his way up the ranks to the office of president at the Crystal City State Bank.

It was no easy matter to be a banker's son in a factory town. As a youngster, Bill Bradley was branded as somebody who was different—somebody who must prove himself to win the acceptance of the other youngsters. Leonard Maul, whom everybody called "Alex," was the bank's janitor as well as the Bradleys' driver-handyman. It was Alex, a gentle black man, who first taught the Bradleys' only child how to play baseball. It was also Alex who installed a punching bag in the family's basement so the boy could learn to defend himself. His mother worried that he would be an inviting target to older boys looking to pick a fight.

Sue Bradley did her best to expose her son to a variety of interests. She arranged for him to take lessons, and there would be lots of them: his schedule was filled with music lessons for trumpet, piano, and French horn, then lessons in dancing and typing. There were still more lessons in swimming, golf, and horseback riding to make him well-rounded. With Alex's assistance, the tall, energetic woman, a former high-school basketball player, installed a regulation-size backboard and pole which was solidly cemented in the backyard and known as "Bill's court." She received immense pleasure in playing one-on-one with her son while he was still learning. It was only a matter of time, however, when she would no longer be a match for the growing boy.

Then Arvel Popp took over. In his book, *Life on the Run*, Bradley refers to Popp as "the only man who would ever be 'the coach' to me." He describes his high-school coach as "a monk, withdrawn personally and unsociable in town circles; rigid with discipline and sparse with compliments; inspiring to boys like me, cruel to those unprepared or unwilling."

Popp, who also coached junior-high football, once had visions of Bill Bradley at receiver—the coach realized that the lad had wonderful hands capable of catching anything that came his way. Sue Bradley, however, did not want her son to risk injury. To Popp's chagrin she vetoed football, so Bill Bradley's large, nimble hands became his instruments for manipulating the big round ball. In time he was a master ball handler—a true master of deception. "He had all kinds of ways of releasing the ball," says Popp. "Off the fingers, rolling, pushing. It doesn't come naturally. You have to practice. But after you're done, it becomes automatic."

Bradley concurs that it takes hard work to be an exceptionally good athlete. Of course it's nice to be blessed with some God-given talent, but an athlete has to make the most of it. "I'm 6'5"," he states. "And other than that, I suppose I had a certain coordination. But everything else beyond height and coordination—and even the coordination to a certain extent—is developed by work and drills and thinking and practicing."

In 1958, Bradley's freshman year, the Crystal City Hornets basketball team became the main event in town; for the next four years it was "The Bill Bradley Show." Of the 3,700 residents in Crystal City, 2,000 of those who were lucky enough to purchase a ticket packed the school's gymnasium for every home game.

Bradley was the star, and while it is true he was blessed with natural ability, he worked hard to refine it. He practiced relentlessly. For hours during the warm weather he would practice fall-away jumpers from the corners of his floodlit backyard court. On weekends and holidays when it became cold, Popp entrusted him with the key to the gym. No player had ever been given the key before or since, nor has anyone ever asked. It was an honor that belonged only to Bill Bradley, and it would have been sacrilege for another player to request the key.

There was one particular rigid drill he'd do during his workout sessions. "I had five spots on the court from where I'd shoot twenty-five shots," he tells. "If I didn't hit twenty-two baskets of the twenty-five shots, I'd start over again. I'd continue this exercise from each of the five spots until I made them."

When asked why he subjected himself to such demanding workouts, he explains, "It was a matter of having the determination to stay there until it was done—and done right. Besides, I loved the game. And I enjoyed practicing. I liked to see what comes from practice. What came was greater proficiency. If you go out to shoot the first day and you don't hit many, you've got to stick with it. Slowly you improve. By the tenth day you're better, and by the hundredth day you're better still. In time you'll be making many shots. And it's very rewarding. Besides, I loved the routine—the repetition, the rhythm of practice."

He loved more than the routine; he had an obsession with the game of basketball. During his early adolescence his heroes were NBA stars such as Bob Pettit, Elgin Baylor, and Oscar Robertson. "They were my *basketball* role models," he says. "I studied their moves so I could pattern my game after theirs." For a short time he even kept a scrapbook on Wilt Chamberlain.

Bradley, who is known for his coolness on and off the court, attributes Coach Popp with teaching him how to maintain an even temperament. "Whether you win or lose," he suggests, "the idea was not to show a whole lot of emotion. In the flush of the moment, during a close game when the pressure is on, you must keep your head. Popp used to say, 'A cool head wins the game.' "

Bradley also learned from Popp how to be a team player. In time he became the ultimate team player, or the playmaker, as they say in basketball parlance. In spite of averaging 38 points per game during his senior year, he was not a hot dog. Not only did he take advantage of passing the ball to another player when he was double- and triple-teamed, he created situations that allowed his teammates to score. "Popp used to say," Bradley recalls, " 'a good player is determined by what he can do *without* the ball.' "

The local gentry still talks about the game that took place on March 15, 1961. In a scene that could have come straight from the motion picture *Hoosiers*, Crystal City was pitted against St. Louis U. High for the state championship. The final quarter was coming to an end and the Hornets were behind 50 to 49—Bradley had 33 points. St. Louis had the ball, and precious seconds were ticking off the clock. Suddenly Bradley stole the ball; the game clock showed eight seconds remaining. He rapidly moved downcourt to shoot the final basket. The crowd was enthralled. To the Crystal City fans it was poetic justice that in their star player's final game he would have the honor of shooting the winning basket. Crystal City could take home its first state championship trophy. At half-court Bradley spotted his teammate, Tom Haley, standing alone at the top of the key. He passed the ball to Haley, who in turn went in to take what appeared to be an automatic layup as the final second of the game elapsed. Unlike the game in *Hoosiers*, however, the ball did not go in and, as the buzzer sounded, the score remained 50-49.

There are certain moments in a basketball player's career that he never forgets. It is probable that Haley and Bradley have each relived the final seconds of this particular high school game again and again. Recalling those final eight seconds, Bradley comments: "It was not that I was this wonderful team player who unselfishly gave up the shot. I was still at half court and there was another player with a dramatically better chance than I to score the winning basket. It's not as if I could have made the basket but instead chose to pass the ball to my teammate and said, 'Here, be my guest.' Sure, Tom missed the layup, and maybe I could have made the shot. I used to replay it in my mind, but I stopped doing that more than twenty years ago."

Bradley had earned three letters in baseball during his high school days, and there was also a brief stint on the track team. As the most celebrated athlete in the history of the school, he was viewed as a sure winner—a sort of a superman with no equal on the playing field. As a consequence, he allowed himself to be talked into running the quarter mile against a rival school. Without practicing for the event, he entered the race and got beat. Not only was he defeated, he was humiliated. An inexperienced runner, he failed to pace himself, and on the last leg of the race, he ran out of steam and fell face down onto the hard surface of the track. The crowd witnessed their fallen hero in disbelief as he forced himself to literally crawl across the finish line. The senator has a scar on his leg that serves as a reminder of his fall on the cinders. While the embarrassment remains with him, so does the lesson about the value of proper preparation. When reminded about the incident, with a faint smile he replies, "It's true, and my spill can be documented." He pulls up his pant leg and adds, "Where's the photographer?"

By the time of his graduation in 1961 Bradley had scored 3,066 points and was being hailed as the best player in the history of Missouri high-school basketball. Twice he was named to *Scholastic* magazine's All-America team. He was a straight-A student and a member of the National Honor Society and was elected president of the Missouri Association of Student Councils. No wonder he received scholarship offers from seventy-five colleges. When all the recruiting efforts were over, he accepted an offer from Duke University, an excellent school with a nationally renowned basketball team. Then, unexpectedly, Bradley announced he was enrolling at Princeton, the Ivy League school in New Jersey, not known for its athletic greatness. Princeton did, however, have a reputation for academic excellence. Most observers were surprised that Bradley would turn down Duke's full athletic scholarship to play basketball at a college where athletes had to pay their own way. While Bradley's father was a bank president, he was by no means an extremely wealthy man; after all, he presided over Crystal City Bank, not Chase Manhattan.

Bradley changed his mind during a summer trip to Europe. "I chose Princeton," he tells, "because I thought, 'If I were not a basketball player, what school would I then attend?' I then determined that Princeton was the school where I would want to go, and, if so, then that's where I should enroll. After all, what would happen if I were to be injured and could not play basketball? In such a circumstance my choice would be a school where I was not an athlete."

In the late summer of 1961 Bradley broke his foot and was unable to play basketball for about two months. The injury reinforced his decision to attend Princeton. By October he was back on the court and continued to improve his game during his first year as a collegian.

In 1961 NCAA rules did not permit freshmen to be members

of varsity teams; it was undoubtedly in the young student's interest that he was not eligible to play at the varsity level during his first year at Princeton. The added distraction very well could have ended his college basketball career altogether. During his first few months at Princeton he had difficulty adjusting to the rigid academic standards at a college that attracted top students from the nation's most elite private schools and public high schools. Bradley was not used to being pitted against such strong competition in the classroom. As a consequence, his first semester's grade-point average had to be raised or he would be ineligible to play on the varsity team the following year. By applying the same discipline he displayed as an athlete, Bradley did improve his grades; he eventually became an honor student.

His athletic and academic excellence seemed to complement each other. If his tenacity on the basketball court carried over in the classroom, his high intellect must be credited for making him a star on the hardwood floor. The flow of his movements, his ability to pass the ball behind his back, his proficiency at shooting from the baseline—each was the result of ceaseless study and practice and caught the attention of the East Coast fans. Reporters wrote about how he would practice each part of his game, most often in solitude, hour after hour, until each action occurred as if it required no thought. He was named All-American as a sophomore and again his junior and senior years. Just as the citizenry of the small community of Crystal City adored him, so did the rest of the country become infatuated with this basketball wizard from Missouri.

Although he was the most celebrated member of Princeton's entire student body, Bradley never seemed impressed with his fame. In fact he acted oblivious to all the fuss and attention bestowed upon him. He joined the Fellowship of Christian Athletes and also taught at a Presbyterian Sunday school. Before games he would regularly play the song "Climb Every Mountain" to get himself psyched up. And after games—even on Saturday nights—he was likely to be seen heading toward the school library. In part the nonchalance that the big kid from the Midwest displayed added to his charm and made him a media sensation.

During the summer of 1964, between his junior and senior years, Bradley worked as a Capitol Hill intern. It was an exciting period in U.S. history. He enjoyed what was practically a front-row seat in the senate gallery where he witnessed the Civil Rights Act signed into law. He refers to his internship as "a major influence on my life. I realized that something had occurred that was very important for the country; something that I thought made America a better place. The thought occurred to me that in the future I would be able to do that. It dawned on me during that summer," he reminisces, "that I would like to someday be in politics and might like to be a senator." After a brief pause, he adds, "It is only in retrospect that I realized it, because after that summer I went on to do other things with my life unrelated to politics."

In the same autumn, when Bradley was captain of the gold-medal-winning U.S. basketball team at the 1964 Olympic games, still more glitter was added to his illustrious athletic career. At a time when the Cold War was at its peak, the team's final victory over the Soviets made the long trip to Tokyo even more meaningful. It also made Bradley a national hero. Probably no other student in the history of the school ever had such high visibility as he had when he returned to the Princeton campus to complete his senior year.

The 1964-65 basketball season was his best ever. He led Princeton to the NCAA's final four, and in the consolation game against Wichita State he scored 58 points, breaking Oscar Robertson's playoff record. It was not as if he were gunning and refused to pass the ball to his teammates. On the contrary, his teammates had decided to get the ball to him so he could end his college career with a big game. "Every time I'd throw the ball to them, they'd pass it back," he explains.

"It took me a while, but I finally got the hint. 'Why not?' I said to myself and let it go."

During Bradley's years at Princeton, Butch van Breda Kolff served as head coach. Bradley describes him as "a man who loved the game and who taught it exceedingly well. Perhaps the most important lesson I learned from him was that there isn't necessarily an end to a particular play or to a particular game or, for that matter, a particular year. Instead, one thing leads to another. On the court this was manifested in the way van Breda Kolff coached because we didn't have plays per se. We had a constant flow in which there were constantly changing opportunities that we had to recognize and take advantage of. It's a valuable lesson which carries over to life in general."

Bradley wrote his bachelor's thesis on Harry S. Truman's 1940 Senate campaign, and in 1965 he received his B.A. degree from Princeton with honors in American history. Named to virtually every All-American team and voted the 1965 college player of the year by the National Association of Basketball Coaches, Bradley was a sure thing to be drafted in the NBA first round. Instead, however, he passed up professional basketball to be a Rhodes Scholar at Oxford University, where he earned a graduate degree after having studied politics, philosophy, and economics at Princeton. At the time his ambitions were to enter either business or law—not a professional basketball career. "Back then, I wasn't much of a professional basketball fan," he says, referring to his undergraduate days. "In fact I rarely watched a game. However, toward the end of my senior year, it was clear that I would be drafted. Interestingly, there was a territorial dispute about who had the rights to me. Princeton was forty-six miles from New York and Philadelphia was forty-eight miles. I was the last territorial pick—even though I was the Knicks' first pick!"

In the summer of 1965, prior to enrolling in Oxford, he led the United States basketball team to victory in the World

University Games held in Budapest. He managed to play some competitive basketball while studying in Great Britain, yet not quite on the same scale as he did in the States. During his first year abroad he commuted to Italy, where he played for a Milan-based team that won the European Cup championship, beating the same Soviet team that the U.S. Olympic team had defeated in Tokyo. "During my second year," he tells, "with the exception of a trip to Yugoslavia to play with the Italian team, I didn't touch a basketball."

In spite of his long hiatus from basketball, the New York Knicks pursued him, but Bradley showed little interest in an NBA career. In 1967, as his second year abroad was coming to an end, an interesting scene occurred in an empty Oxford gym. In Bradley's hands was the first basketball he had touched in nearly a year. "There, I shot alone—just the ball, the basket, and my imagination. As I heard the swish and felt my body loosen into familiar movements—the jumper, the hook, the reverse pivot—I could hear the crowd though I was alone on the floor. I knew that never to play again, never to play against the best, the pros, would be to deny an aspect of my personality perhaps more fundamental than any other."

By this time, at age twenty-four, Bradley was also thinking about life following an NBA career. After all, he knew that there was a relatively short number of years when basketball could be a livelihood. Thinking long-term and looking ahead to a possible political career, he sought the advice of Byron "Whizzer" White, the Supreme Court justice and former All-American football player, and Morris Udall, the U.S. Congressman from Arizona, a former professional basketball player. Both men recommended he play in the NBA, commenting that it would not adversely affect his chances in politics later on. The meticulous approach to studying his options is a particular trait, Bill Bradley observers claim, that reflects his long-term ambitions.

Shortly thereafter he signed a four-year contract with the

New York Knickerbockers. The newspapers reported that he received an amount in the $100,000 range. Bradley won't divulge how much he was actually paid but admits only that he "signed for an undisclosed sum." What he did receive was a large sum in comparison to the average annual salary of $9,500 paid to NBA players in 1967.

Somewhere along the line the sportswriters, and later the fans, began to call him "Dollar Bill." There are several different interpretations of how this nickname was given. The first explanation is that the name was a result of the large rookie contract he received. The second and probably the most accepted theory is that Bradley was a "money player," or the player designated to receive the ball in the final seconds of a game to take the final shot; hence he was considered cool under pressure when the stakes were high. Bradley explains still another interpretation with his tongue in his cheek: "Walt Frazier would say that 'Dollar Bill' was given to provide me with an incentive so I'd go out and buy some clothes."

Frazier, a clothes horse, always sported a high-style suit. Willis Reed and Earl "the Pearl" Monroe were fashion-conscious, and even Dave DeBusschere, Bradley's roommate on road trips, was a stylish dresser. But the man from the Ivy League had no interest in clothes. "We'd go on an eight-day road trip," DeBusschere would tell, "and he'd come out with this little bag, two pairs of pants, some shirts." For the ten years he played as a Knickerbocker, Bradley took a razzing about his clothes from his teammates. It was part of his charm to accept being kidded about how he dressed. No doubt he enjoyed their humor as much as they. He well understood that there was never an intent to be malicious.

The temperamental New York fans were expecting too much of their newly acquired three-time All-American as a highly paid rookie. During his first season as a Knick, Bradley had difficulty making the adjustment to the big league. One of his problems was that he was moved from forward position to guard. "I hadn't gotten the hang of it," he tells, "and I couldn't keep up with the running. Plus my timing was considerably off. I received this giant press buildup—I was going to be the savior of the Knicks. However, in addition to not being the savior, I spent most of my time on the bench. The fans in Madison Square Garden booed me, and they'd throw pennies and garbage on me. Some even spat on me, and in the streets they accosted me with verbal abuse." It was a new and difficult experience for the young man who had been the hometown hero in Crystal City and the biggest of the big men on campus at Princeton. He was used to being cheered, not jeered. The rude reception by New York fans undoubtedly took some of the fun out of his game.

"It was a very rough period," Bradley continues. "The real question was, 'Would I ever succeed in the game?' To my good fortune I had a four-year contract so I never really thought about that first year as a disaster. Instead I viewed it as a learning experience. I was determined to improve, and, with enough hard work, I felt as though I would."

Bradley worked hard throughout the long 1967-68 season. Following his professional debut, he enrolled in summer school. Summer school for NBA players meant playing in the Baker League in Philadelphia, a league consisting of several NBA players plus some talented and tough street players who never quite made it to the big league. NBA stars such as Elvin Hayes, Dave Cowens, and Earl Monroe were there, and so was a determined Bill Bradley. The former Princeton All-American made great strides during the long, hot summer months in Philadelphia. In his own words, "I was able to learn from my mistakes. Consequently I reported to training camp for my second year as a better player. However, I was still a guard, and I did better at the forward position. Then a lucky break happened—at least in one sense it was lucky for me. Cazzie Russell broke his ankle and they moved me from guard to forward.

"This was the last piece to fit in the puzzle," he continues. "We went on that winter to win something like nineteen out of twenty-four games. I was beginning to play decent basketball. This unit [the starting five players] came back strong the following year and went on to win the NBA championship."

It was only a matter of time before Bradley captured the hearts of the fans in Gotham City. During his ten years with the Knicks he played on two NBA championship teams in 1970 and 1973. He became an active participant in the Players Union in a period of major shifting relationships between owners and players. While he is reported to have earned $325,000 a year in his final NBA years, his life-style, unlike that of many stars who exhibited pretentions, was understated and discreet. He continued to wear conservative clothes and drove an old car. In a profession dominated by black players, Bradley was seen as a "great white hope"; consequently there were offers for large endorsement contracts.

When asked why he routinely refused to endorse products, he replies, "I didn't do it for three reasons. First, I didn't want to be viewed as the 'great white hope' by some people for reasons other than my playing ability. Second, I didn't want to be part of the advertising industry that created socially useless personal needs and then sold products to meet those needs. Third, I wanted to keep my experience of the game as pure as possible. In some way, I played basketball because I loved the game. And to have commercialized it would have reduced the purity of the experience for me."

Although he had offers, there were few after-dinner speeches or appearances for Bradley during the off-seasons. Instead he put in long hours in the public service sector. He worked as an assistant to the director of the Office of Economic Opportunity in Washington; he taught reading at an Urban League street academy in Harlem; he promoted prison reform, welfare reform, and environmental protection. He also became involved in national Democratic politics.

When he was not practicing and playing basketball during the long NBA season, Bradley seemed more interested in meeting people—all sorts of people—to learn about their needs, their opinions, and their dreams. He would not only talk to them but interview and study them. It was far more than something to occupy his time. His full-time job as a professional athlete provided him with time between games to observe Americans in all walks of life. He had the opportunity to meet all sorts of people from everywhere—the fishermen in Seattle, residents on Indian reservations, and scores of masseurs, cabbies, waiters, and bellboys in cities wherever the Knicks played. He'd also interrogate his teammates, prompting them to tell stories about their families and personal lives. He concluded, "Above all, I see how much I don't know, and can never know, about black people."

During a few weeks at the tail end of the 1973-74 season he wrote in great detail about his travels, his teammates, and the game of basketball itself. This writing evolved into a book, titled *Life on the Run*, that was published in 1976. It was one of only a few books written by a professional athlete without the assistance of a professional writer and in some circles it is acclaimed as a classic sports book. At the time he was collecting material, Bradley did not intend his writings to be published. "I was an inveterate diarist," he insists, "an inveterate note taker. This occurs out of personal need. I kept a very detailed notebook about people I met and things I encountered. This was the raw material for what in 1976 became *Life on the Run*."

In his book Bradley talks about athletes in general and what he believes is the mental gymnastics that many athletes experience:

> The athletes who succeed in making college teams have the high school experience duplicated on a grander scale. The few who excel on university teams find that

admiration comes then, not from high school friends and adult family friends, but from the national press and from adults they have never met. They begin to see that they can make a good living simply by playing the sport. Self-definition again comes from external sources, not from within. While their physical skill lasts, professional athletes are celebrities—fondled and excused, praised and believed. Only toward the end of their careers do the stars realize that their sense of identity is insufficient.

The above quotation to some degree describes the inner thoughts of the author himself. In 1977, when Bradley retired from the Knicks at the age of thirty-three, he found a whole new identity. It was not enough for him to be simply another ex-jock who would spend the rest of his life reliving the memories of his youth.

To the ex-Knick there is a strong and inseparable bond that exists between a beautiful girl and the pampered athlete. "There is a fleeting aspect of a woman's beauty and one's athletic superiority," he observes. "Both are subject to a dangerous vanity. Both are given credit only for their physical attributes and receive inordinate prizes for them. They are told they are something special, Miss America and the All-American, without understanding what qualities beyond the superficialities of face and body hold importance in life.

"In a matter of time, these attributes change inextricably, and to base your identity on that which is fleeting means continually yearning for what was past as opposed to building on what could be in the future. If you are either beautiful or athletic, you may be pleased and proud about it, but at the same time there must be some basis for more substance to provide inner direction. If not, you will become trapped and forever live in the period when you were once beautiful or athletic. Even if you're an athlete with a professional career, it's a relatively short period, say ten years maximum, before it ends. That's one third of your life, and there still remains two thirds of your life to live. So just on the numbers there has to be more than simply what your body can give you at a particular age."

For a brief time Bradley considered running for state treasurer in Missouri. But then he concluded that Ernestine Schlant, his wife of three years, a German-born professor of literature at Montclair State College in New Jersey, and their newly born daughter, Theresa Anne, should remain in the Garden State. Ten months after retiring from basketball he met with a roomful of reporters in a small makeshift office in Union, New Jersey, and announced he had thrown his hat in the Democratic primary for the New Jersey U.S. Senate seat held by Republican Clifford P. Case. Even though he didn't receive the endorsement of the Democratic party or Governor Brendan Byrne, Bradley won the primary on June 6, 1978, with 61 percent of the vote in a three-way race.

In the meantime Case, who had been in the Senate since 1955, lost the Republican primary to Jeffrey Bell, a candidate also seeking public office for the first time. Bell's credentials were impressive, although mostly academic; he was a Kennedy Fellow at Harvard and an adviser to Ronald Reagan. Because Bell was seen as a conservative intellectual, his entry into the campaign was viewed by some political observers as a test in a major urbanized state of the appeal of presidential contender Reagan's controversial economic program. Because Bradley was labeled a liberal, the race received national attention with both candidates getting considerable out-of-state support. In addition to Democratic leaders backing Bradley, many sports and entertainment celebrities supported his campaign by making personal appearances at fund-raising affairs. Among his Hollywood supporters were such notables as Robert Redford, Robin Williams, Bill Cosby, Goldie Hawn, and Sally Field.

Of the two candidates Bradley was by far the better known, while Bell was definitely the better public speaker. In spite of being 20 points ahead in the polls at the time of the primary, Bradley ignored the advice of his political consultant, Michael Kaye, and his campaign manager, Susan Thomases, and agreed to debate his opponent. His staff argued that Bradley had more to lose and, in particular, he should not share his personal fame with the relatively unknown Bell. Nonetheless, Bradley and Bell engaged in a series of debates—twenty-three in total throughout the state of New Jersey.

Bell came across as a one-issue man who focused only on the "taxpayer's revolt." Bradley favored a tax cut and a strong defense policy, but his far-reaching liberal program also supported increased federal aid to schools, passage of the Equal Rights Amendment, free choice of abortion, and a strong energy policy that also emphasized protection of the environment. On November 7, 1978, Bradley won his first election for public office. He amassed 56 percent of the ballots cast, giving him a margin of more than 220,000 votes. On January 15, 1979, he was sworn in and, at thirty-nine, became the youngest member of the United States Senate.

A fierce competitor, Bradley explains that winning his first election was quite different from winning a world championship in basketball. "When we won the NBA title," he tells, "it meant that we were the best in the world. There was no dispute. Your face aches from smiling for about forty-eight hours, and then it is over. You have been at the top of the mountain and nobody can deny that you were there. But when you win an election, it means you won the right to serve— there is no thought about being the best in the world. The election victory simply means you have gotten over one hurdle that permits you to go to the next level of service to people. Therefore it's more like an entry, while a championship season is the pinnacle."

In the political arena one is likely to witness more name-calling and mudslinging than in the sports arena. After spending twenty-plus years on the basketball courts, Bradley doesn't think there's a place for unsportsmanlike conduct in either arena. He comments: "Being a fierce competitor and being civil are not mutually exclusive. You can be a fierce competitor and, sure, you can go at it and want to win more than anybody else. When it's over, however, you did your best, and your opponent is not evil. Your opponent was just your opponent."

Now in his third term in the U.S. Senate, Dollar Bill has yet to be defeated at the polls, although he regularly experienced defeat as well as victory throughout his long career in sports. "The taste of defeat has a richness of experience all its own," he claims. "Each of us must come to terms with a loss because in each life there will surely be setbacks. Defeat teaches perseverance and perspective. In basketball, it provides a self-awareness about how much you are a part of a group as opposed to your individual effort. For instance, you might be the one to miss the last shot, but the game might have been decided earlier. . . . And then there's another lesson, one that teaches how life goes on. The continuity of life is not one particular moment or contest but how you perform over a period of time."

Bradley also sees an analogy between the pressure that both an athlete and a politician must endure: "Sure, any type of pressure is pressure, whether it's on the foul line in front of a packed field house or it's in the subcommittee. I can draw a definite parallel between a campaign and a basketball season. Both have a certain emotional level, and there are many ups and downs along the way. There is also the media to encounter in both. Each has a game plan that must be executed, and if it fails, you must take a hard look at what happened and analyze what went wrong. Then you must make sure to go to work every day and continue to do the job. This is the way you improve—and grow. A pattern is definitely set in athletics, and it has carried over to my career as a senator."

Once in Washington the freshman senator understood that

there would be some skepticism among his new colleagues in the Senate due to his celebrity status. The same thing happened when he broke into the NBA; again he had to prove himself. During his first months on the job, the former Princeton-Oxford student did his homework well. He spent much of his time learning the ropes; he painstakingly studied the basic issues and relentlessly boned up on minute details. A "facts junkie," Bradley is known now for intensively collecting detailed information before he makes a decision. He was determined to uncover what it took to be an exceptional senator.

"The message came back that there are two types of freshman senators," he reports; "Workhorses and show horses." On the court he was never a hot dog; likewise, it was not Bill Bradley's style to be a show horse. As one staff member who has spent years in Capitol political circles comments: "He has the smallest ego of any elected official I have ever known."

Bradley credits his many years as part of a basketball team—the Crystal City Hornets, the Princeton Tigers, and the New York Knickerbockers—with his ability to work effectively in his present job. "There is a clear transfer," he tells, "where the essence of basketball and legislation is working with people. There is a bringing together of people who have different backgrounds and different personal agenda and getting them to agree on a common objective and then working toward it. In basketball, as a player, you must not hog the ball, nor must you hog the press, and you must give credit where it is due. Well, the same thing applies today. You must recognize that when everyone is working together, the results will be superior to the effort by a single individual. A basketball team is like a five-pointed star. It must function like the Budapest String Quartet, which must play together in complete harmony in order to mesh. Teamwork works essentially the same in many walks of life."

Bradley has won the respect of his fellow senators. He has crusaded to protect New Jersey's environment, stressing that

New Jerseyans have a right to a clean environment which he believes is as important as their right to good health, good schools, and good jobs. Since entering the Senate he has fought repeatedly on behalf of children, pregnant women, parents, and students. He has been active in seeking health-care improvements, expanding Medicare help for the elderly, and fashioning respite-care legislation to relieve the heavy burden on those who care for the infirm. Bradley has continually demonstrated his strong interest in domestic and international trade and finance.

Beginning in 1980 he tackled the tax-reform system. He is now recognized as the prime architect of the 1986 tax-reform code that closed unfair loopholes and took millions of poor Americans off the tax rolls. A book he wrote in 1984 titled *The Fair Tax* is said to have sparked the national movement to reform tax laws.

On October 24, 1990, the U.S. Senate passed the Student Right to Know Act, a bill Bradley had introduced two and a half years previously. This legislation requires colleges and universities that receive federal assistance to publish the graduation rates of their students. The NCAA overwhelmingly adopted requirements modeled on the new law. Bradley claims this right-to-know bill is one of the few things he has done as a senator that is directly related to athletics. "I did it," he explains, "because I felt it is important for families to at least know what schools were going to take their children's education seriously and which ones were going to use them—and then discard them." A study researching the bill revealed that in two thirds of the surveyed schools, fewer than 40 percent of the men's basketball players received diplomas; the figures for football were only slightly better. "Now parents have a chance to make a judgment about which colleges are truly interested in their sons and daughters and others that want to exploit them."

As the father of a teenage daughter, the Senator has a vested interest in the welfare of America's youth. The Bradley family maintains two residences—one in Denville, New Jersey, and the other in Washington, D.C. Ernestine teaches comparative literature at Montclair State College on Monday through Thursday afternoons and commutes by train to the Capitol for long weekends. When Theresa Ann was eight years old, the family decided that she would live in Washington with her father. Each morning the two have breakfast, a time together which, in Ernestine's words, is "sacred." Bradley makes no appointments until 8:15 A.M.; by then, he has dropped Theresa Ann at school and arrived at his office in the Hart Senate office building. Although the split family arrangement has some inconveniences, it appears to be working and has created a close father-daughter relationship, something not all that common in the Washington political scene. The father and daughter enjoy running together at a nearby track. "She can outrun Bill," Ernestine says with pride.

Raising Theresa Ann during the week requires Bradley to juggle his hectic schedule around her and also provide time for weekends when he and Ernestine are together. But then managing his time effectively is nothing new to him; in part it's a carryover from his student basketball days. "When you play sports in an academic environment," he says, "you have to be able to manage your time if you want to do well in the classroom. As a professional, you have your job of playing, which is three to four hours each day, and there's the rest of the day. Being able to use that time effectively requires some discipline to properly manage it. In this area my experience as an athlete has been helpful in the way I structure my schedule today."

With few exceptions the senator brings home a full briefcase each night; while the daughter is occupied with her homework, so does the father do his. Those who work with Bradley marvel at his capacity and willingness to exhaustively prepare himself in advance, leaving no stone unturned and nothing to chance. He tells about a conversation he once had with the treasurer of the Liberal Democratic party in Japan: " 'Who is the best speaker in the Japanese Diet?' I asked, and he replied, 'The worst politician.'

"What most people see in the legislative process is the speech on the floor," the senator explains, "and that's the end process. But what went into that before is enormous. You have to spend time to know your subject. You have to research your particular topic, write the legislation, do the hearings, make changes, pass it out of the committee, deal with the assaults and challenges on the floor, get the bill passed in the Senate, and then it has to be passed in the House. After all of that the whole thing has to be reconciled in a conference committee, and then it goes to the President for a law. Needless to say, preparation is essential. If you are not prepared, nobody listens to you."

People do listen to Bill Bradley. If he has one handicap, it's that he is not a gifted speaker. In an age when people tend to prefer the candidate who delivers the best speech to the one with the most substance, the Senator from New Jersey may be vulnerable. At present he has a reputation as a sleep-inducing orator and has been called such names as "Senator Sominex" and "Boring Bill."

But the record shows that anything he does, he does well; in time it's likely that his speech-making will get better. In fact there are already some signs of improvement. For instance, at a 1987 fund-raising Democratic roast at which he was the guest of honor, Bradley survived an onslaught of good-natured jibes, and when his turn to speak finally came, he exhibited a new dimension of his personality that took his black-tie audience by surprise.

To 1988 presidential candidate Bruce Babbitt, he remarked, "Bruce, God love you, the only time I have charisma is when I'm standing next to you." He waited for the laughs to die down, and then, looking at the man who eventually won the Democratic nomination, Bradley said, "Does anybody *care* if

Mike Dukakis's idea of a good time is straightening out his sock drawer?"

There was more laughter, but the line that really brought the house down was this one: "Well, how *should* we Democrats select the next presidential nominee? Smoke-filled room? Brokered convention? National primary?" He paused and added drily, "Personally, I favor a jump shot from the top of the key."

In a later speech Bradley delivered at Middlebury College on May 28, 1989, he challenged his audience: "America should have a big ambition. So why not a big ambition? Why not every person in America—healthy and educated, an athlete of body and Aristotle of mind?"

Bill Bradley is perhaps the ideal role model for anyone with such a worthy goal.

3

▪ BOBBY BROWN ▪

Baseball Player, Cardiologist, President of the American League of Professional Baseball Clubs

Long before basketball had Dr. J, baseball had Dr. Bobby Brown, a medical student who became a cardiologist while playing third base for the New York Yankees between 1946 and 1954.

While it's never an easy matter to become a physician, Bobby Brown received his M.D. the hard way. He attended medical school and interned during the off-seasons because he played major league baseball beginning in early April and ending in September; during this period 154 regular season games were scheduled. In the case of the Yankees, more often than not additional World Series games had to be added at the end of the season.

When Brown played, baseball was enjoying its finest years. The country had not yet been mesmerized by watching television; the game of baseball was unchallenged as America's favorite pastime. In this era the Yankees dominated the sport. They seemed invincible, and for a while it looked like they owned a franchise on the World Series. Between 1947 and 1953 New York played in six World Series and won all of them. Among the Yankee greats during Brown's era were Joe DiMaggio, Yogi Berra, Mickey Mantle, Phil Rizzuto, Allie Reynolds,

Ed Lopat, Vic Raschi, Tommy Henrich, Whitey Ford, and manager Casey Stengel.

Bobby Brown's story is certainly one of the most interesting in the annals of the sport. He became Dr. Bobby Brown while playing professional baseball, a Herculean task considering the sport's long season. After practicing cardiology for twenty-six years, he returned to baseball as president of the American League.

Bobby was a good all-around athlete during his early boyhood. Encouraged by his father, William, he decided to concentrate only on baseball upon entering the ninth grade. "My dad excelled at sports, and he was good enough to play major league baseball," Brown explains, "but in those days, he could make more money working and playing semi-pro baseball. He loved the sport, and when I showed some interest in the game, like many fathers he relived his youth through mine."

William Brown, a native of Newark, New Jersey, met his wife during the first World War while stationed at Fort Lewis, Washington. The couple had settled in Seattle, where they raised three children. In 1936, when Bobby was eleven years old, the family migrated to the East Coast when his father, an insurance executive, accepted a position with the state of New Jersey.

Bobby Brown tried out for the baseball team as a sophomore at Columbia High School in Maplewood, New Jersey. William Brown was overjoyed. His joy was short-lived, however—the coach confided to him that his son wasn't likely to make the team. "About the same time, my father had a job offer in San Francisco," Brown tells, "and my not making the school team was what finally prompted him to move the family to the West Coast. He was determined I'd be a star baseball player, and by living in California, he figured I'd be able to play ball year round." A faint smile appears on Brown's face when he adds, "As it turned out, I was the first student in the history of Columbia High School to play in the big leagues. Later one of

the other fellows on the team that I didn't make as a sophomore also made it to the majors."

In San Francisco Bobby attended Galileo High School, a
school with a reputation for producing outstanding athletes.
Its graduates include professional baseball players Joe DiMaggio and younger brother Dom DiMaggio, Dario Lodigianni,
Dino Restelli, and Gino Cimoli. Other great athletes to come
from Galileo are Olympic swimmer Ann Curtis, professional
golfer Lawson Little, basketball player Hank Luisetti, and
football star O. J. Simpson.

Bobby's baseball improved during his first summer in California. Not only did he make the 1941 Galileo baseball team as
a junior—he was a star. The new kid in school started at
shortstop and led the league with a .583 batting average. The
following season he was the team's captain and batted .360.
Galileo's baseball team won the city championship both years.

Reminiscing about his two years of high school baseball,
Brown explains the 223 point drop in his batting average.
"While I am sure I improved as a player between my junior and
senior years—I was playing a lot of baseball and, at that age,
a player is bound to get better—anything can happen in a
short season. We only played fourteen games, so it sometimes
happens when a player has a hot streak. Likewise you can have
a cold streak and have a low average. The nature of the game
is that the balls don't always fall or bounce the right way."

Bobby was the student body president in addition to being
the captain of the baseball team. In short, he was a popular
athlete as well as an excellent student. This meant there would
be many choices of colleges to attend, and additionally he had
baseball offers from a few major-league baseball teams to mull
over, including one from the Yankees.

"There was no question in my mind that I'd someday play in
the majors," Brown declares. "It was never a side thought. It
was a major issue and something I always intended to strive
for. My parents shared my enthusiasm for baseball, but they

never had the slightest doubt that I'd first become a college graduate. Although neither of them attended college, they understood the value of a good education. It was always a priority over playing ball in our family."

Baseball's minor-league system was more pronounced in the 1940s than at present, and this worked to Bobby's advantage even as a high school player. "I'd guess as many as sixty to ninety players who played in the minors came home to San Francisco in the winter," he recalls. "On weekends I'd be able to get in a pickup game in the park with some adults that included four or five of those minor league guys. By playing with them, and especially going up against some of those pitchers who later made it to the majors, I realized that I had a chance to compete on their level. This, of course, encouraged me to chase after my dream of someday being a major leaguer."

Brown's brother Billy, younger by two years, was also a fine athlete who was good enough to play college baseball for four years. "My kid sister Beverley probably had as much athletic talent as anyone in the family," Bobby tells, "but in those days girls didn't have many opportunities in sports." William Brown was a big supporter of his oldest son, the family's most heralded athlete, but when Bobby Brown is asked to comment on his father's obvious pride, he says only, "I think he was proud of everybody in the family."

In the autumn of 1942 Brown enrolled at nearby Stanford University to study chemical engineering. Stanford offered student athletes "grants-in-aid" based on economic need. "I didn't qualify for a grant-in-aid," Brown remembers, "but the coach helped me with my tuition and I waited tables for my meals." About a month after starting college, he transferred to pre-medicine. "Chemistry was too dry," he remarks, "and that's what prompted the switch."

On October 25, 1942, Brown's eighteenth birthday, he enlisted in the navy while continuing his studies at Stanford. He played on the school's varsity baseball team during the spring of 1943 as a freshman and had a .460 batting average. "Just another lucky hot streak," he insists. Although he played only a single season, he was voted a member of Stanford's Athletic Hall of Fame years later.

On July 1, 1943, he was put on active duty and sent to UCLA, where he continued to study pre-medicine and play baseball. "I was in the Navy's V-12 program," he explains. "The Navy put a lot of the enlisted college kids into it—a program equivalent to officer's training school. It was similar to being at the Naval Academy in Annapolis. I dressed in a sailor's uniform to classes, and with the country in the middle of World War II, it was an honor to wear a navy uniform. The majority of the guys in the V-12 program were studying engineering, and upon graduating they became ensigns in the Navy."

During the 1944 baseball season at UCLA, Bobby batted .444. The team played in the coast conference and also another league in southern California. UCLA won both championships. Years later Brown was named to UCLA's Athletic and Baseball Halls of Fame.

It took him three semesters at UCLA to finish his pre-med studies, and in December 1944 he enrolled in medical school at Tulane in New Orleans. Although he was a medical student, Brown played on Tulane's baseball team, hitting slightly under .500 for the 1945 season, a batting average which later won him a place in the Tulane Hall of Fame. He continued his studies throughout the war, which ended in August 1945, and in January 1946 the navy discharged him. By this time he had two years of medical school under his belt—and an offer from the New York Yankees.

"I worked out an arrangement with Tulane whereby I was able to enroll in classes after baseball season," Brown recalls. "This was possible because the school's academic year was broken up into six-week rotations. But while it took me two

years to complete my first two years of medical school as a
full-time student, I went four years part-time to finish the last
two years."

When he signed with the Yankees Brown received a bonus
of $52,000 to be paid over a three-year period. At the time it
was the second-largest bonus ever paid to a young player. The
Yankees sent him to their farm team, the Newark Bears, and
there too the medical school student proved his proficiency at
the plate. He led the league with total number of hits—179,
and his batting average of .341 was second only to Montreal's
Jackie Robinson, who batted .349.

Brown was voted New Jersey Athlete of the Year in 1946.
With two weeks to go in the season, the Yankees brought up
four players from the minors—pitcher Vic Raschi, outfielder
Frank Coleman, shortstop Bobby Brown, and his roommate in
Newark, catcher Yogi Berra.

Traditionally the seasoned players dish out a lot of razzing
to their rookie teammates. This was particularly true of the
New York ball club, the game's most famous team. Right from
the start there were several strikes against Bobby Brown.

Some teammates resented his big bonus, which meant he'd
receive a paycheck as a rookie equal to those of veteran players
who had played for five or six years. To the older players the
young medical student seemed straitlaced; Brown didn't
smoke, drink, or chase women. What's more, he was competing with Billy Johnson, a popular player six years his senior.
And, unlike the majority of baseball players, Brown was a
college man. In the 1940s few graduated and fewer went
beyond high school. Less than one in five major league baseball players had ever been in a college classroom.

Although Larry MacPhail, one of the owners of the Yankees,
had good intentions, it proved to be an embarrassing moment
when he proudly introduced his new player at a press conference. MacPhail told a group of hard-nosed reporters about the
fine young man who would be wearing the famed pinstriped

uniform, boasting about the young man's accomplishments not only as a hitter but as a future brilliant doctor. His eloquence prompted one of the reporters to ask, "What are you doing, Larry? Are you hiring a player or a doctor?"

Brown took the razzing, including being christened with the nickname "Quack" by his teammates, in stride. "That year I started in the spring at Tulane and ended up with the Yankees," he says, "which I thought was pretty good." When his rookie season ended in the autumn of 1946, Brown headed back to New Orleans to continue studying medicine. He maintained this hectic year-round schedule for four years. In 1950 he received his degree in medicine.

It was only a matter of time before Brown was accepted by his teammates as one of the boys. They liked him because he didn't try to impress people with his education. But then, with his modest and soft-spoken manner, it would be difficult for anyone not to like him. Above all, he was a fine hitter and a dedicated baseball player—and this they respected.

They also admired his discipline—on and off the field. It was a common sight to see him studying a book when there was time to spare between games. His good friend Yogi Berra comments: "He always had a medical book in his hand. We'd sit in a compartment together [baseball teams commonly traveled by rail before the league's expansion to the West Coast in 1958], and I'd be reading comic books and he'd be reading medical books. Every so often he'd finish one, and I'd say, 'How'd it come out?'

"He wasn't a very funny guy, but he was wonderful to be around," Berra continues; "one of those genuinely nice people you just like to spend time with. Still, at the ballpark, he'd have his medical books with him, and he'd have the team physician give him tests." Berra pauses for a moment and adds, "Bobby was the only person who called me by my proper name, Lawrence."

Brown is equally fond of Yogi Berra. "He was a tremendously

talented baseball player," he tells, "and one of the game's most colorful people. Yogi is a warm human being and is naturally funny. He didn't have much of an education, and as a result he made mistakes in his grammar, which made people laugh— and some of what he said still makes people laugh. Some of his comments were very witty, and he intended for them to be funny.

"Some of his quotes have since become famous. Perhaps the most quoted Yogiism is 'It ain't over till it's over.' It was also Yogi who said, 'You can observe a lot just by watching,' 'If people don't want to come out to the ball park, nobody's going stop them,' and 'Toot Shor's restaurant is so crowded nobody goes there anymore.' There's certainly nothing wrong with the way Yogi's brain works. It works exceedingly well. He has been very successful in most everything he has ever done."

When asked about his studying during the baseball season, Brown replies: "All my life I had been used to playing baseball and studying. I did it all the way through high school and college, so it was something I was quite used to doing. It was part of my life.

"One of the things you learn very early as a student-athlete is that you must pay your dues," Brown continues. "Nothing comes easy, particularly when you're at a highly ranked college or happen to be going to medical school. It's essential to put in long hours because once you get behind it's very difficult to catch up. So every day you have to stay in the swim and exert your best effort. Then, if you continue to play in professional sports, there are always many people trying to take your place. Again, it's the same brand of daily application that keeps you there. If you don't pay the price, you're going to be shunted aside.

"Sure, there are always a few who are gifted with outstanding ability. These are the great students who don't have to work as hard, and there are a few great athletes too. But for the majority of people in competitive colleges, medical school, and professional sports, there is no substitute for just plain hard work. That's what gets you there, and that's what keeps you there!

"Of course it helps to be a good time manager," Brown adds. "When I enrolled at Stanford I had to allocate my time so I could study and play ball, and the same was true when I was in medical school. I simply didn't have one or two hours each day to fritter away. Instead I had to make every minute count. When I was in med school, every day I worked out at baseball. I spent an hour a day playing ball—even when I had nobody to play with. I was running, throwing, and swinging a bat. I was determined to stay in shape.

"People have asked me, 'How did you find the time?' I was able to find an extra hour during those times when the other students were taking naps, talking to their girlfriends, or just shooting the bull. That extra hour was always there—it was just a matter of applying enough discipline to take advantage of it. And the same applies to playing in the major leagues and studying medicine on the side. Of course once the season is underway there's one thing a baseball player has plenty of, and that's time."

Although he had always played shortstop before, when Brown joined the Yankees he was put at third base. "Going from short to third was not that big a problem," he explains. "While I was a fairly good hitter, I wasn't good enough at shortstop to play it for a major-league pennant contender. Shortstop is the most important position on a team, and Phil Rizzuto played the position as well as it could be played. At first I was used as a pinch hitter, substituting at third and second, and on occasion I'd relieve Rizzuto."

It took a bit of adjusting for Brown to be put in a non-starting role. Since tenth grade he had always been the star of every team he played on. "At first, it was terribly discouraging," he admits. "But then it's not unusual for anyone who gets to the big leagues to have always been the best player on any previous team. It was a terrific adjustment for me, and difficult to accept.

"I was determined to become good enough, however, and to improve I'd bring my younger brother to the ballpark with me. He was an excellent batting practice pitcher, so I'd hit for an hour with him and then practice my fielding for another hour before anyone from the team showed up. Although I never had much coaching for my hitting since I was a kid when my father worked with me, I learned a lot from Frank Crosetti, the Yankees infield coach. He'd preach that a ballplayer has to develop the right habits. 'Once you've got the right habits,' Crosetti would say, 'in the game, they'll be instincts.' He was right."

During the spring of 1947 a pitch by the Boston Red Sox's pitching ace, Mel Parnell, broke Brown's finger and sidelined him for a month. Prior to his injury Brown had been platooning at third base for the Yankees, but upon his recovery he was used as a pinch hitter and utility infielder. "A month later, when my finger was healed," he recounts, "the team was on a winning streak, so after my injury I didn't get a chance to play regularly. After having been in the starting lineup and sitting on the bench, just pinch hitting and playing when someone was hurt was awful."

While he was an adequate fielder, Bobby Brown earned a reputation as one of the best clutch hitters in the game. He was the one guy on the bench whom the Yankees liked to use when the pressure was on. In 1947, his first full year in the majors, Brown set a World Series record when he had three pinch hits. It was a pressure series that went down to the wire with the Yankees beating the Brooklyn Dodgers in seven games. Playing as a regular, Brown ripped a triple to right field in the fourth game of the 1949 World Series, scoring Tommy Henrich, Yogi Berra, and Joe DiMaggio. The Yankees won the game by a score of 6 to 4 and beat the Dodgers in five games. Brown's two triples in the five-game series set a World Series record.

To this date Bobby Brown has the highest batting average in the history of World Series baseball for any player with forty or more times at bat. His series average is .439. Among the top twenty players in this category are Lou Brock (.391), George Brett (.373), Lou Gehrig (.361), Reggie Jackson (.357), and Carl Yastrzemski (.352). In the 1949 World Series Brown batted .500 and now shares a record for the highest batting average in a five-game World Series.

During the 1940s and 1950s there were no designated hitters, and a pinch hitter, then as well as now, cannot be put into the game a second time. "Pinch hitting is a difficult job," Brown points out, "because you come off the bench cold, and you haven't had a chance to see any pitching." Brown claims that it was his compact swing that enabled him to make contact with the ball and have relatively few strikeouts.

Undoubtedly Brown's mental attitude was also a contributing factor to his batting success. After all, baseball is a sport in which even the very best hitters fail many more times than they succeed. A player with a .300 average, for instance, will only reach first base three out of every ten times at bat. Just the same he must believe that he will succeed in getting a hit each time at bat. If not, his negative thinking will begin to work against him.

"You must believe you are going to get a hit each time you're up at bat, or you will not," Brown emphasizes. "Baseball is different from other sports because the best players fail seven times out of ten when it comes to batting, and they succeed more than nine times out of ten in catching the ball. So with the batting, you've got to be able to accept the bad times. Those players who cannot don't last long in the game.

"Similarly, in baseball you cannot be king every day," Brown continues. "Somebody gets the best of you a fair num-

ber of times, and psychologically you must be able to with-
stand it. This is especially true when you play for a team like
the New York Yankees. When you fail in Yankee Stadium, it is
very likely that the barber in Tacoma, Washington, knows
about it.

"There is nothing like the highs and lows of professional
sports," Brown adds. "This is particularly true when you play
on a championship team. When you do something extraordi-
narily well during a big game, there's nothing like the eupho-
ria that occurs. Likewise, when you fail under the same circumstance the depression is unmatched. Over the course of
time every athlete succeeds and fails, so I think the trick is to
not be too euphoric when you do well and not be too de-
pressed when you do poorly. You have to try to get that
psychological balance to keep yourself on an even keel."

Just as medical school occupied Brown full-time during the
off-seasons of 1946 through 1950, so did his internships at
Southern Pacific Hospital in San Francisco for the next two
years. In a period when medical interns were compensated $50
to $100 a month and frequently worked eighty to a hundred
hours a week, Brown had an income from baseball comparable
to the salaries of deans in medical schools. "The other interns
thought I was a wealthy guy," Brown acknowledges. His highest annual paycheck during his career as a baseball player was
$19,500.

In 1952 Brown served as a First Lieutenant in the U.S. Army
Medical Corps during the Korean conflict. He was a battalion
aid surgeon with the 160th Field Artillery, 45th Division, in
Korea and was later stationed at an army hospital in Tokyo
where he was used in orthopedics. "While these medical
experiences were good," he explains, "they didn't help me in
what I wanted to eventually do as a doctor."

He returned to the Yankees in 1954 but had not played
baseball for more than twenty months. "I interned during the
off-seasons in 1951 and 1952," he tells, "and was going on

thirty, and I still had not started my residency. I continued to play ball for a couple of months but then I started thinking about my age, and I knew I had other things to do with my life. I was worried that I was getting further and further behind in my medical career.

"I thought that if I postponed going into medicine full time for another three or four years, I'd almost have to start all over again, and I didn't want to do that. I hated to quit baseball, but on July 1, 1954, I decided to devote my full time to my medical career. I had a love for both [careers], but right from day one I knew there'd eventually be a time when I would have to devote 100 percent of my time to medicine."

Baseball experts believe that Brown could have continued playing for a few more years. However, once he made the decision to retire as a Yankee he never returned as a player. His lifetime batting average was .279, which today would place him among baseball's top hitters. "My real regret about my playing days," he says, "was that medical school and interning between seasons caused me to miss a lot of spring training. As a result my playing suffered."

Immediately following his departure from baseball, Brown did a three-year residency in internal medicine at San Francisco County Hospital. During his final year he was chief resident. In 1957-58 he had a fellowship in cardiology at Tulane Medical School.

Brown was a medical student at Tulane in 1947 when he met Albert Goggans, a young resident at the time. "We were great friends," Brown tells. "He went to Fort Worth to practice cardiology, and in August 1958 I joined him in what became a six-person group cardiology practice." Brown practiced cardiology for the next twenty-six years in Fort Worth.

Working so hard as a baseball player and doctor for eight years had molded the character of Dr. Bobby Brown. "I suppose I was used to working hard," he comments, "and the idea of putting in long hours became acceptable to me. It became a

way of life, and I fully understood that hard work was necessary to accomplish my goals."

Brown ponders for a moment and adds, "Something else that
definitely carries over from baseball to medicine is the fact
that you can't become discouraged when things are going
badly. You can never give up until it's over—just like Yogi said,
'It ain't over till it's over.' There are many times in medicine
when a situation looks utterly hopeless and you would like to
throw up your hands and toss in the towel, but you can't do
that.

"No matter how hopeless the odds appear, you make every
effort and keep working as hard as you can to stay with it.
You've got to tough it out and keep battling, and, if you do
that, every once in a while you are going to get a miracle. You
begin to see things turn and somebody fools you because he or
she starts to respond. Somebody will pull through who you
didn't think could. And when that happens it's like winning a
World Series game. That's what keeps doctors going."

Brown believes baseball and cardiology both offered him a
basis for developing self-confidence. "When you do something
successfully over a period of time," he insists, "you begin to
believe that you can do it. In this sense I think confidence
stems from previous success. Of course it gets back to what I
said about hard work. When you work hard at something, you
increase your chances of doing it well."

Brown did not perform surgery as a cardiologist. Instead he
was on the medical end of fighting heart disease. His patients
were those who had suffered heart attacks and heart failure
and problems such as malfunctioning heart valves and heart
muscles. In lieu of surgery, medicines and machines were used
to correct disorders. Cardiology is considered a pressure specialty because it deals with acute medical emergencies that
often involve life-and-death situations. The ex-Yankee clutch
hitter worked well under such pressure.

Former teammates and sportswriters described Brown as an

intense player. When he was brought into a game during a crucial situation, he performed well. Likewise he had the same capacity as a cardiologist. To some degree he attributes his performance under pressure to having an acute sense of concentration. "In the last inning of a tight game," he explains, "with 60,000-plus fans screaming as well as the opposing team's players trying to distract you, you've got to block everything out and do what you're supposed to do—and that's get a hit. The same is true during certain moments in the practice of medicine. You must keep your concentration and do what you know must be done when everything around you is going to pot."

Like a baseball player, a physician must be a team player. Brown explains, "There are many cases in medicine when a teamwork effort requires several doctors to work together. For instance, a case might involve the joint efforts of an internist, a cardiologist, a surgeon, and an anesthesiologist. Each member of the team is responsible to do certain things. Each must do his or her part and, in turn, rely on the others to do theirs. Although certain doctors, like certain athletes, have big egos, they have to realize that they can't always be the star. There are times when a physician must realize that his or her role is not the lead role. It becomes very difficult to deal with a doctor who isn't willing to accept a lesser role because his or her ego gets in the way.

"During the time I played with the Yankees we had some great stars, some of whom are now in the Hall of Fame. Yet there was never one of those players who didn't put the fate of the team above anything he did individually. That went for Joe DiMaggio and Mickey Mantle, right down the line. Everyone did what needed to be done to win the game. You did what was good for the team, not what might help your individual average or increase your image with the fans. As a team player each of us recognized that his contribution to the ultimate result was measured on how it affected the final result—a win for the team. Similarly, when you're a member of a team of doctors, you realize that you have a role to perform, and sometimes it's a supporting role."

Brown was known for an exhaustive dedication to patients during his twenty-six years as a cardiologist in Fort Worth. Doctors who knew him well say that the same compulsion that made him a good baseball player and enabled him to finish medical school remained with him as a physician. One colleague says that Brown didn't know how to relax, and, "even when he wasn't on call, he was calling in all the time." Dr. Goggans says, "When a patient of his died he'd take it very personally. Those of us who knew him for many years could see his practice getting to him."

Dr. Brown and his wife, Sara, had been married in 1951. During the years they lived in Fort Worth and raised three children, his practice occupied the majority of his time. He distanced himself from baseball, rarely watching a game on television, and only took in three or four games a year. "But I did keep in touch with my friends in the game," Brown maintains.

He took up tennis to keep in shape and manages to play three to four times a week. "I play singles and doubles," he says, "and I play at a competitive level so that I get a good workout." He is aware of the importance of physical exercise, and he advises, "pick something like I did that you enjoy so it's not a chore. I look forward to playing tennis, and this, I believe, is the secret of a good conditioning program. If you do something like tennis or swimming, handball and bicycling, for example, you don't have to force yourself into it, and exercising becomes relatively easy."

While Brown put in a full day's work as a cardiologist, he has always made himself available to the community. He is past president of the Tarrant County Heart Association as well as the Tarrant County All Sports Association. He is also a past chairman of the Fort Worth Park and Recreation Board. "Because of my background," he explains, "I felt as though I had something different to offer, and I tried to do my best to improve the parks and recreation system in the Forth Worth area." Additionally, Brown has served as a member of the board of directors of First United Bancorp, First National Bank of Fort Worth, and InterFirst Bank of Fort Worth. Currently he serves on the board of the Amon G. Carter Foundation in Fort Worth.

With his varied background in sports, cardiology, community affairs, and business, Brown was asked in 1974 to serve as interim president of the Texas Rangers Baseball Team. Brad Corbett, a Fort Worth businessman, had purchased the new major-league expansion team in the Dallas-Fort Worth area and thought Brown would be the ideal person to head the organization. Corbett's choice was based on Brown's intelligence and knowledge of the game. Brown was also well connected in the business community.

"Corbett bought the Rangers as an investment, but he didn't know much about running the team," Brown explains. "He asked me if I'd be willing to take a leave of absence from my medical practice for a while until things got settled. I agreed to do it for six months, and then I'd go back to cardiology but be available when he needed me." The Dallas-Fort Worth area was one of the nation's largest metropolitan areas without a major-league baseball team, so Brown's involvement was also a service for the community.

Brown served as president of the newly formed Rangers from May through October in 1974. Corbett credits Brown with the team's smooth startup. "For a new club, we had a good year," the team's owner recalls. "He instinctively knew how to run the team. I was absolutely sorry to see him go." Brown remained on the board of directors after returning to his practice until Corbett sold the Rangers in 1977.

While Brown was considered a success as a baseball club president, he says of himself, "I knew I didn't want to leave medicine." He continued to work at his group practice, once again removed from baseball. In 1983 Brown was approaching his sixtieth birthday and had been thinking about the future, when he would no longer want to work the long and tiring hours that his practice demanded. "I figured that I'd have to do something a little different in three or four years," he explains, "because I was getting tired.

"About this time the new owners of the Texas Rangers approached me and asked if I would agree to be interviewed by a search committee seeking a person to succeed Bowie Kuhn as commissioner. I met with the search committee in New York, but they really wanted a businessman for commissioner. As things turned out Peter Ueberroth, the organizer of the 1984 Los Angeles Olympics, got the job. In 1984 Lee Mac-Phail announced his retirement as American League president, and they asked me if I'd be interested in this position, and I took it. The offer came at the right time in my life, and I've really enjoyed it."

In his role at the league's helm, Brown became one of the few top-level executives in baseball who had had major-league playing experience. Former franchise president Brown was viewed by owners and players as a good person to have in New York because he knew things from both sides of the fence.

When asked to describe what he does, Brown replies, "My responsibilities are simple. I'm in charge of the office that runs the season for the fourteen American League teams." In truth the job is not so simple. There are 1,134 American League games scheduled each season, and as president he must deal with the many different personalities and egos of owners, players, and umpires. In addition to collecting league money and working out disciplinary procedures, Brown has succeeded at keeping the league free from crisis and scandal.

He visits each team at least once a year and talks to each owner and manager frequently. "I believe it's important to meet with them on their turf," Brown says, "so I take in a minimum of sixty games a year. I'm never bored at a ball game. It's a tough job, but somebody has to do it," he adds with a smile.

The Browns maintain residences in Fort Worth and Manhattan. As scores of baseball fans have done for years, Brown frequently rides the subway from the city to the Bronx to take in a Yankee game. He claims, however, that in spite of having been a Yankee, as president he cheers for all the American League teams. When asked what pleases him the most about visiting a ballpark, a sparkle appears in his eye and he exclaims: "Looking at all those kids. I love seeing so many young people at the game."

At the age of sixty-six, Dr. Bobby Brown has plans to stay in baseball for two more years, and for good reason. He's one of those rare and fortunate individuals who is still a key player in a game he has loved since his early boyhood.

4

■ ANITA L. DeFRANTZ ■

Olympic Rower, Amateur Athletic Foundation President, Member of the International Olympic Committee

As a young African-American girl, Anita DeFrantz was an unlikely candidate to become an Olympic athlete and in particular a member of the bronze medal-winning U.S. rowing team. After all, she hails from landlocked Indianapolis, Indiana—a place known for producing basketball players, not rowers. Nor for that matter was she likely to someday be considered by many as the most important woman in America in sports—*all sports.*

In fact, at the tender age of eleven she bowed out of sports altogether in what appeared to be a permanent departure. "As a very young girl, I had aspirations to be a great athlete," she tells. "I was only nine when I joined the Frederick Douglass Swimming Pool team. Our team practiced all summer, and still we were not as good as the swimmers from the Rivera Country Club. It was discouraging.

" 'I've been at this for years,' I once told my father, 'and the white swimmers on Rivera's team are so much faster. Why is that, Daddy?'

"My father explained that the difference was how they trained year round and we only had an outdoor swimming pool, so our workouts were limited to the summer months.

79

'That's not fair,' I would protest. My father, of course, knew we were at a disadvantage. But he also knew what was important about sports. I remember how he would never ask me if I won or lost. Instead, he'd ask, 'How do *you* think you did?' 'Were you able to improve your performance?' and 'Do you feel that you accomplished what you wanted to accomplish in the race?' By asking questions of this nature, he taught me to compete against myself. 'That is your best challenge,' he'd say."

Coming from a middle-class background, DeFrantz was fortunate to have two parents who were professionally trained and who emphasized to their three sons and daughter that a proper education should be their number-one priority. Her father, Robert, was a community organizer who was executive director of Community Action Against Poverty; her mother, Anita, was a teacher and is now a professor at the University of San Francisco. When her competitive swimming days ended, the young girl disengaged herself from athletics and focused on her schoolwork.

"Even as a child, I was a realist," she explains. "Back then there were few opportunities for an African-American female in Indianapolis to participate in sports, so I chose to compete in a different arena. I hit the books. About the closest I got to the playing field was being a clarinet player in Shortridge High School's marching band. I also played the bassoon," she adds with a gleam in her eye.

It's not that DeFrantz had no interest in sports. She was tall and she was strong and she had three brothers. She played touch football and also shot baskets with her siblings. While the attractive girl showed potential, she didn't participate in team sports. As a teenager she was a strong swimmer and spent her summers working as a lifeguard. "I remember a conversation with my fellow guards about the young swimmers who were setting world records back in the late 1960s," DeFrantz recounts. "The consensus was that we were already over the hill because by age sixteen we were too old for the Olympics."

In 1970, following her high school graduation, DeFrantz enrolled in Connecticut College, one of the top-ranked academic colleges in the East. "At the time the New London, Connecticut, campus seemed about as far away from Indianapolis as one could go," she says, "and that appealed to me." Only one year previously, fifty-nine years after it was founded in 1911, the school made the transition from an all-women's college, and, as such, athletics were not a top priority on the institution's agenda. Similarly, participation in sports was far down on DeFrantz's list of personal priorities.

She was determined to receive an excellent education. It was *expected* of her. She grew up in an environment where intellectual discourse was encouraged by both parents and grandparents. Her grandfather, Faburn E. DeFrantz, was a director of a YMCA in Indianapolis that packed its lecture hall with the community's youth to hear such African-American literati as author W. E. B. Du Bois and dancer/choreographer Talley Beatty.

Her oldest brother, David, was the first of the children to leave the nest; he attended nearby Indiana University, her parents' alma mater. Anita became the first of her family to select an Eastern college. Later her younger brothers would head in the same direction; James graduated from Dartmouth, and Thomas was educated at Yale. Each of the four DeFrantz children excelled in the classroom.

As a college freshman DeFrantz stood 5'11", her present height. She was a Hoosier and was expected to try out for the women's basketball team. "I thought it would be fun," she admits, "yet while I grew up around basketball in Indiana, there were no coaches available to teach me some of the finer points of the game. My playing had been limited to pickup games in the backyard. I knew little about the sport except what I observed as a spectator cheering for my high school team. At tryouts I was totally confused when the coach said, 'Anita, take the high post.' Not having the slightest idea what that meant, I looked around for an open spot on the floor and headed to the post under the basket." While she did make the varsity basketball team, her career on the court was uneventful.

One crisp autumn morning during her sophomore year DeFrantz was walking across the campus and by chance passed the school's gymnasium. "I noticed this odd-shaped object on the sidewalk," she recalls. "Being curious and having a few moments to spare, I stopped to examine it. 'What in the world . . .' I started to ask a man standing next to it, who happened to be Bart Gulong, the rowing coach.

" 'It's a rowing shell,' Gulong replied.

" 'Rowing? Shell?'

"He took one look at me and said, 'It's for rowing, and you'd be perfect for it.'

"Quite a line, I thought to myself. I had not been perfect for anything, so after hearing him out I asked, 'When are tryouts?'

" 'Well, you don't really have to try out,' he replied.

" 'I don't understand . . .'

" 'Why don't you come to practice, and we'll teach you everything,' he answered. 'It's a brand new program so we don't expect there to be many women here who have ever rowed before. You can start at the very beginning.'

"What he was telling me was that they needed bodies that could learn the sport," the tall woman explains. "Besides, it didn't make much difference what you ever did before because there is nothing else you do in life that is the same as rowing. As the comedians like to say, 'There is nothing else you can do sitting down and going backwards.' Consequently, each of us who went out for the team started on the same footing because none of us had previous experience in rowing.

"Many rowers, however, are former swimmers. This is true, perhaps, because it too requires considerable discipline and stamina. Swimming also requires its participants to endure some pain, and then too rowing keeps a swimmer close to the water. At least with rowing, however, you get to see some of the scenery."

DeFrantz appears to be a natural for rowing. She is broad-shouldered and muscular. It looks as if her powerful frame would provide an advantage over her competition. "I don't believe anyone is a natural athlete," DeFrantz insists. Then, after a brief pause, she adds, "Or else, I believe that everyone is a natural athlete."

She explains: "To become an athlete, a commitment is required to learning the skills of the sport. Without devoting the proper time and effort nobody, no matter how blessed with physical attributes, will be a top athlete.

"On the other hand, sports is a very natural thing for all of us," she continues. "We're the only species in this world that engages in athletic competition. I believe we have an innate desire to participate in sports. Incidentally, I define sports as the use of the mind to control the body through the dimensions of time and space. As such, athletics is a powerful form of thought. It is also a pleasing form of thought because it involves the entire body. A certain degree of mental capability is required to learn the skills and then execute them again and again. An athletic performance should not be viewed as a reaction, but instead it demands rapid thinking on the part of the athlete."

After a slight pause, DeFrantz adds, "Only we humans are capable of competing in this fashion. Did you, for instance, ever see another species set up hurdles and race over them to see who gets to the finish line first? Certainly other animals fight and play, and they protect their territories. But they don't compete for the sheer joy of attaining satisfaction from performing better than anyone else."

When the Connecticut College women's crew team was originally formed, its purpose was to provide a new sport for the school's athletic program. Rowing would be available to any student, regardless of his or her previous athletic background; therefore, it was an activity that could appeal to many women who were formerly non-athletic. In particular it would be appealing to an individual willing to make a strong commitment and who, through proper training, could become a member of a varsity team. Anita DeFrantz was a perfect candidate.

It didn't take long after Coach Gulong convinced his new recruit to consider rowing before she became hooked on the sport. DeFrantz welcomed the challenge of making the team, and she thrived on representing Connecticut College in competition with other schools.

In spite of the time she devoted to rowing, DeFrantz remained involved in other campus activities. The same year she became a member of the rowing team she was elected president of her sophomore class. During her junior year she became chairperson of the school's judiciary board. While serving in this capacity she wrote the Connecticut College Student Bill of Rights that was later adopted by the entire campus community.

As a senior she represented her class on the Student Academic Policy Committee. She was also an honor student and majored in the field of political philosophy. In 1974, the year she graduated, she was honored by her peers with election to a two-year term on the Connecticut College Board of Trustees. Obviously the discipline required to be a crew member carried over to her non-athletic endeavors as well. When asked about her wide range of extracurricular activities, she says, "My full schedule *made* me manage my time. I could not afford to get behind."

By the time DeFrantz was a senior, Coach Gulong was aware that she was potentially a world-class rower. In spite of her tremendous potential, Gulong demoted his star athlete to the junior varsity during her senior year at Connecticut College. "He did it to teach me a lesson," she confesses. "I wasn't working hard enough, and I had an attitude problem."

He recommended that she begin rowing in the summers at Vesper Boat Club in Philadelphia and try out for the U.S. Olympic women's rowing team. Her reply was, "Oh, I didn't know rowers competed in the Olympic Games."

In all probability DeFrantz was not alone in her lack of knowledge about rowing as an Olympic sport; in fact relatively few Americans are knowledgeable about rowing. A rowing team is staffed by eight members and a coxswain. In international competition there are six lanes that are thirteen meters in width; in 1976 the women's distance in the Olympics was 1,000 meters (since then the women's Olympic distance has been increased to 2,000 meters). "In essence," DeFrantz states, "you hope that nobody passes you and that you pass lots of other boats and get to the finish line first."

There are two categories of rowing. In sculling, each person has two oars; in sweep rowing, each person has one oar. A sculling team has three boats (racing shells); a single scull has one rower, a double scull has two rowers, and a quadruple scull has four rowers. In sweep rowing an eight-oared shell is entered in the race and a ninth person, the coxswain, is the strategist who doesn't row but calls the moves. A coxswain might, for example, give the command: "Ready all, settle!" This means to lengthen out the stroke so there is a little more time between strokes, say, for example, thirty-six strokes per minute.

The coxswain sits at the stern and faces the direction the boat is traveling. The eight rowers, in turn, face the coxswain with their backs toward the bow. In a sport where the expression "pulling your own weight" is taken quite literally, it is advantageous for the coxswain to weigh preferably not more than ninety-eight pounds.

"One of the wonderful things about this sport," DeFrantz

explains, "is that it is not unusual that the coxswain is a person with a physical handicap who would not ordinarily be able to participate in a team sport. I have seen people in wheelchairs, amputees, and dwarfs serve as coxswains. But no matter what his or her disability, he or she must be a leader and have the respect of the crew."

DeFrantz calls rowing the ultimate team sport because every member must work in harmony with his or her teammates. No single person is a star. "Each team member is an absolute equal," she asserts. "It's a sport that demands absolute fidelity to the team. It's egalitarian—no one is more important than anyone else. Our fates are inextricably tied to one another. Reference is always made to the boat that won or lost, not an individual."

She also points out that a rower who competes at the highest level of international competition must have complete confidence in his or her abilities. "Each participant must think, 'I'm the baddest person on the team. Nobody is more deserving or more able than I.' And while it takes this kind of an ego, at the same time one must be willing to compromise in order to be part of the team. Each rower must be willing to accept the pace that the stroke sets.

"Every sport has its moments of magic," DeFrantz tells, "and in rowing this occurs when the whole team is clicking. It's when all of those long hours of practice begin to pay off—everyone is working together as a team with the boat traveling through the water. I would get a real sense of when the boat was moving at a fast speed; it makes everyone on the team want to push to make it go even faster."

After graduating from Connecticut College with honors, DeFrantz was accepted to the University of Pennsylvania's Law School and became a first-year law student in September 1974. By then the young woman had her heart set on two goals. She wanted to make the 1976 Olympic team and she wanted to further her education so she could have a career.

Her choice of graduate schools was limited to two places in the United States where a woman could row at a club—Philadelphia or Long Beach, California. "The University of Pennsylvania was in Philadelphia," she tells, "and the Vesper Boat Club was there." Vesper had a long tradition of excellence in rowing. It had produced several male medalists, and now it was inviting women to train there with the hope that they too would enjoy similar success. "I was delighted to be accepted as a member," she says.

To the uninformed, a boat club in Philadelphia sounds like an elitist organization. "Untrue of the Vesper Boat Club," declares DeFrantz. "In fact it was one of the saddest excuses for a boat club. At one time there were nineteen of us who had to squeeze into this tiny women's locker room, and it never had heat or, for that matter, air conditioning. Our boats were weatherworn and gave the appearance that they wouldn't float. All of our travel expenses came out of our own pockets. Elitist? We were anything but."

While her workouts were long and strenuous, she quickly committed herself to becoming a top-flight athlete. To reach a level of excellence that would make her an outstanding rower, DeFrantz worked out year round—on water and on land. "We competed in the autumn, and when the weather became too frigid and the water froze we'd land train," she tells.

"Rowing requires overall body fitness. If one desires to become an elite rower, it's going to take a few years to develop an appropriate level of fitness. And like the rowing workouts, my land workouts were equally exhausting. I ran, cross-country skied, cycled, and lifted weights. It was a twelve-month, 365-day workout program."

In addition to her law studies and daily workouts, DeFrantz was also occupied with her night job at the police headquarters in Philadelphia. There she interviewed defendants prior to their appearances in court before the judge setting bail. "This is where I learned about real lessons in communicating with people," she says. "I also made up my mind that someday I would work at something involved in the public interest, although I wasn't certain which aspect it would be. What I decided, however, was that I would not be a member of a corporate law firm. That just wasn't my style."

By 1975 DeFrantz's determination and hard work were beginning to pay off. That year she joined the National Rowing Team, and in 1976 she fulfilled a long-time dream by qualifying for the U.S. Olympic rowing team. One hundred women came to the Olympic camp, and eight rowers and a coxswain would be selected to represent the United States in Montreal in the sweep-rowing event. Those who were to compete in the sculling event attended a different camp. In the end DeFrantz qualified and was assigned the seventh seat of the shell, where the team member must assure that the boat has a continuous stroke and a steady flow.

Ten days after selection, the women's sweep-rowing team competed in its first regatta of the Olympic Games. This was the first time the eight rowers and coxswain ever raced together as a team. Five days later, on the final day of the regatta, a strong head wind greatly favored lane one and presented a strong disadvantage to lane six. In a blind draw the U.S. team drew the sixth lane. "It was the luck of the draw," DeFrantz explains, "and what an unfair difference it was!"

While the U.S. women rowers did win a bronze medal, the gold went to the East German team and the silver to the team from the Soviet Union. Had everything been equal, it is believed that the U. S. team would have finished second, "but that's the way it sometimes goes with an outdoor sport," DeFrantz philosophizes.

Recalling her feelings in 1976 she says now: "It's a thrill just to be there at the Olympic Village in Montreal. There I was, in a community consisting of nine thousand people, all of whom had been successful—different sizes, shapes, backgrounds, colors, languages—and I began to understand how significant a movement this was, bringing all these people together, all these people with success in their lives. Of course the welcome you get when you come into the stadium for the opening ceremonies is just beyond words. Maybe if I'd won a gold medal instead of a bronze I would say that was more important. But at the opening ceremonies you hadn't won anything, and yet you were being applauded for just getting there, for just being on the team and *there.*"

Following the 1976 Olympic Games DeFrantz made a decision to continue with the sport for four more years and finish her competitive rowing career in 1980 at the Olympic Games in Moscow. "I decided to do everything possible to be an Olympic champion," she explains. "But after Moscow, that would be it. After all, I'd have my law degree and I'd be obligated to get on with my career. So it was going to be four more years of commitment to training, and I would be out of competitive sports." In the meantime the bronze-medal winner would continue to compete in other rowing events. Between 1975 and 1980 she won national championships six times and also won a silver medal at the World Championships in 1978.

Following her graduation from law school in 1977, DeFrantz served for two years as an attorney for the Juvenile Law Center in Philadelphia. In this capacity she handled caseload litigation in the juvenile courts. She remained a member of the Vesper Boat Club, where she trained daily in preparation for the 1980 Olympic Games. Then, in the fall of 1979, she decided to take a one-year leave of absence from her law career to train in Princeton, New Jersey, where her partner, Cosema Crawford, a graduate engineering student, was attending college.

She and Crawford were planning to team up in the pair event, also called the shell, a race in which there are two rowers to a boat. For a full year the two women engaged in a

rigorous daily training program in preparation for the time
when they would travel to Moscow. They were driven by a
single objective: to win a gold medal—the consummation of a
dream each woman had for many years.

Crawford withdrew herself from consideration for the team
for personal reasons, but DeFrantz made the team in 1980. As
it would turn out, this was a prelude to the heartbreak and
disappointment she and hundreds of other athletes were to
suffer. To retaliate against the Soviet invasion of Afghanistan,
President Jimmy Carter initiated the American boycott of the
Moscow Olympics.

The President's announcement dealt a devastating blow to
the men and women who, like DeFrantz, had devoted thousands and thousands of hours in preparation for the time when
they would represent their countries in the traditional games
between the nations of the world. In what he believed to be a
tactical political move, Carter unilaterally made the decision
to keep the U.S. team at home. The President concluded that
the Moscow Olympic Games would fail without the participation of the Americans.

"When the members of Carter's administration saw those
Soviet troops amassed on the Afghanistan border, they simply
were not prepared to deal with it," DeFrantz recounts. "Certainly they knew that an Olympic boycott would not persuade
the Soviets to alter their Afghanistan engagement. It was sheer
nonsense to think a boycott would make a difference. Carter
acted out of frustration because he didn't know what else
to do.

"At first, an adviser told the President to inform the Soviets
that we would not send spectators. Well, the government
doesn't *send* tourists anywhere. Then Carter announced, 'We
won't send the athletes.' Here too the President of the United
States has never *sent* athletes to any Olympic Games. Not a
single red cent of federal funds has ever gone to the U.S.
Olympic Committee, which at that time was a completely self-

funded organization. Sure, Americans made contributions, and this money bought uniforms and other things, but it was always a totally voluntary effort.

"What right did the President have telling the team to stay home? The members of the team were private citizens, and, as such, each of us had the right to travel and compete in athletics anywhere in the world. After all, isn't this our right as free people? To make matters worse, the U.S. government coerced about thirty other countries including Canada, West Germany, and Japan that they too should boycott the Moscow Olympics."

The young attorney was infuriated and emerged as the leading critic of the boycott. In addition to filing a lawsuit that stated that American athletes' constitutional rights had been violated, she made numerous television appearances to state her case to the public. Her message was loud and clear: "It is the athletes' right to decide whether or not to compete. That right was taken from us.

"The administration is saying that our Constitution doesn't count or, for that matter, neither does the Bill of Rights. And the Sports Act of 1978 [which DeFrantz was active in getting passed] also doesn't count. The decision was a sad chapter in our history. The President had bad information, but his choice was pretty easy. On one side you had most of the nation; on the other it affected six hundred people . . . I was saddened by the ignorance in our nation about the Olympic Games. Furthermore, history shows that an Olympic boycott never works."

Although the Olympic Games were scheduled for July, the boycott movement began in January 1980. The final blow occurred, however, on April 14, when Carter sent Vice President Mondale to address the members of the U.S. Olympic Committee. Mondale made a strong appeal to the committee to keep the American athletes from participating in the Moscow games.

Behind the scenes rumors were aplenty—one such rumor was that the Attorney General would withdraw passports of those who traveled to the games, a power which cannot be invoked unless the nation is at war. When the committee members cast their votes, 30 percent voted to let the athletes decide for themselves, while 60 percent were in favor of staying home.

"At the time, many of the athletes believed that the boycott was the right thing to do," DeFrantz comments. "They believed they were being good patriots. I was angry because the government coerced the committee members to take away something I earned, not what they had earned."

The determined athlete/attorney appeared before the U.S. Senate Foreign Committee to plead her case. With the assistance of local Princeton, New Jersey, attorney Robert Zagoria, DeFrantz even filed a lawsuit against the United States Olympic Committee (U.S.O.C.). To accomplish this the two attorneys eventually joined forces with the ACLU and Covington and Burling, a leading law firm in Washington. Their efforts to stop the boycott were in vain.

It was a stressful time for DeFrantz. The FBI was keeping close tabs on her ("they were following me around"), and she received hate mail and telephone threats with messages calling her a "Commie lover" and telling her to "go to Russia and don't come back!"

"I wanted to believe in the Constitution and the Bill of Rights," she exclaims. "I am all for freedom of speech and the pursuit of happiness. And I would have been delighted to be able to compete in the Olympic Games wherever they were. It just so happened that they were in Moscow."

In spite of the boycott the Soviets hosted the Olympic Games in 1980. While not a single member of the United States Olympic team was present, one did receive an award. The International Olympic Committee had a session in Moscow prior to the official lighting of the traditional torch; at this meeting the committee awarded the Bronze Medal of the Olympic Order to Anita DeFrantz in recognition of her support of the rights of athletes.

DeFrantz was quite vocal in expressing her belief. As time would tell, she was right. The boycott didn't work—it had no effect whatsoever on the Soviet invasion. Eight years after the U.S.O.C. meeting of April 14, 1980, the Soviets signed a treaty to begin to leave Afghanistan on April 14, 1988. "What a shame the Carter administration chose to protest by boycotting the games," DeFrantz sighs. "The message Carter wanted to deliver to the world could have been told just as effectively in Moscow by having the flag bearer appear as the only American to walk out during the opening ceremony."

In 1980 Peter Ueberroth, who would head the 1984 Olympics and later serve as commissioner of professional baseball, invited DeFrantz to join the staff of the Los Angeles Olympic Organizing Committee. In this capacity she developed policy and designed operating plans for the Olympic Villages. Through her efforts she was able to persuade forty-one of the forty-four African nations not to boycott the 1984 games; this participation was a 100 percent increase over all prior Olympic Games.

Later she was given the responsibility of operating the Olympic Villages at the University of Southern California. Her official title was Vice President of the Olympic Villages. She would supervise what was to become home for the summer for an estimated seven-thousand athletes and trainers who participated in the 1984 Games. Food service was available twenty-four hours a day to those housed at the Olympic Villages, in what approximated feeding the population of a small city. In addition to providing room and board, the villages served as a place where athletes could mingle in a relaxed environment. This exposure helped the young men and women from an estimated 160 countries develop a better understanding about different cultures and customs.

To retaliate against the 1980 U.S. boycott of the Moscow Olympics, the Soviet Union and the Eastern Bloc countries refused to come to Los Angeles. This boycott didn't work either; the 1984 Olympic Games were a huge financial success. Of course, large audiences and huge television contracts were contributing factors. Expenses were also greatly reduced because many existing facilities were already available.

At previous games, host cities commonly incurred sizable losses because large public arenas had to be especially constructed for the games. In Los Angeles, however, this was not the case. Olympic events were held at locations such as the Coliseum, the Forum, Pauley Pavilion, and the Rose Bowl. Only two venues needed to be built: a velodrome for cycling events and a natatorium for swimming events. The Olympic Villages used dormitories at two existing sites, the University of Southern California and UCLA campuses, to house visiting athletes and trainers.

At the start of the 1984 games DeFrantz received a noble honor. She was chosen to carry the torch to the opening ceremonies of the Olympics. This honor was bestowed on her in recognition of her role in speaking out against the 1980 boycott and of the contributions she made toward making the 1984 Olympics a success.

Profits generated by the 1984 Olympics totaled approximately $225 million. In accordance with a contract signed with the Los Angeles Olympic Organizing Committee in 1978, 60 percent of this surplus went directly to the U.S. Olympic Committee, with the remaining 40 percent staying in southern California. This meant that a total of approximately $90 million went to the Amateur Athletic Foundation (AAF) of Los Angeles.

In September 1985, the AAF officially opened its doors. This nonprofit organization serves thousands of youths, and has awarded more that $19 million to sports organizations from

1985 to 1990. Grants are restricted to the eight counties in southern California, the area which hosted the games. These grants have ranged in size from $800 to $2 million and cover a wide range of sports from archery to rowing and even a sport native to Malaysia called sepak takraw, which involves two teams of three people kicking a rattan ball over a net.

The AAF initiates programs to meet the needs of the youth in the area and to create models that can be applied elsewhere. Typically the AAF sends representatives into communities to speak with parents and youngsters. It provides the sports equipment, coaching, and guidance needed to develop the programs. But the people in the community ultimately run everything. Among the many activities the AAF has sponsored are SUMMER SWIM, Run for Fun, Beach Volleyball, and Youth Cycling. The AAF is also the home of the Paul Ziffren Sports Resource Center, the largest sports library in North America, with more than twenty thousand books on its shelves, photographs in excess of fifty thousand, and a large collection of videotapes.

DeFrantz joined the Amateur Athletic Foundation as a senior staffer the same year it was founded. In 1987 she was named president. David L. Wolper, one of the most respected producers in the American movie and television industries, serves as chairman of the board. Other board members include Los Angeles Mayor Tom Bradley; Rafer Johnson, a decathlon gold medalist in the 1960 Olympic Games; Peter O'Malley, president of the Los Angeles Dodgers; and Lew Wasserman, Chairman and CEO of MCA.

"I have the best job in the world," DeFrantz declares about her position as AAF president. "We have the privilege of providing the best that sports has to offer to youngsters. Most of our grants focus on organizations that reach large numbers of young people and often a different population of children who may not otherwise be exposed to athletes. For instance, the foundation supports programs that expand sports experiences for girls, disabled children, and other historically underserved young people."

DeFrantz is especially proud of the AAF's Coaching Program. "Too often, especially in the United States, people are of the opinion that they're coaches because they have a clipboard and a whistle," she explains. "But it takes training to work effectively with young people. The responsibility of providing quality coaching is too important to leave to chance.

"A good coach has a tremendous influence on an athlete's life. There's a strong relationship that exists between the individual and his or her coach. For this reason, we believe people must be taught the proper way to work with young athletes. We train coaches to establish programs so their athletes receive maximum enjoyment. We don't want anyone to burn out in the first season. We also host conferences and workshops for coaches that cover issues in sports ranging from drugs to cheating."

DeFrantz thrives on her work at the foundation. In this position the former Olympian has combined her athletic background with her administrative skills as a trained attorney and has become a prominent sports executive. In particular she enjoys the challenge of working with young people and helping them improve their lives.

"Participation in sports plays a vital role for their growth," she believes, "because it provides them with an opportunity to experience success. Success is so important in our society, and yet there are relatively few times to experience success. However, for a young boy or girl, doing something as simple as dribbling a ball provides a sense of accomplishment, and this success is something that can be built upon.

"Once a kid has succeeded in the past, he or she begins to understand that next season can be even better. And the fact that there was a season last year conveys a sense of time which, in turn, provides a history. You see, we live in a fast-moving society in which everything is immediate. Everything is *now*. A good coach helps young athletes understand that things take time. A youngster can learn bit by bit that over the course of a season he or she will be progressively better. Then next season there will be more gains, more improvements.

"One of the great fallacies is that we see professional athletes on television but we never see them training and practicing. We only see the final product, so as spectators we fail to realize the hard work that went into making them so good at their performances. A good coach will direct kids so they realize they are progressing. He or she lets them know that it's a long road and shows them how to travel it with confidence and purpose."

DeFrantz also points out that while athletics promotes physical fitness, it's generally a by-product rather than an actual goal for young people. "There are a lot of flabby kids out there, so adults think by putting them in a physical fitness program, they'll get rid of their fatness. So what do they do? They tell the kids to do push-ups and sit-ups. Now what ten-year-old kid cares about how many sit-ups she can do? Instead, through sports, say a volleyball program, you'll get a kid who is playing well and wants to do better. Then, as part of the warm-up to play better volleyball, she'll do twenty-five sit-ups. Magic! She's doing the twenty-five sit-ups as part of the regimen to improve her volleyball game.

"Sports gives her a reason to be better. It drives her to want to excel. And when a youngster gets used to being the best or wanting to be the best in her particular sport, it carries over. Soon she's saying, 'Well, maybe I can write a better essay,' or 'Maybe I can get all of the questions right on this exam.' It spills over because the individual develops a habit of striving to do well."

There have been many successes at the AAF. Its dynamic president enjoys telling the little, personal stories. One of her favorites is about a young boy who took up the game of badminton when the foundation provided funds to make it available in his community. "One day when he came to school," DeFrantz recounts, "this little boy excitedly told his teacher about a badminton tournament he won. 'Do you have a racket?' the teacher asked.

" 'No, but they provided me with one,' the boy replied.

"The next day, the teacher brought a racket from home and told the child, 'My wife was a national champion and she wanted you to have her racket.'

"Shortly afterward, the boy won another tournament and, as a prize, received a racket. This prompted him to return the one that had belonged to his teacher's wife. From that time on the teacher says that the boy was a different child. He had met with success and had a chance to be proud about what he had done, and he applied it to his schoolwork.

"This is one of the wonderful things about sports," DeFrantz stresses. "It gives people a chance to celebrate their successes, no matter how small they may be. Everybody needs to hear 'Good job. You have done well.' and 'I'm really proud of you. You really went after it this time.' These kinds of comments make you feel that somebody cares about you. They knew you were trying, and that truly helps. We live in a world in which it is difficult to find those moments of praise and congratulations. Sports provides a lot of those moments."

DeFrantz likes to tell about a young girl with polio who had never previously participated in athletics. "She spent much of her time confined to her home and consequently was quite introverted. Once we were able to get her involved in sports, her whole personality changed. She's very proud about her accomplishments as an athlete. She thinks she's the best thing there is now. It's especially evident when you see how she came out of her shell and has become so outgoing around other children."

Another of DeFrantz's favorite stories tells about a telethon to raise money for a rescue mission for the homeless. "During the broadcast, a young boy was presented a pair of athletic shoes," DeFrantz tells, "and the television commentator remarked to him, 'Oh, now that you have these new sneakers, you'll be playing basketball with them.'

" 'Oh, they'll be great for my fencing.'

" 'Really?' asked the surprised commentator.

" 'Yes, I'm learning how to fence.'

"The boy was very self-assured in his reply, and it made me quite proud because the foundation is the only organization that offers fencing for children in our area," DeFrantz says with a broad smile.

Providing the sport of fencing, which otherwise would not have been an option to that young boy, is a single example of what is being made possible to thousands and thousands of youths via the AAF. The AAF is implementing one of DeFrantz's deep-rooted philosophies: that sports belongs to everyone. She believes it is a birthright for every person to be given the opportunity to participate in athletics. Through the foundation's efforts and its financial clout, about sixty-six "dead" parks in the Los Angeles area have been revitalized— these were former oases of greenery and recreation before they were orphaned by deep budget cuts. Many of them have since been used to house park sports programs funded by the AAF. As a result Little Leagues and soccer clubs have sprung up in public-housing projects and low-income neighborhoods.

DeFrantz and her staff are constantly searching for new ways to get children interested in a wide variety of sports and seeking new places to put an array of activities. "Our vision is to have every sports facility being used all the time," she stresses. A basketball tournament she witnessed in her own neighborhood on a Santa Monica parking lot inspired her. "I figured if they could do it, we could. That's another resource— parking lots—where soccer can also be played," she comments.

Schools are another overlooked resource that she believes

can be better utilized because "schoolyards and gymnasiums are typically closed during the weekends, evenings, holidays, and summer months. Most schools are locked up for more hours than they're open," she emphasizes. "The facility is there twenty-four hours a day, 365 days a year, so as long as there is proper supervision there's no reason why it shouldn't be used to accommodate athletics after normal class hours."

DeFrantz continued to serve on the executive board of the U.S. Olympic Committee after the 1984 Games. In 1986 she received perhaps her highest honor yet; that October she became one of only seven women on the ninety-six-member International Olympic Committee (IOC). She is the second-youngest on the committee and was the first African-American to be elected, the first black woman ever selected for membership. Of her role as a member of this prestigious group, the humble woman modestly says: "We are trustees who make sure the Olympic movement continues to flourish."

The list of IOC members is quite impressive and resembles a *Who's Who in the World*. Other members include such notables as La Princesse Nora de Liechtenstein, Le Prince Héréditaire Albert de Monaco (Grace Kelly's son), H.R.H. The Princess Royal (Anne), Le Grand-Duc Jean de Luxembourg, and Seiuli Paul Wallwork (a chief in Samoa). Committee members serve as voting members until age seventy-five. Thereafter their positions are honorary.

Anita DeFrantz will speak out for athletes' rights and fight for opportunities in sports for millions over the course of her next thirty-seven years as a voting member of the IOC. Hence, she will be one of the most influential women in sports for a very long time. It is probable that she will continue to be vocal.

On the controversial subject of whether professional athletes should be permitted to compete in the Olympic Games, De-Frantz comments: "I think Olympians want to know where they stand against the best in the world, not just the so-called 'amateur' athletes."

She adds, "The IOC wants to see the finest athletes in the world represented in the Olympic Games. We have to find ways to support our athletes so they can continue to train and be competitive for as long as they wish. If that means getting paid for training full time, so be it.

"We have separate organizations for sports such as basketball, football, golf, soccer, and so on. And we say that our athletes who receive compensation are not eligible to compete in the games. America has an unrealistic ideal that someone coming from nowhere—a person who is born an athlete—can win a gold medal.

"We are the only country with a dual sports system [amateur and professional]. The rest of the world supports their athletes. I want ours to have the opportunities to perfect their skills to the highest level. The games are for the best athletes in the world to compete against one another—whether they are professionals or not. Every athlete deserves the right to say he or she went up against the best in the world and know where he or she stands. That's what the Olympic Games are all about—a celebration of human excellence."

DeFrantz believes that athletics are for everyone—for everyone to excel and attempt to do his or her best—regardless of the level of competition. She concludes by saying, "Sports is a good test of how just a society is. If you have the opportunity to take part in sports, to learn some skills, to be on a team, it's probably in a community or society that cares about everyone."

5

■ JULIUS W. ERVING II ■
(DR. J)

Basketball Player, Entrepreneur

Some say that Julius Winfield Erving II, known around the world as "Dr. J," was the best to ever play the game of basketball. It's difficult to compare athletes and, in particular, those with diverse skills and from different eras, but during the sixteen-year span that Erving played in both the ABA and NBA, he was unquestionably the most exciting player in professional basketball. He was also the biggest drawing card in the game's history, attracting sell-out crowds in nearly every arena during road trips. Some players are dubbed "the franchise," a reference to a team's star attraction; an ABA commissioner once commented, "Julius isn't the franchise; he's the league."

Erving's popularity was so immense that even non-sports fans throughout America recognized the revered name of Dr. J. It simply translated as "stardom." The nickname is an obvious reference to a surgeon: *The doctor cut up the opposition. He operated on opposing teams. He displayed skill and dexterity on the court comparable to that of a surgeon in the operating room.* Interestingly, he was originally tagged "the Doctor" by a high-school buddy in response to being called "The Professor" by Erving. Only later while playing with the Virginia Squires in the ABA was he christened Dr. J.

Julius Erving was born on February 22, 1950, and grew up in Hempstead, New York, a small community on Long Island about a forty-five-minute commute to Manhattan. His parents were separated when he was only three; his father, an auto mechanic, died in a car accident when he was nine. Julius was a middle child; his sister, Alexis, is three years his senior, and his brother, Marvin, is three years his junior. "My mother was the dominant influence in my life," he tells. "She was and is an intelligent, exceptional woman who was an inspiration and role model to my siblings and me.

"My mother is a strong-willed and humble woman. Her fine character was a tremendous influence that guided me throughout my trials of growing up without a father. As the oldest male in the house, I had to make many decisions. While it was a great responsibility and somewhat of a burden that caused me to miss certain aspects of my youth, I have no regrets because it forced me to mature sooner."

Callie Mae Erving, a sharecropper's daughter, attended junior college in South Carolina, where she taught school before she married and migrated to New York. When she separated from her husband she wasn't licensed to teach in New York. Consequently she did domestic work while training herself to be a hairdresser to support her three children.

"My mother always made us breakfast in the morning, sent us off to school, and, after working a full day, she'd supervise our homework time," Erving recalls. "We lived in a housing project, and each of us had our own key from the time I was eight years old because she wasn't there when we came home from school. My mother was always active in the church, which was an important part of our lives."

Erving began playing organized basketball at the Prospect Elementary School in Hempstead when he was eight years old. "I wasn't very good," he says. "I preferred playing kickball and dodgeball instead, but I gradually leaned toward basketball. Perhaps it was in my blood. I remember once coming across an old photograph of my mother that showed her playing basketball when she attended junior college—her number was 16. I still have that picture. Then too I kept hearing stories about my father, who played basketball when he was in the service.

"The conditions under which we played at Prospect were slightly less than ideal. The school's gym had an extremely low ceiling. It was only thirteen feet high, about the same height as the top of the backboard, and the basket stood at ten feet high. Consequently only low-line-drive shots could be thrown at the basket, and it wasn't possible for there to be any range on your shots."

When her oldest son was thirteen, Callie Mae remarried. Her second husband, Dan Linslay, was a man in his sixties who had retired as a horse trainer and prior to his marriage had worked for the local sanitation department. "He was a highly principled person and, perhaps due to his age, very stuck to his ways," Erving says of his stepfather. "He was a very disciplined man. While he was very helpful to me, the abrupt change in our family caused some slight friction, and there simply wasn't anything I could do about it. I wasn't in control, and that made me feel uncomfortable. Mostly, it made me think how I would like to have control. At a relatively early age I became determined to make sure I'd someday be in charge of my own life."

The family moved to Roosevelt, population 15,000, a community just three miles from Hempstead. It was awkward for a thirteen-year-old boy to be transplanted into a new neighborhood and make friends, especially a quiet youngster such as Erving. Yet it was a smooth transition. The 5'9" boy played on the junior-high basketball team and before long had several new friends.

During his freshman and sophomore years at Roosevelt, he played on the junior varsity team. While he was a good player, there was no indication that he would someday be a star. "Some of the other boys were bigger and more experienced than Julius," says Ray Wilson, who coached at Roosevelt during the 1960s. "And, well, he was somewhat on the frail side. Julius looked like a little doe—all legs and a little body. I recall how I'd think to myself, 'If that kid doesn't grow into the legs he's walking around with, he's gonna look awfully strange!' "

What did impress Wilson, however, was the way Erving handled himself. "He had a certain maturity that I thought was exceptional," the coach remembers. "He possessed an evenness of temperament and was always in control of his emotions. I don't know why, but that's the way he was. I suppose it had to do with his home background, being the oldest boy in a family without a father during those formative years.

"Julius was a quiet boy," Wilson continues. "He always appeared as though he was deep in thought. While Julius never consciously sought to be the leader of his peers, leadership was thrust upon him. He was a good student—the best on the team—and he was popular throughout the entire student body because, well, he was such a nice person."

It wasn't until Erving's third year in high school that he finally played on the varsity team. Even then a senior forward started before him during the first four games of the season. The team was floundering, so beginning with the fifth game Coach Wilson put in his 6'1" forward. Erving never relinquished the position. According to Wilson, he was clearly the team's star by the end of the season.

During his senior year Erving's height reached 6'3" and his weight increased to 165 pounds. Although fragile, he averaged 25 points a game and showed some muscle under the boards, grabbing seventeen rebounds a game. Roosevelt High did not have a championship season, but the team had a champion. Julius was named the most valuable player in the South Shore division of Nassau County and was a member of the All-Long Island team.

According to Wilson, Erving was a coach's dream come true. "He was our star player, and he was always in control. He didn't cry in defeat and he didn't jump up and holler in victory. As his coach, I had to be careful about showing favoritism, and because he was so dependable and obedient he never gave me an opportunity to chew him out. Then one afternoon we were going to Levittown, New York, for a scrimmage, and I instructed the guys to be on the bus between noon and 12:30. Everybody showed up except Julius. 12:15, and still no Julius. Well, I'm thinking to myself, 'Here's my chance to read the riot act to him so I can implant in the minds of the other players that there are no exceptions—we will deal with everyone the same.

"At 12:30 I told the driver to leave—sans Julius. As we started to drive away, Julius was seen running after the bus, and we stopped to let him board. I really laid it on him for being late, much more than I would with another player, but it was an opportunity to discipline him in front of the entire team, and it would be a good lesson for all of them.

"He sat there and took it," Wilson continues, "and never said a word. I don't remember what his punishment even was, and it's not even important, but I do know he took it without complaining. Sometime during his last year of professional basketball the two of us were talking and I found out why he missed the bus that day. He was on his way to the bus and saw a teacher who had a flat tire. He had a decision to make: 'Do I go directly to the bus, or do I stop to help change the tire and miss the bus?'

"He elected to help the teacher and run the risk of missing the bus as well as getting reprimanded. When I chewed him out, he offered no excuses whatsoever. He simply took everything I dished out at him. If it were me, somewhere along the line I would have let it be known *why* I was late. Instead, he only told me years later."

Julius never received the recognition he deserved outside

the Long Island area. It was difficult to determine how good a basketball player he really was. Even he didn't know. "My perspective was strictly regional," he tells. "I never played outside my region, so I had no idea how good our team was or, for that matter, how good I was."

Coach Wilson had a different opinion: "Julius had such a super mentality for the game that I knew he'd be a very good college athlete. However, at 6'3", it looked as if he would be too small to play forward, so it meant he'd be a good guard in college. But then, if he should grow, well, we'd have somebody who is quite different."

Toward the end of his high school senior year, Erving had a single ambition: to get a good college education. He wanted to study business and had no thoughts about a career in professional basketball. Sure, he loved the game, but playing basketball in college was simply a vehicle to provide him with the necessary tools he needed to seek a career in commerce after graduation. "Frankly, I didn't know if I even had what it took to play varsity basketball at a college level," he says, "so thinking beyond that was out of the question."

He received letters expressing interest from nearly 100 colleges. In turn the honor-roll student made the rounds of a handful of Eastern schools, including Dartmouth, Boston University, New York State University at Buffalo, Penn State, NYU, the University of Massachusetts, and St. John's University. After considering a dozen or so scholarship offers, Erving methodically narrowed his choice down to St. John's in nearby Queens and the University of Massachusetts at Amherst, where Jack Leaman coached. Leaman and Ray Wilson were close friends who had been teammates while playing basketball at Boston University.

"Coach Leaman was a major influence," Erving explains, "and I liked U. of Mass. because, while it was big in student enrollment, it didn't seem overwhelming like some of the other campuses. After touring the business school I felt it just looked like the place where I should be. It was also a plus that the quaint college town of Amherst was only a two-and-a-half-hour drive from home. I wanted to go away, but not far enough away so that I couldn't come home if something happened." In the autumn of 1968 Erving began his freshman year at the University of Massachusetts.

He quickly adapted to college life. A close friend from Roosevelt, two basketball players from neighboring high schools, and Coach Wilson's daughter were also enrolled in the University of Massachusetts freshman class of 1968. "With a few friends, I had that base covered for my social life, and athletically, I felt comfortable with my coach, Jack Leaman," Erving recalls. "I had no difficulty with my classes, so the only things that required some adjustments were the New England weather and some of the parochial attitudes. But everybody has to adjust to those things, so they were not really what I'd call problems. Naturally college is going to be different from high school, so I think the best preparation for college is to go to college and live through it. By going, you make decisions as they present themselves."

Everything was going smoothly for the tall, laid-back freshman, and then disaster struck. His sixteen-year-old brother succumbed to lupus after a tough bout. Marvin's death devastated Erving. "I hurt so badly," he says, "and knowing how I was hurting, I tried to multiply that feeling in order to imagine how my mother must have felt. It left me with an understanding about the powerlessness we have in this world on matters of life and death.

"I also realized how we need to grow and understand spiritual existence because it provides us with a hope that our loved ones have been called for and are paving the way for us to someday join them. Through this belief my mother and I gained the strength that helped to put things in perspective so we could cope with our tragedy. In hindsight the loss of my brother made me more mature and focused. Through it all, I

gained strength of character that made me understand the
seriousness of life and how much I needed to appreciate life."

While Erving hurt deeply inside, he was able to overcome
his grief in part by concentrating on his school work and
basketball. First-year athletes were ineligible to play varsity
sports in 1968, yet, to the delight of Massachusetts fans, the
freshman squad went the entire 1968–69 season without a
loss. It was ranked the number-one freshman basketball team
in New England and was considered the fourth-best freshman
team nationally. It averaged 88 points a game. Erving, the
team's star forward, scored 18 points and had 12 rebounds per
game.

When the strong freshman team became sophomores during
the 1969–70 season, U. of Mass. won eighteen games and lost
only seven. The team was finally knocked off in the National
Invitational Tournament by eighth-ranked Penn State. Erving
performed superbly as a sophomore, averaging 27 points and
20 rebounds a game. He was voted the most valuable player in
New England, but he received only minor national recognition.

The first Olympic development basketball camp was con-
ducted in Colorado Springs during the summer of 1970. The
nation's most outstanding recent high-school and college
players were invited to strut their stuff in anticipation of the
1972 Olympic Games. His coach tried to promote the impressive scoring and rebounding statistics of his star player, but
Erving's name was omitted from the list of the top forty-four
players asked to attend the camp. It was believed he played
against a low caliber of competition due to a weak U. of Mass.
schedule, a clear inference that Erving would not have fared
nearly as well against the big boys at the big-time basketball
schools. Consequently Erving was one of four players placed
on the alternate list.

"I was satisfied to spend the summer on Long Island, where
I had a job with the department of parks and would run the

summer basketball league for high-school kids," Erving tells.
"Then I received a call informing me that some players got
hurt and I could go as an alternate. Frankly, I liked my job and
was happy to be home for the summer. Besides, the Olympic
Games were so far in the future.

"I was quite content to spend the summer at home, and, at
the time, I had no visions of ever becoming a pro. So to me it
was just another training camp, and Colorado seemed so far
away. However, my coach was working hard behind the scenes
on my behalf, insisting that I could hold my own against the
big guys. And, not wanting to let him down, I consented to
go."

Recalling his arrival at the camp, Erving confesses that he
was unsure how he would stack up against the highly touted
competition, many of whom were considered America's cream-
of-the-crop candidates for the 1972 Olympic Games and leading NBA prospects.

"I remember sitting in the dorm the first night there,"
Erving recounts, "and several of these All-American guys were
chatting about their future in basketball. I've always been a
good listener, so I just sat back and didn't say anything. Their
favorite subject was what they planned to do when they turned
pro.

" 'Here's what I'm gonna insist be put in my contract,' one
said.

" 'I'm gonna get a $50,000 bonus, and I'm gonna be paid
$100,000 a year,' another boasted.

" 'And I'm gonna buy my mom a $50,000 house.'

"I couldn't wait to get out on the court with these guys.
'Boy, they must be bad,' I kept thinking to myself.

"When we finally got around to playing basketball, I am
basically just playing my game," Erving continues, "and I am
realizing that I am every bit as good as the guys here and
better than most of them. It was the first time in my life that
the possibility about playing professional basketball entered

my mind. I figured if these guys were considering the pros, maybe then I'd have a shot at it too."

The young Olympic hopefuls traveled to Russia, Poland, and Finland that summer, running up a 10-3 record during a hectic two-and-a-half-week tour. Two of their losses were to the Russian national team. Although he came in as an alternate, Erving was the team's most productive player and finished the tour as its leading scorer and top rebounder.

Once back on campus as a junior, Erving had another great year, averaging 27 points and 20 rebounds per game. Again, U. of Mass. went to the National Invitational Tournament and once more was eliminated in the first round. The team finished the season with an impressive 20-3 record. Still, in spite of his sensational performance, Erving received relatively little attention. Although he was selected an All-American by a few minor polls, the major polls overlooked him. His stats, however, were incredibly imposing. After playing two varsity seasons, the 6'5½" forward averaged 26.5 points and 20.5 rebounds per game. He was only one of seven players to ever average more than 20 points and 20 rebounds during an NCAA career.

That Easter, while vacationing at home, Erving received a call from Steve Arnold, an agent who contacted him through his college coach. "He did the talking and I did the listening," Erving remembers about Arnold. "My objective in college had always been to get my degree in management so I could be qualified to become a businessperson. But after hearing out Arnold, the first person I talked to was my mother. Then I met with my freshman coach, Earl Mosley; Ray Wilson, who was now coaching at U. of Mass.; and Jack Leaman. The agent had pointed out that there was a war going on between the ABA and the NBA, and perhaps it would make sense for me to consider signing up with the ABA as a hardship case.

"Back then the NBA was in the process of exploring hardships, and the ABA had no such regulations—it didn't even

PICTURE PORTFOLIO
OF WINNERS

Dave Bing from Syracuse University was the number-two draft pick of the Detroit Pistons in 1966 and became an All-Pro NBA guard.

Today Bing owns Bing Steel and is a Detroit civic leader.

An All-American at Princeton, Bill Bradley was a Rhodes scholar. The New York Knicks won two world championships during the ten-year period he was on the team.

Today a respected United States Senator, Bradley is often mentioned as a Democratic presidential candidate.

Bobby Brown earned his M.D. while playing third base for the New York Yankees from 1946 to 1954.

After practicing medicine for twenty-six years, Brown became the American League president.

Above: Anita DeFrantz started rowing at Connecticut College and was a member of the 1976 U.S. Olympic team.

Today DeFrantz is the president of the Amateur Athletic Foundation of Los Angeles ("the best job in the world") and a member of the International Olympic Committee.

During his sixteen-year pro basketball career, Dr. J played with the ABA's Virginia Squires and New York Nets before moving on to the NBA's Philadelphia 76ers.

Having applied the valuable lessons of sports to the business world, today Julius Erving is a successful entrepreneur.

Gerald Ford was the starting center for the University of Michigan Wolverines in 1934.

The thirty-eighth president helped the wounded nation recover from the trauma of Watergate.

Hard work and Christian faith have led to Betsy King's success on the LPGA tour.

"As good a Christian as she is a golfer," King frequently appears before youth groups as a representative of the Fellowship of Christian Athletes.

Alex Kroll played at Yale and Rutgers before being signed by the New York Titans (later to become the Jets) in 1959.

"I've always been compulsive, driven, and goal-oriented," says Kroll, who worked his way up from research assistant to the chief executive officer of the Young & Rubicam advertising agency.

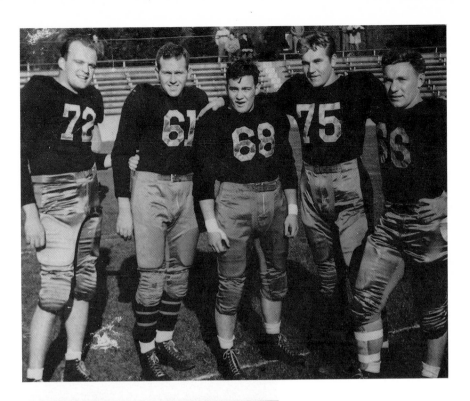

Above: Part of the 1946 Michigan State football team. John McConnell is second from the left.

Never a sports superstar, as CEO and founder of Worthington Industries McConnell nevertheless used the lessons of sports to become a superstar of American industry.

Being on the football and swim teams of tiny Eureka College taught Dutch Reagan to do his best, never give up, and play fair and square.

Ronald Reagan served eight years in the White House as one of our nation's most popular presidents.

Roger Staubach: Heisman
Trophy winner, member of the
Pro Football Hall of Fame,
legendary NFL quarterback
for the Dallas Cowboys.

The competitiveness, tenacity,
and plain old hard work that
allowed Staubach to take the
Cowboys to four Super Bowls
have proved beneficial in his
business career.

Undaunted by setbacks, Randy Vataha pursued a football career and became quarterback Jim Plunkett's favorite wide receiver, first for Stanford and then for the New England Patriots.

Today Vataha is chief operating officer of Bob Woolf Associates, one of the nation's largest sports and entertainment agencies.

"Athletics were my flight to freedom. Through athletics I found myself," says world-class track star and five-time Olympian Willye White.

As Director of Recreation Services for the Chicago Park District, White is spreading her message about the value of sports and recreation to Chicago youngsters.

have a draft—so its teams were just signing up players without regard to whether they were underclassmen. Because the ABA was making such an effort to establish itself, its teams were offering very lucrative contracts—enough money to make me consider leaving college at the end of my third year without my degree."

Erving's "committee" contacted Bob Woolf, the famous and highly respected sports agent in Boston, to seek his advice. Woolf suggested that Erving look at the matter from the NBA's vantage point: "What if you stayed in school another year? Then what offer would you receive? When would you then go in the draft? In the first round? The second round?"

At the time it was predicted that the ABA and NBA would become one league within the next six months. (The ABA and NBA actually merged five years later in 1976.) If a merger were to occur, it was commonly thought, offers made to players would be substantially lower because the bidding war between the two leagues would cease.

Erving's committee had to consider still another angle. From an athletic point of view, what would he gain by playing another year of college basketball? Would his basketball skills improve? Would his team win a national championship, or would it even play in a post-season tournament? Would Erving be an All-American? Would there be a better contract offer?

In the end Erving received and accepted a four-year guaranteed contract with the Virginia Squires in the ABA. His $500,000 salary would be paid over a seven-year period. At the time his was one of the biggest professional basketball contracts ever signed. As late as 1968 only two players had received six-figure annual salaries—they were two of the game's greatest stars ever—Wilt Chamberlain, who had signed for $100,000, and Bill Russell, who, inspired by one-upmanship, received $100,001.

"When I considered the amount of money offered for me to play basketball," Erving states, "I thought about how hard my mother and stepfather worked, and at age twenty-one I'd be paid $125,000 for doing something I loved. It took them twenty-five years to make as much as I'd earn in a single year for playing a game! I studied business in college, so I knew it would be foolish not to consider the offer. Up until I signed, my college education had been my number-one priority—now I had to put it on the back burner so I could focus on my professional career.

"It wasn't that I lost interest in my education. However, I could still attend college and graduate during the off-season. I promised my mother, Ray Wilson, Jack Leaman, and myself that I would someday, no matter what, go back to school to get my degree. It was a vow I intended to keep."

Erving also faced the challenge of playing professional basketball. "It's the ultimate test for an athlete to see if he can cut it as a pro," Erving exclaims. "I knew I could rebound—but this was the pros. I also understood than I did better against the college competition in rebounding and scoring than I did in high school, and yet playing in high school is certainly the easier of the two. That surprised me! Just the same, I wasn't about to predict that I'd do even better in professional basketball than I did in college. After all, the level of competition is far more demanding in the pro ranks."

When Erving joined the Virginia Squires in 1971 he surprised not only the team's owners and the fans, but himself as well. It was as if his style of basketball was tailor-made for the pros and especially for the ABA, which promoted an exciting, wide-open game of basketball. As Erving explains, "My game was suited for the league's style of playing. They didn't have zone defenses. They didn't double-team and triple-team back then, and with the three-point shot, the game started to open up with the press, trap, fire-the-bomb, and a lot of creative types of defensive and offensive strategies. It was a different game versus the old brown-ball league where they'd pound it in, guys beating on each other, leaning on each other, with everyone trying to put in two-foot shots. The ABA made the game exciting and far more fun for the fans to watch."

Erving became the darling of the ABA with his thrilling, driving moves to the basket, amazing shot blocking, flashy passes to teammates, and powerful rebounding. In a league without imposing centers, he was the Doctor; Erving did as he pleased at both ends of the court—and in the middle as well. He'd rebound one-handed with an arm extended behind him to propel himself downcourt to start a break. On the open court he took huge strides, and once near the basket he defied gravity, taking great leaps in the air, slam-dunking the ball through the hoop.

In his first season he averaged 27.3 points and 15.7 rebounds per game. In a playoff game against the Miami Floridans he scored 53 points. When the 1971–72 season came to a close, Erving was voted the runner-up rookie of the year, second to Artis Gilmore; he was, however, named the best rookie in the playoff games. Erving was also a second-team All-ABA player his first year as a professional.

"Of course, I was playing basketball on a full-time basis and was giving it my entire focus," Erving points out when pressed for an explanation for his success in the ABA. Something else had happened during his rookie year. He had grown an extra inch and a half and stood 6'7" tall by the end of the season.

At the beginning of the summer following his sensational professional debut, Erving was back on the U. of Mass. campus for his senior year, taking courses to pick up four credit hours. His game plan was to spend as many summers as it took to earn enough credits in order to receive his degree. On weekends he drove to New York City and played in the summer playground league in Harlem. Only exhibition games were played, and while nobody was paid to participate, the players competed at a level that provided an excellent workout during the off-season. The playground league included many NBA players, the likes of Earl Monroe, Walt Frazier, and Willis

Reed, and those who weren't pros were either ex-college stars or semi-pro players. Between the Harlem league on weekends and school during the week, Erving had a very busy summer.

It was undoubtedly the busiest summer of his life. As a result of some discrepancies in his contract with the Virginia Squires, he signed a $1.8 million contract with the NBA's Atlanta Hawks that included a $250,000 bonus. A squabble developed over the fact that his agent, Steve Arnold, was also representing the ABA. In Erving's eyes this was a conflict of interest.

The Hawks were planning to draft him after his graduating class became eligible in 1972. The Squires, however, did not want to lose their star player and took the matter to court. Erving found himself tangled in a web of lengthy arbitration. "I was thrust head over heels in the business end of my profession," he explains. "Between my legal problems with the Squires, the commercial aspect of being a professional athlete, having recently married, and my physical therapy and training, I had to postpone my studies for the time being." Nevertheless, he again renewed his vow to someday graduate from college.

A New York district attorney, Robert Morgenthau, served as arbitrator and ruled that Erving had to play for Virginia. Additionally the NBA ruled that he could not play for Atlanta; after the draft the Hawks had attempted to select somebody else in the first round and claim Erving as the team's second-round pick. Meanwhile Atlanta drafted another player, and the Milwaukee Bucks selected Erving as one of their two first-round draft picks. Atlanta protested, claiming to already have a signed contract; however, Milwaukee's rights were upheld.

"So there I was," Julius states. "I had a contract with Atlanta but I couldn't play there. Yet the owner insisted that I come to Atlanta and begin playing for them. He said that while I was there, they'd iron out the legal fiasco. I played two games for Atlanta, and the team was fined $25,000 each time.

The fine was paid, and then I was told, 'We want you to stay with us. You'll sit on the bench until the problem is resolved.'

" 'Look, we're going to have to give this thing up,' I said. 'I'll go back to Virginia and play.' I figured if we didn't get it straightened up, I was liable to end up sitting out the season."

The star basketball player was again playing for Virginia, this time under somewhat of a strain. His relationship with the team's owner had soured, and consequently it was mutually decided that he would only play for one year and then move on to another team.

Back in a Squire uniform, however, Erving didn't allow his off-the-court distractions to affect his game. In fact, during the 1972–73 season, Dr. J tore up the ABA. He was the league's leading scorer, averaging 31.9 points a game; the sixth-best rebounder with 12.2 per game; and the third in steals. He was a first-team All-ABA player that season and from then on.

In a complicated deal, the New York Nets signed Erving for the 1973–74 season. This was the result of a decision made by the ABA when it realized that if one of its teams did not acquire Dr. J, the marquee player in the league, he was likely to play for Milwaukee in the NBA. To satisfy the three other teams involved, the Nets traded George Carter to Virginia and paid the Squires additional cash; Atlanta and Milwaukee were also compensated by the Nets for undisclosed sums.

Julius Erving would now play in the Big Apple, and it made good sense. The Nets were in a new arena, Nassau Coliseum, not far from where he grew up. The Nets had not been faring well, and Dr. J would be the drawing card they desperately needed.

During Erving's first season in New York, the Nets had good reason to be pleased with the deal. The team's new acquisition dominated the league and won nearly every honor. He was again the league leader in scoring, with a 27.4 game average. He was third in steals and blocked shots, sixth in assists,

seventh in rebounding, and ninth in field-goal accuracy. It was
no contest when he was chosen as the ABA's Most Valuable
Player during the regular season.

In the playoffs he was even more brilliant, leading the Nets
to victories over Virginia and then the Kentucky Colonels.
Later, in the opening game of the final series, he hit for 47
points against the Utah Stars. The Nets won the ABA championship, and Erving was named the most valuable player of
the postseason. Dr. J drew large crowds in New York as well as
on the road and was on his way to becoming one of the all-time
great legends in sports.

The following season Dr. J continued to be the league's
premier player, averaging 27.8 points a game. In one game
against the San Diego Conquistadors he had a career-high 63
points. During the 1974-75 season he shared Most Valuable
Player honors with George McGinnis.

In the 1975-76 season Dr. J led New York to its second
championship. Once again he was the league's top scorer, this
time with a 29.3-point average. In the playoffs he was devastating, averaging 34.7 points. The Doctor hit 45 and 48 points
in the first two games of the final series against the Nuggets
in Denver where the Nets had been winless that season. The
sixth game was played in New York with the Nets ahead 3 to 2.
It was the last game ever played in the ABA, so it was fitting
that Julius Erving was in magnificent form. With only 5:07
left in the third quarter, Denver was ahead 80-58. It was time
for the Doctor to operate.

During those final minutes of the third quarter, he sank one
of his signature shots. The Doctor drove from the baseline
from the left, but with his path cut off he went behind the
glass, switched the ball from his left hand to his right, and
with a burst of speed reversed direction. He scooped his long
arm under the backboard and spun the ball off the glass into
the hoop.

He narrowed the margin with a layup and followed with two

slam-dunks before the quarter ended. When the game was over, the Nets had clinched the series with a 112-106 victory. Erving scored 31 points. Even more impressively, he dominated the boards with 19 rebounds, some grabbed with his huge hand and passed downcourt in what appeared to be a single motion. He also had five assists and five steals. Erving was named the Most Valuable Player for both the regular season and the playoff games.

All in all the Doctor had five years of play in the ABA, racking up a total of 11,662 points, averaging 28.7 a game. He shot .509 from the floor and .778 from the free-throw line. He averaged more than four assists and twelve rebounds per game.

While the playoffs were in progress, executives and team owners of the two leagues were busy working out the details to merge the seven ABA teams into the NBA. Erving was also involved with the negotiations as a vice president of the ABA players association, representing the players of his league. Unbeknownst to the rest of the ABA, the owners of the Nets and Nuggets—the two best teams in the league—filed applications to join the NBA without notifying either the players association or the ABA's other five teams.

"I felt as though a grave injustice had been done to the players of the five remaining teams," Erving remembers. "From my own personal viewpoint, I wouldn't get hurt. However, I believed it was unfair for the two surviving teams to conspire without regard to the interests of the other players. Furthermore, as a representative of *all* the players, I felt a responsibility to look out for the interests of all the players. I advocated that the merger should include all ABA players. After all, these were guys who worked hard, and there was an obligation to protect their professional basketball careers."

When Erving protested to the team owners, they responded by saying, "You have no choice in the matter."

"What are you talking about?" he questioned. "Your proposal is unacceptable to the players association."

"You do what we tell you," the owners dictated.

Erving read between the lines. "They were telling us that if we don't go along with them, then we don't have a players association. That was a real blow, and I was personally insulted."

Erving was able to use his influence as the darling of the ABA, and as a consequence, following a lengthy series of negotiations, a compromise was reached. Four ABA teams—the New York (later New Jersey) Nets, the Denver Nuggets, the Indiana Pacers, and the San Antonio Spurs—were accepted into the NBA intact; then there would be a dispersal draft among the thirty-six players on the three remaining teams.

"Roy Boe, the owner of the Nets, was the one who spearheaded the whole thing," Erving declares, "and I was really upset with him. I told him that he made a great deal for himself, and now, with the merged league in place, he was going to have to deal with me. We agreed to renegotiate our contract, but we could not come to terms.

"When I made it absolutely clear to him that I was never going to play for him again, he consented to sell my contract to one of the established NBA teams. We agreed to give each other a list of teams that were acceptable, and mine included New York, Los Angeles, and Philadelphia. He said that New York was out of the question, so I selected the 76ers because I had just bought a home in New York and could commute to Philadelphia."

The 76ers bought the contract and, with it, a gold mine. Erving was well worth his seven-figure salary. Record crowds showed up during road trips to see the league's premier attraction, Dr. J, who had been billed in a *Sports Illustrated* cover story as "the 1976 Player of the Year." *Sport* magazine named him its "1976 Performer of the Year"; in its feature article, he was hailed as "the Doctor of the Dunk." In the eyes of many,

Julius Erving was the individual most instrumental in bringing the ABA and NBA together.

The Doctor became one of the NBA's greatest stars. *Sport*'s description could not have been more accurate when it portrayed Erving as a top performer. More than any other player in the history of the game, he transformed basketball into an artistic event. He added a grace that theretofore had not existed. The Doctor elevated the sport from the execution of routine horizontal maneuvers to feats of stunning vertical aerobatics.

He was the first player to realize that basketball is an improvisational sport. With some imagination, a player could achieve more, much more than an ordinary basket. Before Dr. J introduced his innovative style to the game, the slam-dunk was an act of brute strength dependent upon sheer height and power. Erving added a new dimension of creativity and excitement that not only demanded increased competitiveness on the court but also thrilled the crowds. He gave the game both excellence and entertainment.

Erving concurs. "My style of play brought a certain artistry to the game," he says in a soft voice, "which, in time, became acceptable. It not only was entertaining to the spectator, but it aroused curiosity that raised the question, 'How far can you go with it?'

"One artist, for example, puts a brush to a canvas and sees certain boundaries in which he paints circles in the middle, while another artist is not so limited and reaches out to the far corners. I, too, was reaching for the corners, and what happened is that it opened up a wave of players who were also willing to stretch. Like me, they said, 'Hey, I'll let it all hang out, and even if I make a mistake, I've got plenty of opportunity to correct it.' To be an innovator you can't be worried about making mistakes. For this, I give credit to my coach, Al Bianchi, who allowed me to play through those mistakes during my tenure with the Virginia Squires. Had I not initially started my career in the ABA, as an NBA player I probably wouldn't have been able to be the player I became."

As a 76er Erving did in fact adjust his game to suit the team. "We have more talent than your last team had," the general manager told him, "and we don't want one guy scoring 28 points a game. Instead we prefer to have three guys scoring 20 points a game." Dr. J agreed to forfeit scoring opportunities by not taking certain shots; instead, he passed the ball to teammates George McGinnis and Doug Collins. This led one columnist to write: "He was a man blessed with superior physical skills who never forgot he was playing a team sport and never minimized the responsibilities that accompany success and stardom."

During his first season with Philadelphia, Erving scored 30 points in the 1977 All-Star game and received its Most Valuable Player award. Philadelphia made it to the playoffs that same year. In 1981 the Doctor became the first "small man" since Oscar Robertson to be chosen the NBA's MVP.

In the 1982–83 season The Sixers acquired mammoth center Moses Malone, the game's first two-million-dollar player. Once more Erving demonstrated his willingness to blend his skills with another star for the benefit of the team. The addition of Malone proved to be the winning ticket. Philadelphia swept the four-game series with the Los Angeles Lakers, and in the final game the Doctor was clearly in full control, scoring 7 of his 21 points in a ninety-eight-second fourth-quarter burst. When the game ended, the Philadelphia 76ers had won their first NBA title since 1967, and Julius Erving had fulfilled a long-time dream. He now had an NBA championship ring in his possession to go with his two ABA championship rings. It was the last championship team on which he ever played.

When his contract expired at the end of the 1985–86 season, the Doctor agreed to play for the Sixers for one more year. His final one-year paycheck was $1.7 million. Dr. J, perhaps the most loved man to ever play the game of basketball, received a twenty-three-city, six-month farewell. Fans and players paid tribute to a man who had given so much to the sport. Presents were bestowed upon him, including a rocking chair in Los Angeles, a pair of skis in Utah, and a doll hand-made by the Hopi Indians in Phoenix.

He also received oodles of praise. Lakers coach Pat Riley said, "There have been *some* better people off the court, like a few mothers and the pope. But there was only one Dr. J, the player." Isiah Thomas expressed his feelings in a telegram: "You have been an inspiration, a leader, and a perfect role model for me and all other NBA players. You have made the path much smoother for us younger guys to follow." Magic Johnson said, "The Doc went past jumps, hooks, sets, went past everything and made the playground *official*." Gene Shue, Erving's first NBA coach and later a broadcaster for the Sixers, stated, "Our league *needed* somebody like Doc."

With two games to play as the 1986–87 season came to an end, Erving needed 36 points to become only the third player (with Kareem Abdul-Jabbar and Wilt Chamberlain) to score 30,000 career points. He scored 38 points in a game against the Pacers, eight more than his season high. On April 20, 1987, one day after the regular season was over, more than 30,000 spectators lined the streets in the City of Brotherly Love to say goodbye to their beloved hero in a ticker-tape parade.

The Doctor finished his career with 30,026 points. He was named to the All-Star team in each of his sixteen professional seasons, five with the ABA and eleven with the NBA. He had been named the NBA's most valuable player in 1981 and for five years was voted the league's runner-up MVP.

When Erving exited the world of basketball, he was well prepared to step into the world of business. The 3.0-grade-point-average business student had finally received his degree in a graduation ceremony at the University of Massachusetts.

In 1984 he had begun to fulfill his vow to receive his diploma by enrolling in the college's "university without walls." This two-year program allowed him to complete courses away from the campus and thereby pick up a bachelor's degree from the university's school of education. At the 1986 graduation cere- mony he was also awarded an honorary business degree. In the audience were his mother, Callie; his wife, Turquoise; and the four Erving children, Cheo, Jay, Jazmin, and Cory. In 1984 he was granted an honorary degree in dance from Temple University.

Few athletes have ever received such worldwide recognition as Julius Erving. He has also become a wealthy man. Why then, some people ask, did he ever want to go back to college for a degree? "With my sports career behind me, I have a long life ahead of me," he explains, "and nobody can have too much education. Certainly, the more educated one is, the more enrichened is his or her life."

Erving has proven to be a highly successful businessman. Today he is co-owner with his partner, J. Bruce Llewellyn, of the Philadelphia Coca-Cola Bottling Company, a two-hundred- million-dollar firm that employs 2,700 people in eastern Penn- sylvania, Delaware, and New Jersey. He is also the co-owner of WKBW, a television station in Buffalo, New York, as well as Garden State Cable Vision in Cherry Hill, New Jersey. He is the sole owner of The Erving Group, a holding company that serves as the management and administrative arm of his busi- ness interests.

He owns another company, Dr. J Enterprises. This market- ing and public relations firm handles his licensing agreements with the likes of Converse Shoe Company, Dr. Scholl's (a health and foot-care unit of Schering Plough), and Spaulding Sporting Goods Company. Erving serves as a spokesperson for much of Spaulding's sports equipment, including golf and all racket-game products, and, in particular, its Dr. J Basketball division. Dr. J Enterprises also works with NBA International, a worldwide promotional arm of the National Basketball Association, that represents the league, its players, and its product line. An endorsement contract with Coca-Cola Company and Coca-Cola, USA, requires the ex-basketball great to fulfill speaking and personal appearance engagements throughout the year.

For the past seven years, Ray Wilson, the same man who coached Erving at Roosevelt High School, has served as an executive with The Erving Group. Wilson became an assistant coach at U. of Mass. during Erving's college career and went on to become the university's head coach in the early 1980s. Wilson was also Erving's partner in a summer basketball camp called Reach at Morgan State University, which the two men ran during Erving's playing career. The camp was a huge success, with nearly two hundred boys in attendance at each session. The money wasn't Erving's motivation, but the camp did provide extra earnings for his old friend and coach.

Each season a highlight event at Reach was its all-star game featuring many NBA players. This attraction helped the predominantly black college with its athletic fund-raising. Erving enjoyed the closeness the camp provided him with youths ranging from nine to eighteen years in age. He'd tell each group of campers, "There's nothing wrong with dreaming and shooting for a basketball career, but you must strive to receive your education."

He'd also emphasize the high odds against making it to the pros and advised, "Don't put all the eggs in one basket. Be sure to get your education. And even if you do play in the NBA, you'll need to know how to manage your money. Remember too that you'll have a long life ahead of you *after* your basketball career ends . . ."

"Whenever there was a youngster who wanted to talk to Julius," Wilson remembers, "he'd try to find the time. With the tight schedule, it was always a problem. It seems like I was always pulling his arm, saying, 'Come on, Julius, we're going to be late.' "

Erving cared about young people and they could sense it. They responded by caring about him. He was a perfect role model—on and off the court. He cared about family, society, morals, and issues, and he gave back to the community. Erving narrated *Peter and the Wolf* at the Philadelphia Zoo, read the Declaration of Independence at the city's Fourth of July celebration, and lit up the Christmas tree at City Hall. He was loved and admired by children, men, and women of all ages. Youngsters wanted to emulate him; parents wanted their kids to grow up to be like him.

Today Erving enjoys one of the most successful business careers of any former professional athlete. He claims to have learned a great deal in sports that is now applied to what he does in business. "I took risks throughout my athletic career," he states, "because I dared to be great, to be different, and to try new things. And isn't taking risks what being an entrepreneur is all about?

"For example, I took a major risk in 1976 after being named the Most Valuable Player in the ABA playoffs and the regular season, appearing on the cover of *Sports Illustrated*, and then refusing to play because I didn't feel things were right. It was a risk for me to take a stand based on what I believed was a matter of principle. But I wasn't about to sit on my hands and witness so many other players get hosed by the merger of the two leagues. I had tears for those guys and I wanted to support them. Yet at the time my wife was pregnant and my daughter was born that year, and we were in a new house, and I wasn't playing. For a while it was looking as if I would be out of a job. Just the same I was willing to risk my career on a principle."

Perhaps Erving's biggest risk in basketball was the way he played the game itself. In the beginning of his ABA career, many people opposed his style of playing. "The purists believed that anybody who did some of the things I did, like throwing a pass around my neck or behind my back, was hot dogging and didn't belong in the professional ranks. They'd say, 'If you want to do those things, go play for the Harlem Globetrotters.' They didn't like it when I'd grab a rebound, see an open court ahead of me, take the ball, and make the play myself.

"To me this wasn't being selfish—it was a way to win games. And when I'd stand outside and get ready to make a fifteen-foot set shot, I didn't see any point in shooting it from there when I could take the ball in and dunk it, even when some 7'2" guy was there. It wasn't something I had to think about or plan to do. Still I was willing to take the chance that I might get smacked down in the process. I felt as though I had a natural flair, and even though the fans liked it, I wasn't doing it only for their enjoyment. I enjoyed doing it, and I welcomed the challenge. But most importantly, it was a winning style. During the sixteen years I was in the pros, I never played for a team that had a losing season."

Erving emphasizes that an invaluable lesson taught in athletics is how to adapt to change. "Even when I was in elementary school," he explains, "and was playing basketball in that gym with the thirteen-foot ceiling, I discovered something about adapting. Instead of shooting rainbow shots, I shot line drives. Even back then, as a little kid, adjusting was required. When I tell this story about that gym, people say, 'It wasn't fair for the kids in your school to be handicapped with that low ceiling.'

"To these people, I respond, 'Everything is not fair in sports, nor is it always fair in business.' There have been many times when I've walked into a business situation with certain promises having been made, or perhaps specific projections were forecast, and nothing turns out as anticipated. So you adjust and you adapt. You must always be prepared for the unexpected. If you underestimate, you get hurt, and if you overestimate, you get hurt. So don't do either—just estimate!"

Erving simply believes that there is no substitute for talent. "This is applicable in business as well as in sports," he declares. "Of course it becomes quite apparent in an athletic contest because you can readily observe who's performing and who isn't, and it's going to be reflected in the game's score. In business you need talent too, and as a business owner you have to recognize it in others. One individual, for example, might be a numbers person, another excels in administration, another in marketing, and so on. You must then utilize the talent of your people accordingly. To accomplish this, you must communicate and delegate.

"For instance, I might say to someone, 'This is what you're best at and where you should be. I'm not going to interfere. You do it and report back to me. I trust your talent, so I'll go along with you.'

"In the same way, a good coach pools his talent and lets everyone know what he has to do. It then goes back to what I said before about adjusting. In sports every effective coach had a game plan, and if it wasn't working there was a plan B and even a plan C. Kevin Loughery, my coach when I played for the Nets, used to say to us during a timeout or at halftime, 'You know that stuff we talked about and drew on the board ain't working. Somebody is going to have to do something.'

"It's the same thing in business. If it's not working, you have to find out why and then make some adjustments," Erving continues. "Then it's up to the leader to give his or her people the green light and realize it's showtime. When the ball is thrown up, the best coaches sit on the sidelines, sometimes with their arms folded, and they watch. That's right—they do nothing but watch because they've prepared their talent, and now the time has come to execute. Everyone does his or her thing, carrying out the details. This is when you're letting go—in sports and in business!"

When Erving talks about business, he makes it sound so easy. Perhaps he makes everything look easy, like he did when he played basketball—it all seemed so effortless. But as he's quick to point out, "It takes years to be an overnight success."

Ray Wilson, who has worked closely with Erving since the two first met back at Roosevelt Junior High School, says: "As good a basketball player as Julius is, he's even a better person. My wife and I feel Julius and his family are our family. It's been a special relationship that makes us feel blessed."

Wilson's generous comments might sound biased toward Erving had not so many others shared his admiration. In a 1987 informal poll of sportswriters and sportscasters around the country, the *Denver Post* wanted to identify the "nicest" people in sports. It was no contest. Julius Erving appeared on by far the largest number of ballots.

Who says nice guys don't win ball games?

6

■ GERALD R. FORD, JR. ■

Football Player, U.S. President

On December 6, 1973, after he had served in the U.S. House of Representatives for twenty-five years, Gerald R. Ford was requested by President Richard M. Nixon to replace Spiro T. Agnew, who had resigned from the office of the vice presidency. Later, on August 9, 1974, following Nixon's resignation, Ford became the nation's chief executive.

The evening before, on August 8, at nine o'clock, millions of Americans had watched in disbelief as Nixon's familiar face appeared on their television screens. His speech contained the following message:

. . . I have concluded that because of the Watergate matter, I might not have the support of the Congress that I would consider necessary to back the very difficult decisions and carry out the duties of this office in the way the interests of the nation would require.

I have never been a quitter.

To leave office before my term is completed is abhorrent of every instinct in my body. But as President, I must put the interest of America first.

America needs a full-time President and a full-time

131

Congress, particularly at this time, with problems we face at home and abroad.

To continue to fight through the months ahead for my personal vindication would almost totally absorb the time and attention of both the President and the Congress in a period when our entire focus should be on the great issues of peace abroad and prosperity without inflation at home.

Therefore, I shall resign the Presidency, effective at noon tomorrow.

Vice President Ford will be sworn in as President at that hour . . .

The historic speech lasted fifteen minutes. Not once did Nixon concede that what happened at Watergate was his fault. Nor did he ask for forgiveness from the American people. Under these circumstances Gerald Ford pledged his dedication to serve in the country's highest office. He became the only President in U.S. history who was elected neither to the presidency nor the vice presidency.

Taking the helm was no easy matter. There was considerable apathy throughout the country toward White House leadership, and Americans had good reason for their disillusion. Faith in the U.S. government had sunk to perhaps an all-time low in the nation's 198-year history. There was an enormous need for a leader of strength and, in particular, one who possessed the highest character and integrity. Gerald Ford was the man chosen to lead the nation through this difficult period.

Before Nixon had chosen him as his second-in-command, Gerald Ford was a household name only to his constituency in the Grand Rapids, Michigan, area and to those people in the know around the nation's capitol. Most Americans wanted to know more about this man who had been given the awesome responsibility of restoring dignity to the U.S. presidency.

What in Gerald Ford's background provided him with the capability to lead the nation through uncertain and dire times? In part, as Ford himself reveals, his active participation in athletics as a youth played a significant role in molding the man who was to be the thirty-eighth President of the United States.

On July 14, 1913, in Omaha, Nebraska, an infant was born to Dorothy Gardner King and christened in the name of his father, Leslie L. King, Jr. Two years later, the parents divorced and the young mother took her toddler and moved back to Grand Rapids, Michigan. She eventually married Gerald Rudolf Ford, the owner of a small paint manufacturing plant, Ford Paint & Varnish Company. Some time later, formal adoption papers were signed and the child was renamed Gerald R. Ford, Jr.

Although the Fords were poor, the boy was raised in a family that provided both love and parental care. He had three half-brothers, yet not the slightest hint of partiality was shown by "Dad" Ford, a family man who was very devoted to his four sons. In addition to teaching the boys to fish, he would routinely toss baseballs and footballs to them during their toddler years. When they were older he encouraged them to play team sports. His adopted son excelled as an athlete. During his sophomore year at South High School in Grand Rapids, young Gerry was named starting center on the city championship football team. He was also a member of the all-city squad.

"In those days," Ford recalls, "we played a double-wing formation. It was more difficult than the T-formation, because, rather than looking straight ahead and virtually handing the ball to the quarterback, I was forced to view everything upside down. That gave a jump to the opposing lineman, so I had to move very quickly to carry out my blocking assignment. Then too I had to perfect different ways to snap the ball to the different backfield players and, of course, the kicker."

About playing the unglamorous role of offensive linesman,

he has this to say: "Every offensive play begins with the center, so it's a fairly responsible position. If I were to start a play with a poor pass to the backfield, the team would lose yardage or even lose the ball. In those days we played both ways, so I also played as a linebacker and participated in a lot of action on defense too."

Ford was a standout in track, basketball, and swimming, but his main interest was football. During his senior year South High had an undefeated season and won the state championship. Ford captained the all-state squad. He did not fare as well in the political arena. "I was one of three candidates for my senior class presidency," he tells, "and I lost. Sure, it upset me, but the loss didn't shake my self-confidence. First, I had enough successes as an athlete to believe in myself. Second, I played in enough games and we got beat, so I had a clear understanding about the risk of losing when you compete against others."

After graduation Ford was invited to visit the campuses of schools such as Northwestern, Michigan State, and Harvard. But University of Michigan's coach was able to persuade the Grand Rapids football star to come to Ann Arbor. "He showed the most genuine interest in me as an individual," Ford recounts. "He talked about the fine education I'd receive at Michigan, and I was impressed by the fact that he personally drove me to the bus station for my return trip home. Besides, not only was the university nearby to Grand Rapids, but Michigan had an excellent reputation for academics and athletics." In 1931, the year Ford enrolled, the Wolverines were ranked among the nation's top teams. Michigan's football team was so revered that a new stadium had been constructed to accommodate record-breaking crowds of ninety thousand people.

Then came the Great Depression, and feeding a family of six took priority over paying the cost of one son's education. South High's principal, Arthur Krause, a dyed-in-the-wool

Michigan football fan, however, came to the rescue when he arranged for a "bookstore" scholarship in the amount of one hundred dollars to be awarded to its former star player—this was enough to pay Ford's tuition for a full year.

The determined young athlete saved another hundred dollars during the summer by working in a paint factory—additional funds he earmarked for his education. Aunt Ruah and Uncle Roy LaForge faithfully sent two dollars every week to their bright and handsome nephew. The ambitious student also waited tables in the university hospital dining room for three hours a day in exchange for meals. Ford was able to make ends meet by sharing a four-dollar-a-week third-floor room measuring ten feet by ten feet with a basketball player. Once every two or three months he supplemented his earnings by selling blood at the hospital for twenty-five dollars.

During Ford's freshman year at Michigan his studies, part-time work, and football left him with little time for anything else. That first year he showed promise on the gridiron and was presented the school's Meyer Morton trophy, a silver football, for outstanding freshman player in spring practice.

"Back then first-year students weren't allowed to play on the varsity," Ford explains, "but after having a good freshman year, I had high hopes of playing as a sophomore. There was only one problem. I played behind Chuck Bernard, who was an All-American center. Consequently I spent a lot of time warming the bench. While I got in enough time to earn my letter, it was frustrating to be a second-stringer. It was something I wasn't used to and, in particular, after having received star status as a high school player and then having such a good freshman year.

"That same year the Michigan varsity team had an undefeated season and won the national championship," Ford continues. "We had a perfect season again in '33 and for the second consecutive year were ranked number one in the nation. While it was a source of pride to be a member of those two championship teams, I didn't like sitting on the bench. While some people would have been discouraged by not getting in there, I kept telling myself that I was competing against an All-American. I knew that my day would come after Bernard graduated because I still had another year of eligibility."

Michigan was still ranked among the nation's top ten during the preseason polls in spite of several team members graduating—and starting at center was Gerald R. Ford. "I had high hopes that we'd repeat as contenders for the national title once more," Ford tells, "but before the season started our quarterback, Bill Renner, broke his leg and was out for the season and John Regeczi, our punter, met with a similar fate when he injured his knee."

These key injuries were decisive blows to the style of football Michigan played. In those days sportswriters wrote that the Wolverines had "a punt, a pass, and a prayer strategy." In short, their game plan stressed that a team with a good punter, a good passer, and a strong defense would always win, so whenever the Wolverines won the toss of the coin, they elected to kick.

A good kickoff would put the other team deep into their own territory; the defense would contain them and try to force them to make mistakes. When the Wolverines took over with good field position, they would throw a long pass and pray for a completion. Whenever they received the ball in their own territory, they'd punt—sometimes even on first down. With a superior punter they'd pick up ten to fifteen yards with every exchange. If the passer connected with a long pass, they'd score.

With both its star passer and punter sidelined, Michigan's 1934 season was doomed for certain disaster. The team started with a 16-0 loss to Michigan State followed by a 27-0 defeat by the University of Chicago. The third game, against Georgia Tech, presented a problem because Michigan's best pass receiver was a track star named Willis Ward. Ward, Ford's close friend and roommate during road trips, was black and the South was segregated. Tech's coach threatened to call off the game if Ward played. A compromise was finally reached when Georgia Tech agreed to sideline one of its star white players to even things up, and the game was played.

"I was distressed," Ford recalls, "so I called my stepfather and asked him if he thought I was justified in refusing to play. He replied, 'You ought to do whatever the coaching staff decides is right.' I still wasn't satisfied, so I asked Willis what he thought was right.'

" 'Play,' he advised. 'The team is having a bad season, and we could end up losing our remaining games. We could beat these guys, and the team needs you.' Willis inspired us, and as a result we played our hearts out. We beat Georgia Tech 9-2."

It was the Wolverines' single victory of the season. During the team's next five games, Michigan was outscored 98-12 by Illinois, Minnesota, Wisconsin, Ohio State, and Northwestern.

Ford's best performance occurred during a close 7-6 defeat against Illinois. On a wet afternoon in Ann Arbor the game became a kicking match; each team punted fifteen to twenty times.

"Despite the slippery ball," Ford smiles, "I had a perfect day, never once having a bad center. Our athletic director, Fielding ('Hurry Up') Yost did something after the game that he rarely did—and what he did made the whole season seem worthwhile. Yost put his arm over my shoulder and said, 'Ford, that was one of the finest exhibitions of centering I have ever seen.' Well, getting a compliment from somebody like him was the ultimate in praise. It's something that I have never forgotten."

After the season ended Ford was voted the most valuable player on the Michigan squad, and on New Year's Day 1935 he played a total of fifty-eight minutes in the annual Shrine

Crippled Children's Hospital game in San Francisco. "We got beat 19-13, but I was pleased because I had played well," he comments.

Another thrill came that August when Ford played his last football game as a member of the College All-Star team against the Chicago Bears. Even though the collegians lost 5-0, Ford considered it an honor to have been selected for the All-Star team and to compete against one of the great legends of football, Bronko Nagurski.

Ford received offers to play professional football from both the Green Bay Packers and the Detroit Lions. "Each team said they'd pay me $2,800 for a fourteen-game season," Ford remembers. "At the time that was big money, and it was tempting, but my mind was set on studying law. I didn't think pro football would lead me anywhere."

With a check in the amount of $100 that he had received as an All-Star player, Ford headed for New Haven to visit Yale University, where he intended to attend law school. The purpose of his trip was to secure a job as an assistant line coach as well as the position of freshman coach for the boxing team. With the annual wages of $2,400 these two positions paid, Ford would have enough funds to study law.

"It was the first time in my life that I was actually able to save money," he tells. "By January 1936 I had accumulated enough savings to repay a two-year six-hundred-dollar loan made to me by some friends of the family. It was a debt I still owed from my days at the University of Michigan."

Among the football players whom Ford coached during his days at Yale were Bob Taft and William Proxmire. Among his law classmates at Yale were Cyrus Vance, Potter Stewart, and Sargent Shriver. Despite the tough competition and his grueling full-time coaching jobs, he graduated law school in the top 25 percent of his class.

Ford returned to Grand Rapids in January 1941 and began the tedious job of studying for the Michigan law bar examination. After passing the bar he and an old fraternity brother, Phil Buchen, took a bold step by hanging up their shingle rather than electing to join an established firm.

"We were impatient and ambitious," Ford recalls. "While we had good vision, we didn't have clients. Our first work was a routine title search for which we charged fifteen dollars. However, after the client balked that it was too high, we reduced the bill to ten dollars."

In time more clients came and the law office of Ford and Buchen took on work involving pension trusts, wills, labor disputes, separations, and divorces—it was a thriving practice. Then, on December 7, 1941, everything changed when Japanese planes attacked Pearl Harbor.

In early 1942 the young lawyer became Ensign Ford of the U.S. Navy and was sent to V-5 preflight school in Chapel Hill, North Carolina, where he served as a physical fitness instructor. He wrote many requests for a transfer to participate in a combative role.

In the spring of 1943 he received orders to report to the light aircraft carrier USS *Monterey* with a dual assignment of athletic director and gunnery division officer. That November the *Monterey* joined the aircraft carrier USS *Enterprise*, another light cruiser, and six destroyers, and engaged in extensive combat in the Pacific. The *Monterey* was almost lost when a severe typhoon hit it and a serious fire on board killed a number of crew members.

Ford was discharged in 1946 as a Lt. Commander. Upon his return to Grand Rapids he joined the law firm of Butterfield, Keeney, and Amberg. Two and a half years later, at the age of thirty-five, he ran for Congress.

"After World War II, I had some strong feelings that the country should take an internationalist point of view," Ford tells. "The district's congressman, Bartel Jonkman, was an isolationist and also a senior Republican on the House Committee on Foreign Affairs. He was doing his best to veto constructive foreign aid legislation such as the Marshall Plan. I didn't like his positions on these issues, so I decided to run against him in the primary. In 1946 he had no Republican opposition, and he was a shoo-in in the general election. The last time a Democrat was a representative was back in 1912.

" 'Jonkman can't be defeated,' everyone advised me. 'He's a nine-year incumbent and he's much too strong. Besides, you're only thirty-five and he's sixty-five.'

"I was determined, and I figured that because I was a new, fresh face who had been away in the military, I had a chance to beat him—in particular if I worked day and night.

"The big issue was our difference of views on foreign aid," Ford explains. "I blitzed the district, talking to anyone who would listen, and expressed my opinion on how I thought it was necessary and morally right for the U.S. to provide aid to rebuild war-torn Europe and Japan. Jonkman strongly opposed any aid whatsoever.

"I challenged him to a debate and he refused. This was his first mistake. Next he alienated Leonard Woodcock, the United Auto Workers Representative in western Michigan, and, as a result, the union supported me. Then, due to his isolationist views, Jonkman lost the support of the Grand Rapids *Press*.

"His fatal mistake was when the newspaper endorsed me for the primary and he blasted the editor instead of directing his wrath at me. The two of them got into a personal feud and it worked to my advantage. The tide shifted to me, and that's when Jonkman made a desperate effort to attack me and my supporters with a flurry of ridiculous charges. On election day, I beat him by a two-to-one margin. Once I got the nomination it was pretty much a foregone conclusion that I'd win the general election—and I did."

The novice Republican captured 61 percent of the vote. Six months previously Ford had been given no chance to win the election. During the next quarter of a century Ford won twelve more elections with an astounding average of 64 percent of the vote.

A secret to Ford's success in politics, he claims, is a lesson taught to him as an athlete. "Any good football team has to have a strategy. This means the team must be prepared to execute the most effective offensive plays based on its personnel. Likewise each team member has a specific assignment, and he must be prepared to execute it properly on Saturday. The same applies to the defensive unit.

"In politics, prior to each campaign, I had to prepare myself about certain issues," Ford continues, "and as I did in football, I made it my business to know where my opponent stood. If I wasn't knowledgeable on his views, I'd put myself in a position where I'd be vulnerable to his attack, and at the same time I'd have no ammunition to go after him.

"Likewise, I would be an ineffective representative if I didn't do my homework in advance and walked on the floor of the House without knowing what the issues were. There'd be no way I could cast an intelligent yes or no vote. So whatever it took to study the background of each piece of legislation, I'd make certain to come prepared. To do otherwise would have been irresponsible."

As President, Ford had to prepare himself in advance so he could understand important issues and thereby be equipped to approve or veto scores of legislation. Similarly, as the nation's chief executive officer, Ford had to review large stacks of "homework" assignments prior to meeting with heads of states, foreign diplomats, and domestic government officials. On issues regarding the Cold War, the security of America and of the free world was at stake. Here again, like a well-coached football team, success depended on teamwork.

"Beginning with the chief of staff," Ford says, "which supplied me with a steady flow of information that passed my desk, I found it necessary to continually critique data so I could make the right decisions. There was far too much reading material for me to cover on a daily basis . . . without relying on others to get it ready for me in advance. If I couldn't rely on my staff, I'd never have the time to do it on my own."

A large portion of the information to which the former President refers was prepared by his White House staff and presented to him in a briefing book—a thick-bound, single-spaced report that often contained a hundred pages or more. Like other modern-day American Presidents, Ford would extensively review this material to prepare himself for his presidential duties.

Frequently it required a monumental effort to stay well-informed on so many issues; however, failure to be fully prepared could be devastating for the entire nation. There simply was no other alternative to President Ford; he *had* to do it. During the month of November 1974, for example, Ford was required to study several briefing books when he journeyed to Tokyo on the first leg of a lengthy Far Eastern tour.

When Air Force One landed at Tokyo's Haneda International Airport the eighteenth of November, it marked the first time ever that an American President had set foot on Japanese soil. Here meetings were scheduled at the Imperial Palace with Emperor Hirohito and Prime Minister Kakuei Tanaka. The Japanese emperor is head of state in name only and, accordingly, does not discuss politics or major issues. Hence Ford brushed up on his marine biology, a subject about which Emperor Hirohito was an expert and on which he had authored four books. Later the two men discussed baseball—the Emperor was a devout fan.

Ford's conferences with the prime minister were of a more serious nature. Subjects discussed included U.S. assurances to sell its agricultural commodities, the need to reconvene the GATT (General Agreement on Tariffs and Trade), the pooling of energy resources, strategies to combat the recession, and the role Japan would play in the economic stability of South Vietnam.

Briefing books on each of these subjects—from marine biology to economics—were thoroughly prepared in advance and meticulously reviewed by President Ford. More briefing books were prepared for his trip to South Korea, where Ford discussed the subjects of military aid and human rights with President Park Chung Hee.

The final stop of the tour was the Soviet port city of Vladivostok. Soviet Premier Leonid Brezhnev and Foreign Minister Andrey Gromyko had journeyed more than four thousand miles across seven time zones by train from Moscow to meet with President Ford on the morning of November twenty-third.

In the beginning their conversation was informal. Brezhnev talked about his soccer days as a young man: "I played the left side. I haven't played in a long time." "I haven't played football for a long time, either," Ford replied. "I wasn't very fast, but I could hold the line."

The dialogue between the two world leaders became more serious when the subject of the arms race was brought up. This was the first meeting between the two nation's heads of state since May 1972 when the two countries reached an agreement on strategic arms limitations (SALT). That accord included a freeze on the numbers of land- and sea-based ballistic missiles, both those in existence and those under construction. The first SALT agreement was due to expire in October 1977, so it was essential that a permanent and more extensive accord be reached.

While the meetings with the Soviet leader went smoothly and set the format for the signing of SALT II, Ford received some distressing news from home from one of his aides. On a missed field goal Michigan lost to Ohio State in Columbus that Saturday afternoon by a score of 12 to 10. While the President felt bad about his alma mater's defeat, "There were more important things that demanded my concern," he tells.

The day-to-day schedule of a United States President moves at a demanding pace even when he is not jetting around the world to attend meetings with heads of state. Back at the White House every day, beginning early in the morning and continuing into the late hours of the night, the job consists of grueling work. In short, the position of President of the United States requires an individual with a high level of energy.

Gerald Ford attributes his abundance of energy to keeping in excellent physical shape. Ford stands an even six feet tall, and his weight is the same at 198 pounds as it was during his football days at Michigan. The former high-school swimmer still swims a quarter of a mile each morning and again in the late afternoon. While his basketball, track, and football days are long behind him, he now plays a good game of golf—and he's an avid skier.

Other than some knee trouble left over from his football days, the former President is in tiptop shape. "Taking good care of your body goes further than simply doing it for health reasons," Ford asserts. "When you're in good shape, you're more mentally alert."

During his tenure as President, Ford had a swimming pool installed in the White House, which he used on a regular basis. Every morning he arose at 5:30 and began his day with a series of calisthenics in an exercise room located in the residential area of the White House. "It's a discipline that long ago became part of my routine," he explains. "It goes back to my participation in sports.

"When a team effort is required in a game like football, it takes a lot of practice to get the offensive and defensive units to jell. It doesn't happen overnight, but the amount of time put in during the week is reflected in the team's performance on Saturday. And you've got to keep it up for the entire season.

"A lot of players viewed practice as drudgery, but I always looked at it as part of the game. To me it was a challenge, not a dreary way to spend a couple of hours each day. Later I carried this attitude over to my studies in law school. Again, to a certain extent, the drudgery is there, but it's part of the learning process to become a successful attorney."

Whether or not to pardon Richard Nixon was one of the most difficult decisions Ford had to make during his presidency. Millions of Americans across the country were bitter about the Watergate scandal—they viewed the break-in and the cover-up as a national disgrace. They were angry and bitter and wanted nothing more than to see Nixon put behind bars. It was certain that several of his aides would be sentenced, and for him to remain free represented a dual system of justice. After all, he had given the orders for the break-in.

"The country was in a turmoil," Ford explains. "It was an awful time. In my first month as President I was spending about 25 percent of my time listening to lawyers in the Department of Justice and the White House staff telling me what I should do about Nixon's tapes and Nixon's papers. At the same time the United States was faced with growing economic troubles as well as problems with the Soviet Union. I finally decided that my obligation as President was to spend 100 percent of my time on those problems rather than spending 25 percent of my time on the problems of one man.

"The only way to clear the decks was to give Nixon a pardon. I wanted to get the entire controversy out of the White House and out of the front pages of the papers all over the country. The continuous court proceedings from indictment to conviction to appeal would have lasted two to three years, and those headlines would have gone on and on. The only way to get it off the agenda was to do what I did. It was my own decision. The majority of my staff didn't agree with me but I thought it was right, and I think time proved it to be. But it wasn't very popular for a long time."

The Nixon pardon was one of many decisions Ford made during his political career that he knew would be unpopular.

Nonetheless, he did what he believed was best for the country. On matters of principle the former President is simply not a man to give in to the critics. Here too he cites his athletic days: "As a football player, you have critics in the stands and critics in the press. Few of them have ever centered the ball, kicked a punt, or thrown a touchdown pass with 100,000 people looking on, yet they assume they know all the answers.

"Their comments helped me to develop a thick hide, and in later years, whenever the critics assailed me, I've been able to let their jibes roll off my back. In most cases the critics are not qualified to pass judgment on whether the team played well or whether it was well coached. Sure, they get emotionally involved, but as a participant on the playing field a player must accept the criticism and go ahead and do his or her job.

"It's a sign of strong character to do what you think is right. Conversely, if you allow the people in the stands to upset you, you can't play well. The same applies to allowing a sportswriter who criticizes you in the newspapers to bother you. You have to be oblivious to their negative comments. I believe my participation in competitive sports was very important training for my later experiences in politics."

Recently Ford wrote a letter to his good friend Jim Murray, the renowned sports columnist with the *Los Angeles Times*. "I told him that I still read the sports section first because, at least there, I have a 50-50 chance of being right," Ford laughs. "Those are better odds than a politician has on the front page or any other part of the newspaper. While sportswriters can be tough, I think they're basically more fair than other writers."

Throughout his term in office, President Ford was depicted by comedians as clumsy and consequently bore the brunt of their jokes. Yet, in truth, Ford is unquestionably the finest athlete ever to reside in the White House. He is an agile man, but tens of thousands of photographs were taken of him on ski slopes and golf courses—he was bound to take an occasional spill or slice a golf ball that landed behind a tree.

"Sure, I took my share of spills," he says. "Anyone who ever put on a pair of skis has, and I've also had my share of bad balls—let's remember, I'm not a pro. Well, with enough photographs of everything I do, the odds were high for some to be printed in the newspapers. For the most part they were humorous photographs and I got a good laugh out of them. I never let it bother me. There were far more important things to worry about as President than being criticized for a bad golf shot or a fall on the slopes."

Gerald Ford took the razzing in good spirit because, as everyone who knows him well will testify, he is a good sport. He has a keen sense of humor and has never been one to take his own importance seriously. This is not to imply that the former President lacks self-esteem and confidence. "Undoubtedly, my success as an athlete in high school and college developed my self-assurance," he states. "Yet I had enough losses along the way that I never became overconfident or arrogant."

In the political arena as well as the sports arena Ford proved to be a winner. Beginning in 1948 with his first political election, he was the victor in thirteen consecutive congressional races. His White House loss to Jimmy Carter in 1976 was, in fact, his only defeat as a candidate for public office.

After the Republican party's 1976 convention in Kansas City, the polls showed that Ford was trailing Carter by 33 points. This prompted Ford to challenge his opponent to a series of debates on national television. "We had to do something dramatic to catch up with Carter," he explains, "and I figured the debates were one way to narrow the margin. I was never apprehensive about going face-to-face with Carter. First, I knew the issues, and second, my in-depth experiences at the federal-government level provided me with a background that

I believed gave me, at minimum, a better than even chance to prevail. And I'm sure . . . my competitive spirit that I developed in athletics was what got my juices going. And when those juices get going, it gets *me* going."

Gerald Ford is a man who doesn't quit when he's losing— even when he was getting beat by a lopsided margin of 33 percentage points. In the end Jimmy Carter won the November 1976 election with a narrow 1½-point margin. Ford's never-give-up attitude, however, made it a close race. Political experts claim that the Nixon pardoning was the determining factor that cost Ford a second term in the White House. "I did what I had to do because it was the right thing to do," Ford states. "I'd do the same thing all over because I believe it was right."

He then adds, "When you're in a competitive situation, whether it's an athletic event or non-sports-related, you have to make hard decisions. You can't second-guess yourself. And once it's over you must go on with your life. Now, did I mind losing the election? Of course I did. I never like to lose anything."

Ford says that since he stepped down from the presidency, he and Jimmy Carter have been good friends: "I have always respected my opponent when I competed in athletics, and it's the same in any contest. I don't believe in dwelling on a defeat." In a telegram acknowledging his loss in the general election, Ford wired the President-elect:

Dear Jimmy:

It is apparent now that you have won our long and intense struggle for the presidency. I congratulate you on your victory. As one who has been honored to serve the people of this great land both in Congress and as President, I believe that we must now put the division of the campaign behind us and unite the country once again in the common pursuit of peace and prosperity. I want to assure you that you will have my complete and whole-hearted support as you take the oath of office this January. I also pledge to you that I and all members of my Administration will do all that we can to ensure that you begin your term as smoothly and as effectively as possible. May God bless you and your family as you undertake your new responsibilities.

Gerald Ford

After Chief Justice Berger administered the oath to Jimmy Carter, the new President's first words were: "For myself and for our nation, I want to thank my predecessor for all he has done to heal our land."

In his interview for this book, Ford stressed: "I strongly feel that being a good team player is more important than being a star. Sure it's nice to be a star and a good team player. But I would always want my reputation to be primarily a good member of my team." He then added, "By doing this, your prospects for being a star are enhanced."

President Ford served our country well. In this capacity, he was, perhaps, the ultimate team player. As such, he shined as a star.

7

▪ BETSY KING ▪

World-Class Golfer, Witnessing Christian

Betsy King breaks many of the molds from which the public expects its superstar athletes to be produced. Arguably one of the greatest performers the world of women's golf has ever produced, King, in point of fact, needs to be explained. She is almost always found among the front-runners of today's major tournaments, but she frets about becoming too competitive.

Win, lose, or draw, she rarely shows emotion. There is no "high-fiving" or throwing her visor in the air when the putt falls for her, just as there is no pouting when the drive goes awry. To her chagrin, King has been called "the Ice Lady."

"Reporters and fans have always had a hard time understanding Betsy King, just like they don't understand most athletes who don't brag when they win, cry when they lose, admit they spend more time reading the Bible than thinking about major championships and halls of fame, and who can't come up with a better explanation for their success other than the fact that they practice a lot," commented *Golf World*, which named her Player of the Year in 1989.

Few would have predicted stardom for King during her early days as a professional, although she earned her tour card on her first attempt at qualifying. She got off to a blazing start in her maiden outing as a professional, the Long Island Charity Classic, and held the lead after thirty-six holes, only to falter later and finish in fifteenth place.

Her lack of experience and what the professionals saw as a flawed swing were to continue to take their toll. She didn't win a major tournament for seven years. Her only victories were one tournament in Japan and a team event on the tour. "I don't recall ever thinking of quitting golf, but I did think I might never win a major tournament," she says.

She was sustained by the knowledge that there are many people who never win but still have a comfortable life-style playing professional golf. She felt she could live with that situation so long as she knew she was making her best effort: "For me the turnaround came in 1980. I had just dropped to fiftieth in the LPGA [Ladies Professional Golf Association] rankings, after being nineteenth the year before. It is interesting that I became a Christian at the beginning of that year."

Also in 1980 she began her long and mutually rewarding coach-student relationship with Ed Oldfield. Oldfield had been successful in coaching a number of top women golfers, including Jan Stephenson, and is known as a perfectionist who will not back away from changing every facet of a player's game from A to Z. Not the least bit short on self-assurance, Oldfield declares, "I am confident I can make a player successful, but it's not magic, and there aren't any shortcuts. It takes a player who is patient and determined."

He had the ideal student in Betsy King, a lithe 5'6" blonde who wanted to learn and was not the least bit afraid of hard work. Coach and student labored through long practice sessions on golf courses around the country. They broke her game down into its multiple parts and put it back together. Following each session King would take endless practice swings in front of a mirror to perfect what she had been instructed to do. The determined young athlete missed a lot of tournament cuts that season, but both she and her coach could see progress was being made.

After the 1980 season she moved to Phoenix to join several other women from the LPGA Tour who were also Oldfield's students. Sportswriters reported that she would hit as many as eight hundred practice shots a day, working on the changes she and Oldfield agreed were necessary to improve her game.

The King-Oldfield partnership has been described by one sportswriter as "golf's most successful and most enduring teacher-student relationship since Jack Grout taught a young kid named Nicklaus to swing as hard as he could." King says of those turnaround days, "I was never a natural. I've always had to work hard, but that is easy when you know you're working on the right things. I'd been to fifteen teachers in my life, but the things Ed said made the most sense."

All the hard work and sacrifices began to pay off. By the next season she moved her LPGA rating from fiftieth to twenty-second. She was rated number one in 1984 when she won $266,000 and again in 1989 when she won the United States Women's Open, worth $80,000 in prize money and even more in prestige and confidence.

For the year of 1989 as a whole, she won six major tournaments including the Jamaica Classic and the Nestlé World Championship, where she was up against sixteen of the best players in the world, including Patty Sheehan, Nancy Lopez, Beth Daniel, and Juli Inkster. King's annual earnings exceeded $650,000, making her the first woman golfer to win more than one-half million dollars in a single year.

By the middle of the 1990 season she had won more than twenty official LPGA titles, plus the Women's British Open and a tournament in Japan, to claim a total of well over $3 million in prize money.

King says that she will continue to take lessons throughout her career. "The thing a lot of people don't understand is no matter how good you get, you still need to take lessons, always trying to improve," she declares.

"I am a firm believer in aiming for perfection—accepting, however, the fact that none of us will ever be perfect. Before you begin to win, you are apt to think you have to play perfectly in order to beat the competition. No room for mistakes. But you do learn after a while that you can make a lot of mistakes and still win. It's like that in golf and anything else in life.

"You also have to accept the fact that there are many things in life to enjoy without being perfect at them."

Gesturing toward an old-fashioned organ in her home, King says she took a lot of lessons and spent many hours practicing on that instrument. "I reached a certain level, far from perfect, and I knew I would never get a lot better. But I keep playing for myself and my friends when we sing hymns. That provides a lot of enjoyment," she relates.

While perfection is neither possible nor necessary, error-free play has to be the constant goal, King believes. "If you don't keep trying to get everything just right, particularly in golf, a lot of people are going to pass you by." This means lessons, discipline, and practice, practice.

"The biggest thrill I get is when I have practiced a particular thing—still learning from my mistakes and my lessons— then go out in a tournament and do it right . . . a hook around a tree or a low punch shot or something like that," she observes, "because that's something new I have learned and practiced and put into play."

Practice leads to good mechanics and that, in her opinion, is the key to the improvement of her game. "I think the mental part of golf is overplayed," she says.

"Pardon me?" one is tempted to reply. What kind of heresy is that when books and videotapes on positive thinking and the visualization of success in every endeavor from golf to selling to weight control are falling like rain on an April afternoon?

King's response goes like this: "Having a mental image of success is fine, but I can beat any 18 handicapper in the world—I don't care what the person's attitude is. He can picture hitting a golf ball 250 yards all he wants, but if he hasn't worked hard at developing that swing—if he doesn't have it, he can't do it."

She proceeds to tell an interviewer that it is just the law of physics at work—not emotion, not visualizing the swing and the ball sailing long and far against a clear blue sky. When you make a good swing, a good shot follows.

"There certainly are people who have unorthodox swings, but they get away with it. It's almost like they hit good shots in spite of the swing, not because of it."

King admits that she is always thinking about how to do the one or two things she is working on. "That helps me a lot under pressure. Instead of thinking, 'I have to make a good shot here,' I am free to concentrate on what I must do to make the swing I need to make at that time. I am not really thinking as much about the goal of doing well on that hole or winning the round as I am about what I have to do right then and there with the club."

She has found that when a golfer is trying to undo a bad habit he or she can't get it done by hitting balls on the driving range for an hour and then forgetting the problem when it is time to play a match. "The easiest way to change a bad habit is to think about it while you practice at the driving range. Then think constantly during the match about what you learned to do to correct the error. Keep at it until doing it right becomes natural," she advises.

In fact, King is likely to spend more time thinking about a bad shot she made than the good ones. Her reasoning is simple. If you don't recognize your problems and think about them, how can you correct what you have been doing wrong?

King notes that a great many people have a problem with taking lessons to undo mistakes and learn new things, to say nothing of practicing until the improved skills are ingrained into the total game. In other words, they are reluctant to sacrifice short-term for the longer term gain.

"One thing young people have a hard time with is sacrificing for now, realizing that down the road there is going to be a benefit," King insists. "Also there is a big problem with the examples a lot of kids see in adults. They see too many adults leading lives that say, 'I want it right now.' As you mature, you learn you can't have everything right now. Immediate success, immediate improvement—it usually takes time and patience."

As King speaks, she recognizes that a visitor to her home in Scottsdale, Arizona, could see a contradiction. The house, by any measure, is stunning. The 3,200-square-foot structure sits on about an acre of land some eighteen miles north of Phoenix. King describes it as semi-modern with a Southwestern influence. It is one-story in construction, yet its high, vaulted ceilings, supported by four sturdy but graceful columns one encounters upon entering the front door, give it a special feeling of spaciousness. Its interior walls are a muted white; the decor is in soft shades of blues accented by a range of pastels.

Looking through tall glass doors at the back of the main room out onto a large patio, one is struck by the glistening swimming pool and high stucco wall beyond which, in the far distance, rise the rugged brown mountains of Arizona.

"Here I have this house, but I waited for it," King says. "I know when I had my first good year I waited before I bought anything major. I had seen people who did well in professional sports spend money, and then later they didn't have anything left. That put extra pressure on them. They had to continue to perform well to keep up their life-style. I knew that I didn't want to do that. I have just tried to be patient and move up gradually. It is good for anyone, especially young people, to learn not to overstep their bounds."

In her frequent appearances before youth groups as a representative of the Fellowship of Christian Athletes, King speaks to the point of life goals. She maintains that people of all ages should think of being the best they can be in all things at all times instead of trying so hard to be number one.

"I want to be mentally, physically, and mechanically prepared when I begin each tournament, and then I want to give 100 percent effort on each shot," she declares. "The rest will take care of itself.

"You know in your own heart if you have given 100 percent of your best effort. You know if you are loafing or if you haven't performed as you should in some situation.

"We also have to keep it in perspective. When we have done 100 percent of all we can do, that is it; that's all we can do in that situation. Then leave it alone, spend time in relationships with others, trying to help people who are less fortunate than we are. That's what God calls us to do."

When it comes to goals, King firmly believes that it is never wise to set an objective over which one does not have 100 percent control. "I try not to set goals that don't depend solely on my own individual efforts," she explains.

Applying this idea to golf, she declares, "To say my goal is to win the U.S. Open is to take on a mission that is impacted by a lot of other factors. There are 150 other players out there who influence the outcome. And there's the weather and a million other things I cannot control or even have much influence over. What you can do, though, is make it your goal to be prepared and give your best on every shot."

She believes it is the same in every endeavor. The salesman shouldn't have as his goal winning the gold cup as top salesman of the year. Competing salesmen and products, economic conditions, even the weather and world affairs, will go a long way toward determining who wins that award. Instead, he should be aiming toward a target of being the best he can be each day.

Given the widespread folklore of winning athletes' attitude toward competition, it is interesting to hear King express her concern that she may become "too competitive" and explain how she tries to keep emotions out of her play.

King acknowledges that when she went on the LPGA Tour in 1977 she was too competitive for her own good. These were tough days for her when she was trying to come to grips with her own shortcomings and resented the success of others. She began to accept the fact that there are people with God-given talents who have a better chance at winning.

"I came to believe that, as a Christian, you are called on to be the best you can be with the talents you have been given, whatever they are. For me that was a big liberating factor. I don't have to compare myself with other people. What counts is what I am achieving with the talents God has given me.

"I think everybody is going to have a different walk in life; you just have to do the best with where you are and the situations that come your way," she says. "And, when you do that, you are free to enjoy the good in everyone else or what happens good for someone else.

"You have to be competitive in golf, but only with yourself and the golf course, not with other players. When I go out and play, I certainly want to beat everybody else, but it's almost like I get into an analytical mode about myself and my game."

King recalls that she didn't follow her own advice in a match at Lake Knona Club in Orlando, Florida, against golfers from Europe. "A lot of emotion had built up. On the last day I was playing against a girl from Scotland," she relates. "I was two up with four holes to play. There were a number of other Europeans following us around; they were really rooting for my opponent. That upset me a lot and I got far too competitive. I tried too hard. Instead of taking it one shot at a time and just trying to hit each one the best I could, I started worrying too much about what she was doing. I ended up tying the match."

Those who follow King's play say that it is just about impossible now to read the difference between her highs and her lows. If she loses, she will most often put it aside by saying it just wasn't her day and it wasn't meant to be. If she wins, there is no big celebration—it's off to practice to improve her game for the next tournament.

She attributes the progress she has made in controlling her emotions and in pointing her competitive instincts in the most constructive direction to her deep religious faith. "I pray to be a good witness," she says. "I pray for peace. I pray for perspective. But patience comes up more than anything."

It is clear that King is not pleased with the media's reference to her lack of emotion, particularly the "Ice Lady" tag applied by at least one writer. "You get tired of that; it's kinda tough," she admits. "It is true that I am always fighting to control my emotions. So they say, 'Ice Lady.'

"Every sport is different. In golf the best players aren't the most emotional ones. It is different, say, in basketball and football. In those sports it helps to get psyched up. In golf you have to think more and stay calm to do what you're doing the best way possible. So I've made it a goal of mine to control my emotions."

King believes she has become more patient as she has matured. She describes patience as a major part of her Christian faith. "I don't know how many times I have prayed for patience before I go out to play in a tournament . . . and in everything I do, for that matter. Oftentimes I don't succeed. Sometimes I can be very patient, then not patient in other things. We all fail at some point to achieve a mature life, but I keep trying."

A visitor does not spend much time in King's presence before it becomes crystal clear that the most important thing in her life is her Christian faith. It is obvious that the blessing of the close, sustaining relationship she enjoys with her mother and father provides another important underpinning for her approach to life on and off the golf course.

King was born in 1955 in Reading, Pennsylvania (population 80,000-plus), fifty-miles northwest of Philadelphia. Her family soon moved a few miles outside of town to settle near Limekiln, Pennsylvania, a community composed of a country store and fifty mailboxes.

She grew up in a happy and secure Christian home composed of her father, Weir, a practicing doctor now in his seventies; her mother, Helen, a homemaker; and an older brother, Lee, an attorney in the West Palm Beach area of Florida. The family lived in a sprawling country house on a hill overlooking thirty-two acres of farmland. King is drawn back to this place from her past as often as her heavy schedule will permit. "I like to go back there during the summers when I take a little time off. It is such a contrast for me," she explains.

The King family's life was strongly oriented to sports. Her father, a Canadian by birth, attended Dickinson College in Carlisle, Pennsylvania, on a football scholarship. After serving in the Canadian Air Force in World War II, he earned his medical degree at Thomas Jefferson University in Philadelphia. Her mother was captain of the women's varsity basketball team and played field hockey at the University of Rhode Island and was later named to that institution's athletic hall of fame.

Both of King's parents are avid golfers and her brother was active in almost all sports. From an early age, Betsy King was an all-around athlete, playing softball, basketball, and field hockey. By her early teens she was competing in out-of-state golf tournaments.

"I was a typical tomboy," King remembers. "Our whole family was into sports. My brother is a year older. We did things together. We were very fortunate because our parents exposed us to a lot of opportunities, but they never pushed us.

They let us pursue what we wanted. I took lessons to learn to play the organ and the clarinet. There were lessons in ice skating, swimming, horseback riding, ballet, and golf. I took all sorts of instructions."

King soon found that she was more inclined toward athletics than music and some of her other pursuits. Besides, with athletics, she liked to practice. She and her brother would often spend the day at the country club playing golf. Many hours were devoted to shooting baskets at home.

By the time King graduated from high school she had won all-county honors in basketball, softball, and field hockey. Ironically, she did not play golf as a part of the high school program. "That was the era," she points out, "when women couldn't play with the guys and there wasn't a girls' golf team. So I just played softball instead as my spring sport."

She started playing golf at the age of ten, the year she took her beginning lesson from the pro at the Reading Country Club. Her first experience in serious national competition came at age sixteen when she entered the U.S. Golf Association Junior National Tournament at Augusta. "There may have been as many as 120 girls there for the two days of qualifying rounds," she recalls. "The tournament takes the top thirty-two, and they go into match play. I didn't make the cut."

Two years later she beat a star golfer thirty years her senior to win a Central Pennsylvania title. In 1972, while still in high school, she got all the way to the semifinals of the USGA Junior Girls Championship before losing to Amy Alcott, who turned professional soon after the tournament.

Meanwhile King had done quite well in the classroom and graduated in the spring of 1973 among the top ten in her class. What with sports, lessons in a variety of fields, and study, hers was a busy schedule. Didn't she feel somewhat set apart from her classmates because of the discipline required by such a regimen?

Not really, she thinks, because things were so different then.

"When I was in high school a lot of people played everything," she explains. "You didn't specialize the way they do now. I almost think that it's bad that kids are forced to pick an activity and concentrate on it almost exclusively. Each activity takes so much time that they almost make you drop other things, where when I was in high school you could still do a lot of things. I think that is the way it should be. You can specialize when you get older, but at high-school age I think it is better to be exposed to a lot of different things to find something that you enjoy doing and that you are good at."

Furman University at Greenville, South Carolina, where King enrolled as a freshman in 1973 on an athletic scholarship, was an excellent choice for the young athlete. Founded in 1826, Furman is the oldest Baptist college in the South. Small, with an enrollment of about 2,500, and conservative, it insists on strict academic standards while supporting a healthy sports program. The institution is nestled on a beautiful, wooded campus, encompassing 750 acres. A challenging golf course borders the campus.

King continued the same kind of busy schedule at Furman she had pursued in high school. "I started out thinking maybe I was interested in history, because I had liked the subject so much in high school," she says. "But I didn't enjoy the first history course I took at Furman, so I decided to switch majors. At the end of my sophomore year I moved into physical education." She flourished in this environment, devoting many classroom hours to studying subjects related to sports while competing in intercollegiate basketball, field hockey, and golf.

During her second year at Furman she suffered a knee injury, first in field hockey and later in basketball. This was to set the course of her life.

"I didn't have surgery at the time, but I did have to have an operation about eight years later to repair torn cartilage on both sides of my knee and some other damage," she explains. The net result of the injury midway in her college career was to cause her to focus her attention and energy on golf, which placed different demands on her knees than other sports did.

Furman was beginning to assert itself as a national power-house in women's golf. With King playing a leading role, Furman's team won the National Collegiate Championship in 1976, her junior year. That year she was low amateur at the U.S. Women's Open. The next year she was selected as Fur-man's Athlete of the Year.

King was also winning in the classroom. She graduated cum laude in physical education with an overall 3.4 grade-point average. The college recognized her accomplishments in the classroom by naming her Woman Scholar Athlete of the Year in 1977.

King says that her heavy schedule of sports and classroom work probably caused her to suffer socially. "I didn't go out as much as a lot of people did," she recalls. "Even in college, I felt that when we were going on a golf trip on the weekend I had to make up for it in studying. I remember going to the library many Friday nights. There weren't a lot of other kids there.

"It was interesting the way the academic side of my time at Furman turned out," King muses. "I took these tests in high school, and they predicted my grade point in college would be 2.6. I don't know how they came up with something like that. I was near the top of my high school graduating class. It just goes to show how hard it is to predict what someone can do when he or she tries."

It was clear that King had a shot at the professional golf tour, and she went after that objective with a determination that paid off. But it was a rocky start for her. At this point religion entered her life in a serious and significant way.

King had grown up in a reserved kind of denominational

church, which she describes as "a church where no one brings a Bible." Of those years she says, "Religion just wasn't a priority with me."

At Furman, attendance was required at a chapel service each week. It really wasn't a religious service; it was more about the humanities. "On Wednesday mornings they had what they called a 'Religion in Life' course, where they brought in speakers like Dr. Joyce Brothers and former President Jimmy Carter," King remembers.

She resisted attempts by other students to entice her to join their evening Bible studies. "I just wasn't interested at that time," she says. But King found a different world in professional golf. She was becoming too emotionally involved in her game. She was troubled by the fact that her emotions fluctuated with her performance. Her peace of mind off the course suffered; her play was being hampered.

By 1979 she recognized that she needed some power beyond herself in order to succeed. She accepted an invitation to attend a fellowship of Christian Athletes Golf Day in Florida. She studiously considered what she heard the speakers say about what Christ had meant to their lives. She questioned the other women about their faith. What she heard and experienced caught her attention.

The next year King was invited to a Tee-Off Conference by Margie Davis, who was soon to be named chaplain for the women's tour. This event featured an opportunity to play golf and to learn what it means to have a personal relationship with God. "I have to admit I was as much attracted by the practice time for golf as I was to the morning and evening discussion sessions. I had never been to one of these fellowship things. I figured the worst that could happen would be that I could work on my game," she related in the book *Grace & Glory,* which recounts the stories of the Christian faith of a number of women athletes.

The closing speaker for the conference was Bruce Wilkerson, from a ministry known as Walk Through the Bible. His message boiled down to the simplest terms: "You need to say a prayer, to invite Christ into your lives and accept him as your Savior." According to King today, "That was the first time I had ever heard how to invite Christ into your life. I did just that."

The change in her life was not as if a blinding light had been turned on—it wasn't as if she had been on the wild side and had to be converted from a life of sin and depravity. She explains: "I am thankful that I didn't have to get to the point of being in the gutter, in real trouble, before I saw the need for God. It was just that I realized something was missing. I wasn't being the best I could be.

"As a Christian, I recognize the fruit of the spirit that should be in my life. Love, joy, peace, patience, kindness, goodness, gentleness, faithfulness, and self-control. These are the attributes of a mature Christian, so that is something I want in my life and that I am striving for. The Lord is the one who enables you to achieve things. It's not just your self-effort going forth; He empowers you. So sometimes if you try too hard yourself alone, you don't achieve your goal."

King believes that a substantial number of highly visible athletes in college and in the professional ranks exhibit strong Christian faith because of the pressure they live under. "I think sometimes the pressure of athletics makes people think about things more," she declares. "Lots of times people try all their lives to get to the top, thinking that is going to satisfy them. When they reach the top they realize that's not all there is to life; something is left out. At the same time there is a great move toward evangelism in athletics, so the need and the answer come together."

King is happy to see more and more athletes becoming involved with religion. Because they are among the most admired people in our society, they have a platform from which to influence other people.

"She's as good a Christian as she is a golfer," according to
Bill Lewis, a retired U.S. Navy captain who leads a ministry
among golfers for the Fellowship of Christian Athletes (FCA).

Principally through the FCA King has become involved in a
number of public service and humanitarian works, including
Habitat for Humanity, which is perhaps best known because of
the involvement of President Jimmy Carter. In the fall each
year King and as many as a dozen of her friendly competitors
from the tour go into the Appalachian Mountains of Tennessee
to actually build housing for the destitute people who are
struggling to live there.

"I know nothing about building a house," she admits. "I'm
not very mechanically inclined, but they have us do different
things. We are basically servants for a few days. It is so different, and neat. I am completely away from golf."

She describes the life as "spartan," the food as "plain." "It
is hard work. I have put in insulation, swept up the workshop,
laid tile flooring, and installed sheetrock. I have even done a
little painting.

"We enjoy it, being together and working as a team. But we
still compete as to who can drive the most nails or get the
most work done."

Her alma mater, Furman University, is another beneficiary of
King's good work. Each year, along with another golfer, Beth
Daniel, she hosts a pro-am tournament to raise money for the
golf program at Furman. She invites twenty-six of the best
pros on the women's circuit. Together, they have raised over
$50,000 each spring since 1981 to provide for the endowment
of a permanent golf scholarship.

Other recipients of King's public service include the FCA,
Easter Seals, and numerous local charities for which she has
organized and played in pro-am tournaments.

It is significant that of the numerous trophies tastefully
displayed in her Scottsdale home, the one that first catches a
visitor's eye is the Good Samaritan Award presented to her by

the Good Samaritan Hospital of Phoenix and Standard Register, a business reference service. "It is given to one player each year who has done the most for charity," she explains hesitantly. She declines to say more than that she's not sure what year it was presented and that she believes it was given for her work on behalf of Habitat, FCA, Easter Seals, and Furman.

What does the future hold for Betsy King?

"First, I expect to keep playing competitive golf for some time to come. Then I don't know. I have tried to use the tour time for putting myself in a position financially so that when I retire, I won't have to make a decision based on money. I am fortunate. There are not many people who are able to do that.

"I have thought at times of maybe going into some sort of Christian work full time. But I don't know. People I have met in the ministry are usually very people-oriented. I'm really not that much of a people person. Frankly, I like going out by myself and practicing. I don't necessarily like sitting around all of the time talking and socializing.

"I feel that a lot of my skills are administrative in terms of organizing such things as the pro-ams. I could see myself in athletic administration like an athletic director, as opposed to coaching."

Betsy King faces life with confidence, backed by great personal assets that have been nurtured and honed by participating in athletics.

"I know that you definitely can learn a lot of lessons about life from athletics," she says. "For me, personally, I believe the Lord had me out there so that I would be brought to recognizing my need for Him, just because I had a hard time handling the pressures of the game—the ups and downs.

"I am a little bit dismayed when I look at athletics now because the money side has almost taken over too much of the academics. The kids don't have enough chance to get an education, because they have to spend so much time on a sport. For me, personally, I never felt that sports were a detriment to my studies. My involvement just helped me to better organize my time. And I played because I love to play. If kids are not playing because they love the game, then they shouldn't do it."

King's message to athletes, young and old alike, is simple and to the point. "I have learned that it takes a lot of hard work and practice to be successful in athletics," she says. "I also have found out that the same kind of effort is demanded in whatever field you pursue. You just have to put in so many hours to give yourself a chance to perform well. There aren't any shortcuts to reaching your full potential."

8

■ ALEX KROLL ■

Football Player,
CEO—Young & Rubicam

When freshman Alex Kroll tried out for Leechburg High School's football team, he stood 5'6" and weighed 113 pounds. The only thing big about him were his size-twelve feet. "My feet were my toughest opponent," he tells. "They resisted me every step of the way." The lanky, awkward teenager was an improbable candidate for football stardom.

Leechburg (population 3,000) is located on the Kiskiminetas River, about forty miles northeast of Pittsburgh. The steel-mill town had a well-deserved reputation for growing big, strong athletes. The valley had produced several football players who went on to star at major colleges; some even made it to the professional ranks. During the summer of 1953 not a single person suspected that Alex Kroll could someday be one of them. In spite of his oversized feet, it appeared he was destined to be small. His father, a local steel-mill worker, stood at a mere 5'7".

When asked why he chose to play center, Kroll explains: "I was thin and not very strong, but in Leechburg, where football was the king in the hierarchy of sports, I wanted to be on the team. Football wasn't an elective in my hometown; it was a requirement.

"Upon carefully analyzing my competition in the freshman class I found that no one was interested in playing center. After all, it's a sort of awkward position that requires looking at the world upside down and throwing the ball backwards. I have since been told that having spent so many years looking at the world upside down has served to my advantage as a creative director of an advertising agency," Kroll says with a laugh.

"Well, my plan was simply to practice, practice, and practice, and through sheer repetition, I'd eventually master it. So that's what I did. I set up a rubber tire in my backyard and spent hours hunched over a football, continuously tossing it at my target."

August 18 traditionally marked the first day of football practice in western Pennsylvania, and in 1951 it was young Kroll's debut as a football player. On this particular day the temperature stood at 90° Fahrenheit and the humidity was perhaps even higher. Kroll was confident that his practice was about to pay off—that is, until a much bigger freshman from a nearby farming community also showed up to try out for center.

"This kid had real shoulders," Kroll recalls, "and really big muscles. Even his name was intimidating and perfect for football—*Shellhammer*. After taking one look at him, the only thought that raced through my mind was, 'I'm going to be the second-string center for the rest of my high school career.'

"The practice took place on the dirt infield of the baseball diamond. The coach didn't want us to wear out the grass on the game field," Kroll continues. "For starters he put us through a series of calisthenics. Next we did eight laps around the field which totaled two miles, then, about an hour into the workout, we did hundred-yard wind sprints. These generated enormous clouds of dust.

"People were crawling off the side of the field; many were throwing up, and still others were trying to. I was in considerable pain. In addition to the fatigue, my shoes were too big and so was my helmet, which partially blocked my vision. But I kept running, and when it came time to do the ninth wind sprint, Shellhammer, who was lined up next to me for the first eight sprints, had disappeared. He was walking off the field heading back to the locker room.

"He had quit! I was stunned and elated. I had endured something that a bigger, stronger, and apparently tougher guy could not. Suddenly the aches ached less and the pains were less painful. I decided that I could finish the morning and, after that, another, and another, and another."

The scrawny kid with the big feet worked hard for the rest of the summer and throughout the autumn months. By the end of the season he had made his way up to second-string center on the Leechburg varsity football team. "I was clumsy and I wasn't much good," Kroll confesses. "It was simply my good planning that the team was short on centers so I did play a lot."

Kroll's young analytical mind concluded that he had two options. One was to quit the grueling sport altogether because it was too punishing; the second, to become a lot stronger and faster—as soon as possible. He chose the second option.

"It sounds like the dumbest cliché in the world," Kroll tells, "but I read one of those Charles Atlas ads that appeared in my comic books, and it started me thinking about buying a set of barbells. By lifting weights I could develop my body and come back the following year with some muscle.

"My father, who had dropped out of school in the fourth grade, was employed as a laborer in the mill. I knew he worked hard for his money, and I didn't have the heart to ask him to buy me a set of weights. It's not that we lived on the proverbial wrong side of the tracks, but where we did live was kind of a family joke. We tell people that we lived next to the tracks, next to the main highway, and next to the river, which was polluted and dead.

"Down the road was the gas company, which had piles of scrap metal and automotive and railroad parts stacked in an empty lot in the back. It offered me a large selection of rusty wheels of trucks and railroad cars, and together with bits of broken-down machinery I assembled my barbell set.

"Every day after school I'd go behind the gas company on the side facing the river where nobody could see me, and I worked out. Not only would I have been embarrassed if anyone saw me lifting wheels and pipes, but back then people thought bodybuilding would make you muscle-bound. I didn't know a single person in the entire valley who lifted weights, and I didn't want to make it known that I did.

"In the meantime, I saved all my money from my newspaper route, and by Christmas, I amassed enough money to buy a real barbell set—a 100-pound set. I worked out on the second floor of our frame house, and whenever I'd drop the barbell, dirt and soot were jarred out of the ceiling. It drove my mother crazy, so she gave me permission to lift downstairs. By my senior year, I'd sometimes work out three times a day—with weights in the morning, running after school, and then more lifting in the evening. I was determined to be an excellent athlete. Once, about 5:30 A.M., I actually fell asleep after doing a bench press, and sometime later my mother came downstairs and rescued me. When she first saw me lying there, she thought the barbell had killed me."

At the beginning of his sophomore year, Kroll weighed in at 150 pounds. The following year his weight shot up to 175 pounds. He claims to have learned a valuable lesson from his weight lifting. "What I was doing," he explains, "was setting incremental goals and, little by little, increasing them. It required a lot of discipline to stick to the routine. But it worked."

During his junior year in high school, while he wasn't a star, Kroll did make the starting lineup. Although Leechburg was a small high school, it beat Baldwin Township in the

Pittsburgh area for the western Pennsylvania championship.

"Playing on a winning team did wonders for my self-confidence." Kroll admits. "And this confidence carried over to my academic life as well. As a freshman I had been encouraged by my relatives, who were conservative people, to enroll in a trade course. They wanted to make sure I'd know a trade after I graduated so I could get a job. I even took typing in a class of thirty-two girls in which I was the only boy—it was embarrassing but, at age fourteen, also tantalizing. Actually, learning to type was a valuable skill in later years.

"Gradually it dawned on me that at best I'd someday end up as a clerk at Allegheny Ludlum, the local steel mill. I thought I could do better than that, so I switched over to academic courses, requiring me to double up on French and Latin in order to graduate on time.

"Perhaps it was my success with my weight-lifting program which triggered the idea that I could do better," Kroll considers, "but I started to experiment with all sorts of self-improvement programs. In my spare time I began reading the Harvard classics, which my father had bought for me when I was born. For years those books had remained unopened and had stared at me from the shelves in my room. In the beginning I started with the easier books—novels—and eventually I worked up to Montaigne and Plato. I'd even buy books like *30 Days to a Better Vocabulary, How to Think Clearly, How to Run Faster*, and other self-help books.

"I've always been compulsive, driven, and goal-oriented," he continues. "I had a need to do the best I could all the time. I was determined to be a great football player, and I always knew that somehow, no matter how inferior a physical start I had, I could make myself good. I'd go to sleep many nights and picture exactly what I was going to do on the field—how I'd make certain moves, perfect blocks, and perfect tackles."

By his senior year Kroll was 6'2" and weighed 215 pounds. He was named captain of his baseball team as well as the football team. As a standout linebacker and center he was named to the All-Western Pennsylvania football team.

His desire to excel showed up in other areas too. He was editor of his high school's newspaper and graduated second in his class, finishing only behind his cousin Rita Ziegler, who he says was "not only smarter but more personable and far more attractive—and she still is."

There were still more cousins in the valley. His father was one of thirteen children, so many Krolls lived in Leechburg and the surrounding area. ("Our family has the distinction of having the only Polish name that was lengthened when our grandparents came to America," Kroll smiles. "It was originally spelled 'Krol.' ") And most of his mother's nine siblings lived nearby as well. Consequently young Alex had a large extended family with aunts, uncles, and cousins everywhere. "I could go 150 yards in any direction," he smiles, "and there'd be an aunt looking out a window, sitting on a front porch, or hanging the laundry to dry.

"They were always looking out for me, and, when I was little, affectionate ladies were always picking me up and giving me kisses and hugs. I couldn't tell if we were rich or poor. I had a wonderful built-in support system. Family members came to watch me during practice sessions, and at the actual games I even had my own small cheering section. Of course everyone in the town supported the football team—we were the main event."

While Kroll was fortunate to come from a supportive community, he also realized that his ability to excel as an athlete and a scholar was his ticket to someday leave Leechburg. To him there was no other choice. The one thing in life he didn't want was to end up working in the local steel mill.

During his senior year he was offered a slew of full athletic scholarships. He was pursued by colleges such as Maryland, Penn State, Colgate, and Indiana. However, he elected to enroll in Yale, an Ivy League school that did not offer athletic scholarships.

To the ambitious young man, Yale represented the biggest challenge. First, in his mind, the school's outstanding academic reputation was unsurpassed, and, second, in 1956 *Look* magazine picked Yale's football squad as the third-ranked team in the nation. Although Kroll did not receive an athletic scholarship, he did receive one based on need, and as he recalls, "I certainly needed it. I had to get a job to have a little spending money." He adds, "At the time going to Yale was the hardest and most aspirational thing I could think of doing. So I did it."

At Yale the young freshman enrolled in an experimental course called Directed Studies, considered the most testing course for freshmen and sophomores in liberal arts. He studied the arts, history, literature, and the science of each progressive Western culture. "Simultaneously, we studied such subjects as Greek art and literature, then the Romans, followed by the Middle Ages, and so on. Each week we were required to write a paper and we had to give a talk in class every week. It was a challenge, and I was ecstatic. I thought I was doing the most exciting thing I could be doing at that period of my life."

Kroll also excelled as an athlete at Yale. He was captain of the freshman football team, played on the school's first rugby team, and lettered in wrestling. During his sophomore year he started at center and played as a linebacker on a Yale team that was nationally ranked; it lost only a single game to Colgate and beat arch-rivals Princeton and Harvard to win the first official Ivy League championship. It was the last Ivy League football team to finish in the top ten of any poll for major universities.

In Kroll's mind, life could not possibly get any better. Then an accident changed everything. In May of 1957, after several months of hard studying and the winter doldrums, he and several friends went off campus for a few beers to let off a little steam before exams. On the way back the car in which Kroll was riding crashed into the back of another automobile. There were no injuries, but a large crowd assembled, and there was a lot of pushing and shoving.

As Kroll climbed out of the backseat of the car, a figure came rushing toward him. Instinctively Kroll threw a powerful right cross that broke the man's jaw. To make matters worse, the man he struck was a young associate professor of zoology. The university made it perfectly clear that Kroll would not be welcome back in the fall. "It was a regretful and appalling thing to do," he comments. "My family was crushed, and I was sort of stunned that I had thrown away this wonderful opportunity to study and graduate from Yale."

After a brief period of soul-searching, Kroll enlisted in the Army and served two years in the military police. "The army and its discipline helped me grow up emotionally," he acknowledges. "I also had a chance to play football for Fort Campbell on an exceptional team, the Screaming Eagles.

"General William Westmoreland was the post commander, and he wanted a team that would be a source of pride for the entire post. The general was very demanding, and when we lost one of our early games he insisted that we keep playing until we had a record he'd be proud of. We achieved that when we beat Fort Bragg for our twenty-second victory. That's when he said, 'Okay, you can stop.' Thank God! We thought we would be playing through Easter."

Although Kroll reapplied to Yale, the school refused to take him back. In the summer of 1959, with the encouragement of army teammate Art Robinson, an ex-captain of the Rutgers football team, Kroll enrolled at his buddy's alma mater. He attended Rutgers in spite of receiving an offer to play professional football for the Los Angeles Rams.

"I was happy being back in college," Kroll tells, "and, in

particular, studying English literature. Having only played one year since 1956, I had to really work to get my speed and timing back. I did okay and played on a great Rutgers team that finished the year with an 8-1 record."

After being elected team captain the following season, Kroll delivered an inspiring message at a farewell dinner attended by a large crowd of alumni in honor of the graduating seniors. He vowed to his audience that the following year would be even better than the past 8-1 season. In his emotional speech he made a promise that the 1961 team would deliver the school's first undefeated season. If the team delivered on Kroll's promise it would be the first ever for Rutgers—and that dates back to 1869 when the school played Princeton in the first intercollegiate football game.

"It was one of those spur-of-the-moment things," Kroll recalls, "a very ambitious goal that one doesn't normally announce in front of an audience. But on the other hand, stating such a goal in public added pressure on my teammates and, of course, on me too. We were committed."

Rutgers' record going into the last game of the 1961 season was 8-0. The team needed a win over a formidable opponent, Columbia, to clinch the Ivy League title. It was the twenty-fifth of November, and Kroll's parents were at the game celebrating their twenty-fifth wedding anniversary. Also in attendance was Kroll's girlfriend, Phyllis Benford, to whom he planned to propose after the game. He had given the engagement ring to Abe Sivis, a team trainer, to hold for him until after the game. Kroll refers to the ring as a neo-emerald because "it was green and *looked* like an emerald. Of course it wasn't, because I couldn't afford to buy an expensive ring. If we won, I wanted to propose as soon as possible because I concluded I would have a great psychological advantage that would make it extremely difficult for her to turn me down."

The game was played before a home crowd in a packed stadium on a picture-perfect day for football. The temperature was 60° Fahrenheit with a slight breeze and an azure sky. In the final quarter everything was perfect with one exception— the score. With twelve minutes to play, Columbia was winning by a score of 19-7. Rutgers' first undefeated season was on the line.

"Then we got the ball on our own 20-yard line," Kroll says, "and in the huddle I began screaming, 'We're not going to let these guys take our season away from us.' From that point I don't remember much. I was exhilarated and energized, and I think it might have spread to the other members of the team. We were unstoppable from that point; our defense devastated Columbia's offense, and we scored every time we got our hands on the ball. The final score was 32-19. To me it was very poetic—the perfect day—the twenty-fifth of November, my parents' twenty-fifth anniversary, and we scored twenty-five points in those final twelve minutes of play.

"As soon as the game ended, I quickly showered and dressed. Abe gave me the ring and I met Phyllis on the field. We strolled around the stadium, and the setting was just as I dreamed it would be. Everything was so serene; the mid-afternoon sun was just going down, the band had stopped playing, and the crowd was on its way out. The odds of her accepting my proposal were in my favor. 'How could she possibly say no?' I thought to myself. Thank God, she accepted."

In the young couple's eyes, the only problem with getting married was the actual wedding. The Benfords were Episcopalian and the Krolls were staunch Roman Catholics. The father of the bride had visions of walking his daughter down the aisle in Leechburg's one and only Episcopal church; the mother of the groom had her heart set on a full-blown Roman Catholic wedding at Leechburg's St. Martha's Church. The couple's solution was to elope.

Phyllis accompanied her husband-to-be to Miami for the North-South game, and in what Kroll describes as a perfect ecumenical setting the nuptials were performed by Miami Beach's mayor, who was Jewish. The night before, in the bar of the Sheraton Hotel, Michigan State's coach, Duffy Daugherty, gave a premarital pep talk to the bride in the absence of her mother. Rutgers' coach, John Bateman, an assistant coach for the North team, walked the bride down the aisle. Players from both the South and North teams, several pro scouts, and a handful of New Jersey congressmen were in attendance. The honeymoon took place in Tucson where an East-West game was played and continued when the couple traveled to the Senior Bowl where the young groom also played. "It was just Phyllis and me—and forty-five football players," Kroll adds.

Named as center to all seven All-American teams in 1961, Kroll was definitely material for the pros. He had been chosen in the twenty-seventh round of the NFL draft by the Los Angeles Rams in 1959, the year he was scheduled to finish his four years at Yale. However, after the 1961 season the New York Titans (later to become the Jets) of the two-year-old American Football League selected him in the second round. Kroll says, "I had a choice of either playing for the Rams in the NFL or the Titans in the newly formed AFL. I chose the latter because I wanted to stay in the East where my friends and family were. I even tried to convince the Rams to trade me to the New York Giants in the NFL. I appealed directly to their general manager, Crazy Legs Hirsch, but he ignored me."

Meanwhile Kroll graduated from Rutgers in early 1962 and took a job in the research department of Young & Rubicam, the big New York advertising agency. He had considered seeking a law degree but was persuaded to work at Y&R because he could play football and also work for the advertising agency.

"Y&R was very straightforward with me," Kroll recalls. "They said, 'Why don't you work here for a couple of years *while* you play football? Then you can decide whether you are an advertising man or a football player.'

"It was the first indoor job I ever had. I started in the

research department, and I hated it. I lasted four and one half months until it came time to play in the All-Star game. From there I went straight to the Titan training camp without any intention whatsoever of ever returning to the advertising business."

Although he had played the position of center, Kroll started at tackle during his first season with the Titans. While the rookie thrived on playing professional football, he was turned off by the mismanagement of the team. The Titans were poorly financed; as a result it was not unusual for the players' paychecks to arrive several weeks late. Finances were so low that the team lacked the funds to hire an offensive-line coach. It was up to Kroll to learn on his own how to play tackle. The team finished the season at 5–9, marking the first time Kroll had ever played with a losing record.

After the 1962 season ended Kroll went back to the advertising agency and, in what he describes as a naive way, asked: "I don't think research is for me. Do you have anything else around here that might be?"

He was told: "Yes. Can you write?" He was then given a copywriting test.

It was a fortunate day both for Kroll and Y&R. He passed a writing test and began what was to be an outstanding career as a copywriter and creative director.

At this point Kroll really began to focus on the inevitable fact that his career as a football player could not last a lifetime. He knew he must begin to prepare himself for life after the sport. "Besides," he says, "I didn't want to tell my children I made my living by bending over in front of Joe Namath."

It was a tough decision to make. He received $13,500 a year for playing football, a large sum for a lineman in those days. Working full-time as an apprentice copywriter would pay him about half that amount.

At 6'3" and weighing 245 pounds, Kroll was an anomaly among his fellow copywriters in the bullpen. His broad shoulders and crew cut didn't fit in with the petite Vassar woman who occupied the seat to his left and the recent Mount Holyoke graduate at his right. When he walked into meetings, the oversized cub copywriter gave the impression that it was his job to move the furniture. "I didn't look the part," Kroll smiles, "but no matter how I looked, I really liked it.

"This was different from anything I had ever experienced," he explains. "Football—any sport—after a while becomes somewhat repetitive. Sure, the people you play against get bigger, stronger, and faster, but so do you. However, the motions and the moves are essentially the same. Now I was in a field where everything was constantly changing. There was no limit to the problems that would arise or the challenges to be faced. There were so many different facets to advertising. It was part science, part art, and part theater."

In March 1963 the Titans received a second life when the team was purchased for $1 million by a five-man syndicate headed by David "Sonny" Werblin. The team's name was changed to the Jets and the new white and green uniforms were issued. Weeb Euwbank, who coached the Baltimore Colts in the late 1950s and won the 1959 NFL championship, was hired to head the Jets.

Playing in the NFL had been Kroll's ambition from early boyhood. To be paid for a game that was so much fun was a dream come true. "I had planned to play professional football for at least ten years," he comments, "but after that shoddy experience I had with the Titans, I was vulnerable to making a change. Once I began working as a copywriter, I became so enamored that to even my own surprise, when Weeb Euwbank called me to come back, I found myself faced with a moment I had been dreading for months. 'Coach, I've decided not to come back,' I said with a slight quiver.

"After I hung up I had an empty feeling in my stomach. Not playing in this game was unimaginable. Yet I felt good about my decision—I felt good even though I was starting off at a low entry position at Y&R. Sure, there was a feeling of anxiety. I had a wife and a child to support, plus I didn't know if I could succeed in the advertising business. But the challenge was there, and it was clear that I had to try it."

What excited Kroll the most was the high level of competition he encountered. Although he had competed against world-class athletes during his football career, he believed the new arena he had entered was equally competitive. "The quality of people is so good that on any given day anyone who competes for a new piece of business needs to score a minimum of 99 against the five other agencies that are in the running. It might take a score of 99.6 to be the winner. The margin is so slight that the difference is the intensity, the extra effort, and the tearing up of copy and doing it a dozen more times until it's perfect. There's so much competition in this field that you must continually get better and better. You've got to grow every day and can never let up."

After playing professional football, his new position being put behind a desk and removed from the game's excitement could have seemed somewhat dull. "Not true," he declares. "To a person with eclectic interests, there's nothing quite like this industry. However, if you don't love it, you will never learn to like it. There are so many frustrating situations, and the possibility of rejection is always there. But when you excel in this business, you have some wonderful opportunities to work with exceptional companies. One day a client might be Colgate, and the next day it's Time, AT&T, or Ford, or it might be an airline or perhaps a branch of the federal government. So while an NFL career might sound glamorous, I never felt that advertising was less intense than professional athletics."

As a copywriter, Kroll faced the possibility of having his ideas rejected. It is not unusual in copywriting to spend days or weeks on a particular ad only to have it changed or rejected by the agency's creative director. "A powerful determinant that inhibits people from presenting truly great ideas is fear," Kroll acknowledges. "They are afraid they'll get hurt or laughed at, so they avoid taking risks. When they have an outlandish idea they often freeze up and keep it to themselves.

"Fear tends to constrict the creative arteries. By giving into it, people lose the confidence to express themselves. The main lesson of football is to get up again and again. When you get knocked down, you get up. When you lose the game, you know that there will be another game. So the individual who gets up and keeps going toward the goal line eventually does well. I think getting knocked down and getting up again is good training for business life.

"In addition to the turndowns a copywriter receives internally, he must also face rejection by the client. You must remember that, in the end, it's the client's money," Kroll points out. "He is the client, and while somebody once said that the customer is not always right, *he is always the customer*.

"The customer puts his money into the ad or the commercial—we are agents, not principals. A long time ago Ray Rubicam said, 'You owe your client your very best idea. If he cannot be convinced to accept it and support it, then you owe him your next best idea.' "

The list of Y&R clients is quite impressive. It includes such blue-chip companies as Colgate Palmolive, AT&T, PepsiCo, American Home Products, Johnson & Johnson, Kraft General Foods, the United States Army, and the United Negro College Fund. Y&R is the firm that put the bull in the china shop for Merrill Lynch; it also linked Bill Cosby with Jell-O Pudding.

There are also clients who got away, such as Eastern Air Lines and Chrysler. When Eastern decided to go to a new agency after seventeen years with Young & Rubicam, Kroll actually threw a "celebration" the following night in the ballroom at the Pierre Hotel with four open bars and two bands. The affair was attended by more than one thousand staff people.

"Losing Eastern after having the account and doing such

great work for seventeen years was devastating," Kroll admits. "My reason for having the party was so our people would remember the great things we had done over so many years and not the last painful weeks."

Young & Rubicam also lost Chrysler, its biggest account. "Lee Iacocca was fired at Ford, and when he came to Chrysler, he decided to fire us," Kroll explains. " 'I like you guys,' he told us, 'but I know some other guys better and I might only have ninety days in this job.'

"Iacocca gave the business to Kenyon & Eckhardt. It took him only four minutes to convey this message to us. We represented Chrysler for twenty-one years, so that conversation broke down to about one minute for every five years. But Kenyon & Eckhardt had to resign the Lincoln-Mercury account to take Chrysler, and forty-nine days later we were fortunate enough to win this business. So while we lost our biggest account, we didn't roll over and die. Instead we focused on the opportunity to win a better account."

A slight smile appears on Kroll's face. "I remember how Dick Bouch, an ex-marine who was my football coach in high school, used to have one solution for everything. He had only one motto, and that was to run it off. I used to think he was a sadist, but the older I get, the more I like it. If you lie there, your bruises just congeal and you feel bad. If you get up and run, you're moving toward something else."

Perhaps Alex Kroll's greatest strength in his capacity as an advertising executive is his ability to motivate people. He's an inspiring leader, and he expects everyone to do his or her work right. This attitude makes people work hard for him. As one associate states: "Alex creates an atmosphere where you *expect* to win. High expectations, not fear or threats, are a strong motivating force." Somehow Kroll has been able to transfer to the world of business the same quality he exhibited as captain of the 1961 Rutgers team during the last game of its only undefeated season.

Kroll credits much of his success to his ability to "make teams." He insists that in the advertising business, "it's not the individual but the team that wins. When I served as the agency's creative director, I would take a team of people and, from what I imagined, I'd try to create a field of play in their imaginations. It was an imaginary field of play that had boundaries, and with this I'd establish a strategy and create a goal. I'd tell them, 'This is the goal. This is what we have to accomplish,' and I'd try to get them excited about it. While it is not my intention to make this business sound frivolous, my approach was to make a game out of every problem. By doing so, a lot of the fears, tension, and inhibitions were removed. If not, these negative factors become a drain on people's energy.

"In this business there is a pressing and continual need to provide each client with our best effort," Kroll emphasizes. "The effectiveness of a particular advertisement can vary so vastly that its value to the client is subject to extreme fluctuation. As a consequence the creative element in an advertisement and its impact on the audience play a crucial role in determining a client's success."

Kroll points out that the crux of the advertising business is understanding what people truly need and want. "We must determine what their true hopes, dreads, and dreams are," he explains. "The object of the advertising is to dramatize the real human value of our clients' products and services."

Once Kroll made up his mind to pursue a career in advertising, he made a commitment to himself to devote his best and fullest effort to his work. His meteoric rise to the top of his field has long since become legendary. In 1969 he was tapped for the senior vice-president and associate creative director's job at Y&R. The following year, on November 23, 1970, the day of his thirty-third birthday, he was named executive vice president and creative director of the firm. This promotion made him the youngest person ever to serve as creative director of any major advertising company—anywhere in the world.

Six years later he was tapped for the presidency of Young & Rubicam, U.S.A.

"It was a very difficult decision to make the move from creative director and step up to become the manager of the U.S. company," Kroll tells. "I thought being creative director was the world's greatest job. But once again I was curious about myself. I was attracted to the challenge of subjecting myself to a whole new set of tests and stresses."

In March 1985 he became chairman and chief executive officer of the worldwide organization that today employs more than twelve-thousand people in 322 offices in forty-five countries around the world.

Interestingly, while the vast majority of U.S. multinational agencies have become publicly owned corporations, Young & Rubicam has remained privately owned. Only active employees can own stock in the firm, and 10 percent of them do. Founded in 1923, Young & Rubicam is the nation's only major advertising agency still operating under its original name. Most advertising firms have been merged with others, have been acquired by holding companies, or have since folded. The firm is headquartered at 285 Madison Avenue in its own twenty-six-story office building, making it the only major agency remaining on Madison Avenue, a street that has long been synonymous with the advertising industry.

"It is a great source of pride to me personally," stresses the CEO, "that we neither have any aspirations to be the world's largest firm nor, for that matter, publicly owned. I don't see any particular advantage of going public. The quality of the work we do for our clients is what matters. A public company has two clients—one is its anonymous stockholders and the other is the real clients. The interests of each may be quite different. What is important to those two separate clients can diverge.

"We only have one client—it is Ford, or it is AT&T, or it is Colgate and *every one* of our clients. Our long-term thinking is that we intend to be in business forever, and we want to do our business *our* way. It's our opinion that a creative enterprise such as ours should not be subjected to the whims of public ownership. As a private company we have more flexibility to do things our way.

"Furthermore, it puts us in a position to think long-term because we don't have to be concerned about how some anonymous stockholders will react on a quarterly basis. Imagine, for instance, how such public stockholders would feel about our opening a Moscow office. Similarly they'd take a dim view about our establishing an office in China in 1986 after a ten-year negotiation. So far, we haven't made a dollar. The total amount spent on advertising in China is only around four-hundred million dollars. We're gambling that when the sleeping panda awakens, Y&R's clients will be uniquely situated to penetrate the largest untapped market in the world."

As a privately owned firm, Young & Rubicam has been able to invest perhaps even more than its share of time and money into being an outstanding corporate citizen. A priority of Y&R's philanthropic involvement has been its commitment to America's educational crisis. Like so many other leading CEOs, Kroll believes that the nation's future ability to compete in the world marketplace is directly dependent upon providing all of America's youth with a good education.

He also thinks that vast improvements in the nation's educational system are necessary in order for Americans to enjoy a quality of life that is otherwise certain to deteriorate. In 1989 Kroll started a unique program within the firm to tackle the problem head-on. A team of bright and capable Y&R people were given the eighteen-month assignment of analyzing what is wrong with America's school system and what must be done to fix it. During this period as much as 50 percent of their normal work assignments was devoted to the project. They visited inner-city schools in New York, Philadelphia, and New Haven and on the West Coast, attended many conferences across the country, and interviewed education innovators as well as those people who were viewed as obstructions to the system. When the assignment was completed, the team presented a report with recommendations about what changes are necessary to fix the system.

"As an organization that has long been involved in public-service communication," Kroll points out, "Y&R is in a position to make a valuable contribution. After all, our work revolves around understanding people, what motivates them, why they learn, and why they don't, so we can take a new approach because we're a private company that's dedicated.

"You see, there's a wonderful potential in all kids," Kroll continues. "The real issue is figuring out how we can stimulate them and release their potential. Sure, some of us were lucky and something turned us on and made us want to learn. In my case, growing up in a small town, I had a large family who was rooting for me to do well. That's a lot different than the poor kid who's left off at the school and, when he gets home at the end of the day, his or her parents aren't there.

"I was blessed to receive a fine education," Kroll adds. "As a high school sophomore, it was my good fortune to have a marvelous teacher, Mike Dzvonik, who taught me to love studying algebra. That was quite a feat because to this day I don't care for algebra. But he had a way of making the subject come alive and seem exciting and important. He injected an electricity and enthusiasm to the course that, to my surprise, inspired me to also take geometry and trigonometry from him. I liked those courses even less, but I took them because I liked to be around him. He showed me the joy there was in learning. What a contrast Dzvonik was from the nuns who taught me in parochial school. They terrified me! He made a lasting influence on my life. To this day I see him when I'm in Leechburg."

Kroll started another education-related program at his alma mater in Rutgers' speech and communications department. "I have always been concerned about the athletes who don't make it after their college or professional sports careers have ended," he explains. "So I met with Rutgers and they devised a program aimed at helping athletes get more out of their college education.

"My concern is for the gifted athlete who is particularly articulate with his or her arms and legs and is excessively competent between the yard markers but is not doing well in the classroom. After meeting with Dick Andersen, who at the time was their football head coach, and Joe Bolen, who ran the program, we concluded that one reason why some athletes fail in their schoolwork is because their fundamental communication skills are relatively poor. While they have confidence in physical activities, they do not possess it in the classroom.

"Well, I sponsored this program with Rutgers in setting up a credited course to teach these skills. It instructs them on how to competently express their ideas in every kind of environment, and it even includes talking to the media. A real value of the program is to teach them to express their ideas, which helps them do better in their other courses. About fifteen students enroll each semester, and to date more than a hundred have taken the course. I've visited the class and talked to the kids, and the program is working reasonably well. At some point it could be used as a model for other schools."

Y&R has a long history of commitment toward education in America. Twenty years ago, when Kroll was serving as creative director, the agency became involved with the United Negro College Fund. At the time the agency was engaged in a campaign for the Urban Coalition and coined a powerful slogan: "Give jobs. Give money. Give a damn."

"Maybe the use of the word 'damn' stimulated him," Kroll speculates, "but a young copywriter recommended as a theme for the United Negro College Fund: 'The mind is a helluva thing to waste.'

"I told him, 'I don't think so. I don't think the use of profanity will work with academic institutions.'

"I'm sure rejecting his idea hurt him, but within twenty-four hours he bounced back with a much better line: 'A mind is a terrible thing to waste.' Since then this theme has become a classic advertising campaign that has raised hundreds of millions of dollars. It's a magnificent testimony to what public service can accomplish in this country."

Running a giant advertising firm requires Kroll to maintain a stiff pace. His duties as CEO include visiting clients and agencies in marketplaces around the world. His day often begins at 5:15 in the morning, and he commutes to and from Redding, Connecticut, located sixty-five miles from Manhattan, where he also has an apartment. He rarely leaves the office before 6:30 or 7:00 each night, and frequently there are dinner meetings with clients. He also serves on several civic and business boards.

The energetic executive undoubtedly has tremendous stamina, and, in spite of spending 50 percent of his time traveling, he stays in excellent physical condition. "Even though the pressures are considerable," he concedes, "and the travel schedule is strenuous, I always find time to exercise. I think you have to do that to keep your sanity."

At 6'3" he weighed 240 pounds when he played for the Titans in 1962. He weighs 210 pounds today. To keep in shape, he rides both stationary and mobile bicycles and also plays tennis and cross-country skis. "When I'm on the road," he says, "I'm more interested in staying at a hotel with a good workout room than an elegant restaurant. I have jogged in practically every city where we have an office, including Budapest, Shanghai, and Moscow. It's something you have to do. I believe keeping physically fit is enormously good for your mental health."

In addition to maintaining his hectic work schedule, Kroll has taken the time to be active in several professional and civic activities. Currently he is chairman of the American Association of Advertising Agencies (4 A's), a member of the Advisory Board of the Center of Advertising History of the Smithsonian Institution, a partner of The New York City Partnership (New York Chamber of Commerce), a trustee of the United States Council of International Business, and a member of the Board of Directors of the United Negro College Fund.

To what does Kroll attribute his success? Much of it he credits to Phyllis, his wife of twenty-nine years. "I have been blessed by being married to a woman who is not only smarter but more creative than I," he says. "She turned that talent mainly to raising our three children, Alex, Jr., Michael, and Alicia, and supporting my efforts. I am lucky to have such an ally."

In honor of the twenty-fifth anniversary of receiving his All-American award from Eastman Kodak, Kroll was asked to address the present crop of All-Americans gathered at a banquet held in the Century Plaza Hotel in Los Angeles. His audience howled when he said: "At your age I could barely imagine life after football. I figured I'd keep playing until my knees turned to Jell-O. I never thought I'd end up selling it."

The young men listened intently when the former All-American talked about his transition from football into advertising. "The same sport that leaves scars on your knees, leaves patterns in your mind. Even as a novice, you find you know a lot about something important, winning. And that is a formidable advantage. Everybody likes to win. Few are willing to take the pains to win. Football not only teaches the rewards of discipline but the necessity for it."

And they nodded in agreement when he told them: "I'm reminded that years after Sam Clemens gained worldwide repute as Mark Twain, the storyteller, a schoolboy chum of his once declared, 'I knew just as many stories as Sam Clemens. He just wrote them down.' Writing it down, getting it done, executing, is what football is all about."

His audience was listening intently when he concluded: "All-American. It is the stuff of which millions of young men's dreams are made of tonight, tomorrow night, and the night after. All-American. You will always have it. It will be there to lean on, on some tough nights and long days—to pick you up when you lose a few. I know. You can always say, 'If I did *that* once then I can do *this* now.' You, like all All-Americans, will not be able to play football always. But you can always win."

When asked about his message to young athletes, each of whom will someday leave the playing fields and hope to go on to excel in even larger arenas, Kroll philosophizes: "Football is not a sport that only teaches how to block, tackle, run, and pass; it teaches how to win. It teaches how much must be sacrificed and how you must discipline yourself. Then, when you do win, you find out how really good it feels. It's not just physical. It's psychological. The knees and legs won't last. And after the skills of blocking, tackling, running, and passing are long gone, what is left is knowing *how to win*."

9

▪ JOHN H. McCONNELL ▪

Football Player,
CEO—Worthington Industries

John McConnell is living proof that the American dream is alive and well. The West Virginia native went to work at the local steel mill as a ninety-cents-an-hour laborer after he finished high school. After World War II he entered Michigan State University, where he played football. Although he might not be considered a sports superstar, McConnell learned lessons as a tenacious and competitive athlete that enabled him to become a superstar of American industry. Today he is the founder and CEO of a billion-dollar enterprise that is recognized as one of the best all-around performers on the *Fortune* 500.

The John McConnell story begins in a small, quiet town of 100 in West Virginia called Pughtown. "They changed the name to New Manchester sometime after I left—and for good reason," he chuckles. Located at the tip of the state on a narrow strip of land about five miles wide, the town rests between Ohio and Pennsylvania not far from the Ohio River.

For as long as anyone can remember, residents who were able to find employment worked in the valley at the steel mill, at the pottery, or in a coal mine. McConnell's grandfather was killed in a mine when McConnell's father was only thirteen years old. "My father went to work after finishing grade school, and when he was old enough he got a job in a steel mill and worked there for his entire career," McConnell says.

Nobody ever had much money in Pughtown, and when McConnell was growing up there during the Depression the region was particularly hard-pressed. Nonetheless, he claims to have enjoyed a wonderfully wholesome life. "Those were happy times," he tells, "and we developed good values. There was no television back then, and without money we never traveled too far away from home, so we made our own good times. Once, for instance, I made a pair of skis out of barrel staves. Another time I made a boat. The skis and the boat barely functioned, but making them provided me with a sense of accomplishment.

"As a young boy my favorite recreation was playing tackle football in pickup games. We never had any equipment so we'd play in our street clothes. However, when I was in fifth grade I was given a pair of shoulder pads from a relative in Pittsburgh who I thought was my rich uncle. Actually it was a hand-me-down pair that his son outgrew. The first day I had them, I wore the pads in school for the entire day. The teacher thought I was somewhat strange, but seeing how proud I was she let me keep them on."

McConnell went to high school in Chester, West Virginia, just a few miles north of Pughtown. As a freshman he weighed 150 pounds, which in those days was considered a decent size for a lineman. He was also a pitcher on the baseball team. By his senior year he weighed 185 pounds, which made him the third-biggest player on the football team; fullback Herb Coleman, one of the bigger boys, later went on to achieve All-American fame as a Notre Dame center.

The school district was so poor that there was only enough money to provide jerseys for fifteen of the football players. The rest of the team wore old white sweatshirts. When asked how good he was during his high school football days, McConnell modestly replies, "I was one of the guys who got a school jersey."

During his senior year he received several scholarship offers for both football and baseball. He and his younger brother, Bob, even had an opportunity to attend a summer baseball camp with the Pittsburgh Pirates. But after graduating from high school in 1941, McConnell put to rest all his dreams about being a star athlete and did what was expected of him. Like everybody else in the area whose father had a job in the mill, he went to work for the Weirton Steel Company.

"I was supposed to visit the University of West Virginia in Morgantown," McConnell recalls. "That same week I received a call from the mill that there was an opening for me. I asked my father what I should do, and he said, 'If you want to go to college on a football scholarship, that's fine. But if you get hurt and they don't pay your way, don't expect me to help.'

"Well, at the time that ninety cents an hour looked like a lot of money to me. It was—in comparison to the forty cents an hour I earned during the summers working for the state road commission. As far as going to college was concerned, back then I always knew I'd never go. No one in our family had ever attended college, and I was certainly not what you'd call a motivated student. My grades were only average. While I made As and Bs in the courses I liked—I loved history—I did poorly in the math courses, particularly algebra, which I barely passed. I thought it would be great to know how to type, so I took typing, and it's something that really came in handy later on. But with no ambition to go to college, I had no desire to excel in those courses that didn't interest me."

The young steelworker labored in the mill for eighteen months and, with raises, was making ninety-six cents an hour in January 1943, the month he left to enlist in the U.S. Navy. After spending eight months at service school on the Great

Lakes, he traveled by rail to Fleet City in California, a naval base that served as the marshaling area for the entire fleet in the Pacific Theater.

"When I arrived, I asked if the base had a football team, and they did, so I tried out for it and became a starting tackle," McConnell recounts. "I was surprised but very happy to have made the team because with thousands of guys on the base the competition was very difficult. Most of the guys were former college players, so the level of playing at Fleet City was comparable to playing collegiate football. For instance, Harry Huber, who the year before had played at Michigan State, was the other starting tackle. Harry and I quickly became good friends. As football players, we were given soft jobs. I was put in charge of cold storage, and in this capacity I handled all the food that was sent to the mess halls.

"After the season ended Harry and I sat down and had a serious discussion. Although we could have stayed at Fleet City and played football, we decided the right thing to do was fight the war. So, in 1943, just a week before Christmas, we boarded the USS *Saratoga* and spent nearly two years in combat in the Pacific. I was in gunfire control, which was a technical job that involved working with the ship's computers and radar systems.

"The *Saratoga* was pretty badly beat up at Iwo Jima and had to come back for repairs, so in March 1945 we were given a thirty-day leave," McConnell continues. "Huber took me to East Lansing and introduced me to Michigan State's head coach, Charlie Bachman, and on his recommendation things were set up for me to play there after the war ended. Then we were back in uniform in the Pacific again."

When the war ended in August 1945, the *Saratoga* returned to Pearl Harbor. Admiral Thomas J. Hamilton, the U.S. Naval Academy's head coach from 1946-49 and the University of Pittsburgh's athletic director from 1949-59, announced he was forming a football league in which all branches of the service in the Hawaiian islands would compete—the navy, the air force, the marines, and the army.

Huber and McConnell tried out and made the team. They spent the next four months playing football in Hawaii. Some of the better teams in the league had ex-professional players including several All-Americans. "There were ten games on the schedule," McConnell remembers. "When the season ended in December, we were shipped home the following week. It was a great way to end my time in the military."

After his discharge from the navy McConnell married his high school sweetheart, Margaret Rardin, who had just graduated from West Virginia University. In March 1946 he enrolled at Michigan State in time for spring football practice.

Although he could have received an athletic scholarship, McConnell elected instead to go to college with the assistance of the GI Bill. "While the school talked to me about a scholarship," he tells, "paying somebody's way was frowned upon if he was able to get by on the GI. As far as I was concerned, the GI was all I needed to get my education."

After the war freshmen were eligible to play on the varsity squad. That fall McConnell played guard for a mediocre Michigan State team that ended the season with a 5-5 record. During McConnell's days on the squad, Michigan State was an independent school and played a mishmash of opponents such as the University of Michigan, Boston College, Iowa State, Washington State, the University of Kentucky, and Mississippi State. In 1953 Michigan State played its first season as a member of the Big Ten Conference, which it won that same year.

During his freshman year in college McConnell's study habits had not improved from those he had in high school. "I simply didn't apply myself," he confesses. "I never bothered to study, and I rarely took a book home. Homework was something *other* students did. I was able to get by with hardly any effort in high school because I was blessed with a good memory. I have total recall of the spoken word. If somebody told me something fifty years ago, I can repeat it today.

"Unfortunately what worked in high school wasn't enough at the college level. During the summer term between my freshman and sophomore year I became ineligible for the football team due to poor grades. It's funny because that summer I took conversational speech—the easiest course I knew of—just so I could raise my grade average, and the instructor gave me a C. About a month later I bumped into him on campus and he inquired about how my football was going.

" 'Because of your course, I am no longer playing football,' I said.

" 'Why didn't you tell me?' he replied. 'I would have fixed it.' It was too late, however, and that was the end of my football career.

"It was a real downer," McConnell continues. "I was ashamed of myself. But it made me apply myself, so I started to study and eventually became a decent student. Our daughter, Margaret, was born in 1948, and being a father had a settling effect on me. I could see myself losing my GI Bill if I didn't get my grades up. Once I became determined to graduate, there was a noticeable improvement in my grades."

The money from the government made it possible for McConnell to attend college, but it was not enough to support his young family. Consequently he took on odd jobs ranging from carpentry to house painting. He also worked a night shift at an Oldsmobile axle plant. "The only qualification it took for a student to get the job was that he was a veteran and married," he explains. "About two hundred of us qualified. It was a union shop, and production schedules were set for every machine.

"During the war not many automobiles were being manufactured, and afterward the production schedules remained unchanged. This meant that I could get my work done in five hours and have three extra hours to study. I took my books to the plant and studied in the cafeteria during this free time. I wasn't the only one—the other guys did it too.

"Although the company's managers let us alone, the union was mad at us because we worked too fast. Consequently the union insisted that we spread our work out over an eight-hour shift. I couldn't believe it!" he exclaims. "How could there be quotas that encouraged workers to be unproductive? I told my wife that if there was ever a time in my life when I owned a company, I would never permit such waste to exist.

"I have never had anything against unions. But I always believed that management organizes plants—unions do not organize plants. If you run your operation properly, and if you're fair, honest, straightforward, and keep your people informed, your employees will never want to be represented by an outside party."

By attending school for three straight summers and working nights at the Oldsmobile factory, McConnell graduated as a business major in December 1949, two quarters early. Following his graduation he went to work as an order expeditor at Weirton Steel. His starting pay was $225 a month.

"I was the first person ever put on that job who had not worked down in the mill as a clerk or at something equivalent," McConnell points out. "Even though I had worked in the mill after high school, nobody was ever brought in right out of college. I worked in the order department, which was part of the sales department, so I was in direct contact with the district sales offices as well as customers. However, the job didn't involve any outside selling. Even though my title was order expeditor, the position was mostly clerical.

"The good thing about the job was that I was in direct contact with customers. They'd call in, and by talking to them I was able to learn a lot about customer service. It was good training because on one side, I was working with the mill people, and on the other, I was working with customers."

During the eighteen months McConnell worked for Weirton Steel he received two raises. He was making $275 when he left to take a sales position with Shenango Steel, a small steel processing company in Farrell, Pennsylvania founded by John Clark, a former employee of Weirton Steel.

"Clark would visit the mill about every three months to expedite orders," McConnell says. "He'd check out what was being scheduled and what was not. Once he said to me, 'John, if you ever decide to leave Weirton, give me a call because we're going to put some salesmen out on the road.' I could see that Shenango was a growing company, so in the fall of 1951 I went up to see if he really was serious about hiring me. He offered me a straight salary of a hundred dollars a week, plus a car. I was in heaven. It was like finding gold.

"At Shenango I was given a territory covering upper-state New York up to Buffalo that included Syracuse and Rochester. Also included was northern Pennsylvania. While we lived in Youngstown, Ohio, I was on the road most of the time for the next three months.

"Then the central Ohio territory became available and I was told it was mine for the asking," he remembers. "Although the company didn't have a single account in the area, I'd be doing the same sort of selling I had been doing—calling on all manufacturers who bought processed steel. I took it so I wouldn't have to spend so much time driving."

Two years later McConnell was put on a straight commission. By then the hard-driving salesman had enough active accounts and sales experience under his belt to be confident that his commissions were likely to exceed his fixed weekly salary. It was a calculated gamble, but with hard work McConnell knew the job change would pay off. Even though he now had to pay his own travel expenses, his monthly earnings increased from $1,200 to $1,500, which, as he puts it, "was a lot of money in those days." In July 1954 the McConnell family moved to Columbus, which they have called home ever since.

In January 1955 McConnell made the bold decision to start his own company. "As hard as I was working," he says, "I thought I might as well be in business for myself. I figured I could broker steel on my own, and I'd just continue making calls like I did working for Shenango. After all, I had been chasing smokestacks all over central and southern Ohio for three years—I went into places where a steel mill guy would never even go. I made some good contacts so I felt comfortable selling them as a broker.

"By this time I had developed enough confidence in my knowledge of the steel business and my ability to sell. Of course not everyone shared my confidence. My father, for instance, thought I was crazy. Every time my parents would visit us, he'd say, 'Boy, I think you're making a big mistake.'

"He was rooting for me, but there had never been anyone in our family who was ever self-employed," McConnell explains. "He just didn't want to see me get hurt. Interestingly, my brother, Bob, is a successful independent geologist in Houston. As it turned out, both my father's sons ended up venturing out on their own."

McConnell's goal was to find a niche in the steel industry. "I observed that the major mills were gearing their operations toward large-tonnage orders," he recounts, "while many steel users had a growing requirement for smaller, more specialized purchases. I saw that a need and an opportunity existed for an intermediary between the steel producer and the steel user, so I set up a desk and telephone in our basement and I was in business.

"Shortly afterward I received my first order from Ohio Thermometer Company in Springfield, Ohio, a city about forty miles directly west of Columbus. After I made the sale I had to purchase $1,800 worth of steel from Weirton to fill the order.

I only had $1,200 but I figured—no problem—I'll get thirty days to pay for the steel, and in the meantime, Ohio Thermometer would pay me. To my dismay, however, Weirton's credit manager said, 'No, you're not incorporated, you have no assets, and our strict credit policy demands you pay for your order in advance with cash.'

"I was taken aback by what he said. 'What am I going to do?' I asked myself. After thinking it over, I jumped in my 1952 Oldsmobile and drove over to a City National Bank branch office and asked to speak to a loan officer. By handing over my car title as collateral, I was able to borrow the $600 I needed to close the deal."

McConnell was off and running. Working as an independent broker, he served as a middleman between the customer and the steel mills. The novice entrepreneur continued to make sales calls to, as he puts it, "anyone who appeared to be a prospect for buying steel. At first I concentrated on making calls close to home—between Columbus and Dayton and Cincinnati, and all the small towns in between, as well as those southern Ohio river towns bordering West Virginia and Kentucky.

"It's no easy matter to open new accounts, and more often than not I couldn't even get my foot in the door past the receptionist to see the buyer. If I learned anything from my football days, it was—is—to get back up after I got knocked down. My coach used to preach, 'You only have to get up one more time.' What a wonderful lesson for a salesperson!

"I must have called on some customers at least a dozen or more times before I finally got in to make a sales presentation. And even with the ones I did see, I would be told time and time again, 'We're not interested. We're satisfied with our present sources.' It takes guts to keep going when you're always running into stone walls. It's no fun, but you've got to do it."

At times what appeared to be a solid sale would turn into bitter disappointment for the young steel broker. "I was thrilled when I landed a big order for a couple hundred tons of steel," McConnell recalls, "which, as a broker, meant that I'd first purchase steel from my supplier, Elliott Steel, a plant in New Castle, Pennsylvania. Then, after I shipped it to my customer in western Ohio, I received a call that took all the wind right out of my sails. 'We can't use it,' I was told. 'The steel is too soft.'

" 'What do you mean?' I asked. 'There was nothing in the order that specified a particular temper. You just ordered commercial quality, four temper.' [Four temper encompasses everything unless specified otherwise.]

" 'Sorry, Mac, but it's too soft for us to use to make tubing. We don't want it.'

"I was sweating," McConnell says. "I was going to make fifteen hundred dollars on the deal, and now I was stuck with all that steel that I had no idea what to do with. As it turned out, Rube Elliott, the owner of Elliott Steel, saved me by finding a tube company in Indiana that agreed to take the order. We made no profit on the transaction, but at least we were off the hook."

The tenacious steel broker made dozens of cold calls during the course of a seventy-hour workweek, and, in addition to working hard, he worked smart. "Sure, I called on companies who didn't know me from Adam," he declares, "but *I knew something about them.* I always had my black book with me— sitting in my car next to me. I kept notes on both the company and the individual I called on. And I did my homework in advance to increase my odds of getting past the gatekeeper. This is something else I attribute to my athletic career. Most football games are won prior to when a team steps on the field on Saturday afternoon. The team that wins is generally the one which is the best prepared. This comes from hours and hours of practice."

In the mid-1950s most steel mills were purposely moving away from smaller tonnage, instead focusing on larger, high-speed production equipment. However, McConnell was determined to buck the trend and be a specialty steel company. Simply put, he would buy steel as a basic commodity and add value to it. To do so, McConnell decided to invest in a slitter, a machine that cuts rolls of steel into specific widths according to a customer's needs. The purchase was a bold but important decision for the six-month-old company.

A slitter was an expensive piece of equipment, and considerably more than McConnell could possibly afford on his own. "The owners of Columbus Stamping and Manufacturing," McConnell explains, "were not only customers but good friends. So when I told them about my ambitions to process steel, they said, 'You'll need someplace to operate, so why don't you move into the new plant we've just built.'

" 'That would be fine,' I replied, 'But I only have about $5,000 or so in my checking account, so I don't have the money to buy a slitter and pay the rent.'

"Not only did they agree to guarantee my credit, but they each invested $5,000 in my company and in June 1955 with $15,000, my business was incorporated and became the Worthington Steel Company."

At the time of the company's incorporation, the McConnell family had two children; Margaret was now seven years old and John was two years old. McConnell worked out of a small office in his home. As he tells, "I was blessed to have an understanding spouse who let me start a business. My workweek typically ran eighty hours a week. Without my wife Peggy's support, I don't know what the outcome would have been. Most importantly, she took care of everything at her end so I would be free to concentrate on my business."

The same month the business was incorporated a slitter was purchased at the cost of $54,000 with the $15,000 investment in the newly formed corporation and with the personal guaranties of the three owners. In the meantime Worthington Steel moved into the new building, and there was rent to pay on a

7,200-square-foot lease. Five employees were hired in anticipation of the scheduled delivery in September of the slitter.
With the added overhead, the company suffered a loss of
$2,000 during the month of August, a large sum for the small
firm. "It made my partners very nervous," McConnell recalls,
"and they wanted out. They didn't understand my business, so
I couldn't blame them.

"The slitter arrived on schedule, and we cut enough orders
during the last week of September to wipe out our loss. We
even managed to show a small profit. With that my two partners came to me and said, 'Well, maybe we ought to think this
over after all . . .'

" 'It's too late,' I said. 'I already lined up five other investors.'

"One of the investors was my father-in-law, a pottery plant
worker, who took out a second mortgage on his home and put
$3,000 in the company. He had no idea what my business was
about. He just wanted to help me, that's all. The other investors were two of my cousins; Jim Purdy, my first salesman; and
his father-in-law."

These original stockholders profited handsomely from their
investments. McConnell's father-in-law passed away in the
early 1970s, but it is estimated that today's market value of his
$3,000 investment is $26 million for his heirs.

By the end of its first year, Worthington did $342,000 in
sales. The company made a profit of $11,000—it was a begin-
ning. As orders began coming in, still more equipment was
purchased. Sometime later, a squaring shear and roller leveler
were acquired, "all used equipment from the Weirton mills,
old junk that they considered obsolete," according to McConnell.

By 1959 the company had grown enough that it was necessary to install a second slitter. "In the beginning we took jobs
that the big steel companies wouldn't touch," the steel executive explains. "Those orders were either too small or too

exacting, in dimensions that nobody wanted to do. We simply found a niche."

Old-timers recall the long and hard hours their employer worked. "It was nothing for him to drive to Dayton in the early morning to make a call on a customer," one employee tells, "be back in the plant by mid-afternoon, roll up his sleeves, and work side by side with everyone else to get an order out the door late that night."

Employees routinely describe McConnell as that rare CEO who treats everyone in the company as an equal, no matter if he or she works in the plant or in the executive suite—to him, everyone is important and makes a contribution which is always appreciated. McConnell shows a genuine concern about each employee's welfare—and he makes a real effort to communicate with all employees and listen to what they say.

"Our employees have never been treated as hired hands," McConnell explains. "Going back to my college days when I worked in an automobile plant, I saw how productivity can suffer when employees don't share the company's goals. Too often in American industry, employees and management act like opponents rather than teammates. I don't feel this will occur when people are treated fairly and with respect—instead of working against the company, they feel a part of the company. There are amazing things that can be accomplished when people work together for the good of all."

Long before Japanese manufacturers came to the United States with what were deemed revolutionary innovations promoting teamwork in the work force, John McConnell was working with his employees in what today is called an egalitarian environment. Back in the 1950s, however, a business owner rarely would treat employees with the kind of respect and fairness shown to those who worked at Worthington. Unions were in their prime and, as such, there was a well-defined line drawn between management and labor. As a consequence, a strong adversarial relationship existed between the two, most evident in heavy industries such as mining, automotive, and steel. Hence McConnell was sometimes viewed by many businesspersons as a maverick entrepreneur.

Today it is in vogue for managers to proclaim that they treat their employees with respect and fairness. However, talk is cheap. Several subtle differences practiced at Worthington demonstrate that management and labor, can, in fact, work in harmony in steel manufacturing. At Worthington a statement is made to its work force: *Everyone* is respected regardless of position or title. There is, for instance, a noticeable absence of private dining rooms, executive bathrooms, and flexible hours for managers.

Furthermore, there are no time clocks that workers must punch. Every employee is a salaried employee. McConnell says that he never forgot the waste he witnessed at the Oldsmobile axle plant. "It used to make me so mad," he exclaims. "The workers would begin to wash up and stand in line to punch out twenty minutes before the shift ended. Frankly I thought it was degrading to stand in line to punch out. It was as if the company didn't trust its people."

Worthington does not have job descriptions either, McConnell points out. "They're self-limiting and give rise to an 'it's not my job' attitude. People are given the authority to determine how best to do their jobs, and they accept individual responsibility for quality and productivity. Our steel processing operations have no quality control inspectors, yet the product acceptance rate exceeds 99 percent."

There are no coffee breaks at Worthington. "We give our people all the coffee, tea, and hot chocolate they want," the CEO explains, "but we tell them we're not going to shut down a machine just because it's ten in the morning. This method says to people, 'You are a responsible person. When you feel you have the time, help yourself.' We do, however, have breaks where our people work on an assembly line such as our cylinder plant. At certain times departments within these plants shut down for a fifteen-minute break. But at our steel plants, breaks absolutely do not exist."

Since 1961 all Worthington employees can get a three-dollar haircut in company barbershops—and on company time. When asked about the bargain haircut, McConnell replies, "it's our way of saying, 'Thank you for your efforts—we are going to make a personal chore more convenient for you.' When we put these programs in place, skeptics told us they would not work. They were wrong. A little trust goes a long way."

Employees are given all sorts of recognition for production records, and everyone is eligible to participate in a stock purchase plan. Recognition in the form of company stock is presented to employees who miss one day or less each year; one employee who hadn't missed a day in seven years accumulated $8,000 of the company's stock.

"We started to give awards for attendance back in the 1960s," McConnell recalls, "and it did wonders for reducing absenteeism. Our current rate hovers at 1 percent. That's incredibly low compared to other companies'." These numbers are particularly remarkable because all employees are salaried, so virtually all absences are paid 100 percent.

Most impressive is how Worthington employees are provided a financial stake in the company's success. "Since day one," McConnell explains, "we have had some sort of incentive pay. The current plan, which dates back to 1966, allocates 17 percent of our pretax profit to a pool that is divided among all employees based on each individual's base pay. And even before this figure is paid out, 2½ percent is taken off the top and invested in a deferred plan for the employees' retirement. In good years these bonuses based on performance have been as high as $4,000 a quarter per employee! They can be as high as 50 percent of an employee's base wages.

"In addition, fringe benefits run approximately 30 percent of our employees' base wages. Our executives also participate in a bonus plan that's tied into profits. In fact, two thirds of their compensation is based on profits. If profits are down 15 percent, for instance, bonuses go down 15 percent. For the top managers, however, it's a little more discretionary, and if a plant manager in Louisville, for example, has a big quarter, we might boost up his bonus a little bit."

Productivity figures positively prove that Worthington Industries has a highly motivated work force. The company registered $431,000 in sales per employee in 1989 compared to $135,000 in the metal manufacturing industry overall and $111,000 for all U.S. manufacturing.

Executive Vice President Bob Klein was impressed with McConnell's philosophy on profit sharing when he originally interviewed to join Worthington. "Mr. Mac emphasized the fact that if people work hard," Klein recounts, "make the contribution, and pay the price, plus they're willing to do the little extra things and make sure the quality is good, the company is willing to share the profits." Klein, who began his career as a sales rep, has adapted well to his boss's philosophy.

Worthington's wages are considered highly competitive in the steel and automotive industries, and perhaps even more attractive because the company does not lay off people during poor economic periods. "When times are bad," McConnell says, "our people paint, clean, do maintenance work—anything. In the past when we've had a slow period, we've taken the opportunity to do our expansion work. So we have our people do all kinds of jobs. Nobody objects because they're working. In a union shop they'd be sent home—union job descriptions would not allow them to do that. But here it gets back to teamwork again. Everybody helps each other and everybody pitches in."

The company was thirteen years old in 1968 when it became a publicly owned corporation. In 1971 the company made its first attempt to diversify when it purchased a small pressure-cylinder business. That same year its name changed from

Worthington Steel to Worthington Industries. The company has since expanded and made its biggest acquisition in 1980 when it acquired Buckeye International, a large manufacturer of steel castings and a producer of custom-injection molded plastic products and precision metal components. Based in Columbus, Ohio, Worthington Industries presently operates twenty-five manufacturing facilities in ten states and Canada and employs more than six thousand people. Additionally, seven distribution centers are located throughout the United States.

McConnell is quick to attribute Worthington Industries' enormous growth to the effort and hard work of many individuals. When the CEO speaks about his company's achievements he rarely uses the word *I* but instead speaks in terms of *we*.

John McConnell has built a billion-dollar corporation with an emphasis on teamwork, and what's more he did it without the benefit of the scores of management books that were written in the 1970s and 1980s. Nor for that matter did he emulate another company in the steel industry.

When asked what inspired him to instill teamwork as his company's bedrock philosophy, McConnell modestly responds: "If I learned anything in sports, it was that nobody can do anything alone in this world. In football you're taught to function in a team environment. Without each of the eleven players working as a unit, the team does not succeed. This is true in so many walks of life and especially in business. I don't care who you are—you must have the cooperation of other people. People can assist you, and if you treat them right, they are going to give 110 percent."

McConnell sits back in his chair to reflect; a slight smile appears on his face. "You know, if you're driving down an old country road in West Virginia and you see a turtle sitting on top of a fence post, you can be sure that it didn't get there by itself. He had a lot of help."

Much of McConnell's help has come from within the company itself. Worthington Industries believes in promoting its own people rather than seeking management from the outside. "Our senior management team is homegrown," he explains, "with the exception of specialists—say, an engineer or metallurgist—our people are given the opportunity to advance as high as they want to go.

"When an organization brings in management from the outside, I think it's bound to have a bad effect on morale. Employees get the feeling that no matter how hard they try, the company is apt to pass them up for somebody else."

McConnell pauses for a moment and adds, "I'd estimate more than 90 percent of our foremen and plant superintendents have worked their way up through production. All of our salespeople have gone through a training program that has them working six months doing physical labor on a series of jobs in the plant. Afterward they're in inside sales for at least six more months. This way they don't go out and take bad orders, because they know the process. They also understand what it costs to take bad orders."

Don Malenick is a prime example of how people can advance at Worthington Industries. Malenick started as a laborer with the company at age nineteen upon graduating from high school. Over the years he attended night school and today, thirty-two years later, he holds the position of president and chief operating officer.

In its 1990 annual report Worthington Industries listed the average age of the company's senior managers at only fifty-one, yet these same individuals averaged twenty-two years of experience with the company.

While many *Fortune* 500 companies recruit graduate students fresh out of the business schools, McConnell states, "We don't go after those guys. Instead we put our people through *our* training program so they learn *our* business. Naturally, if somebody has worked here for a while and then wants to get his or her MBA, we'll go along with that."

Instead of recruiting business school graduates, Worthington Industries places a priority on hiring individuals who demonstrate the potential to make good team players. While there is not an actual policy to actively seek out college athletes, there is no doubt that the company employs more than its share. Perhaps as many as twenty key employees have played varsity sports at a college level.

Ohio State University is located in Columbus not far from Worthington Industries. Under the direction of the legendary Woody Hayes, Ohio State has long been known to develop athletes who are also quality people. Bob Klein, for instance, starred as a right halfback for the Buckeyes in the early 1960s. One of his teammates on the 1962 national championship team was fullback Dave Francis, who also works for the company. A two-time All-American linebacker for Ohio State in the mid-1960s and a Philadelphia Eagles standout for seven years, Ike Kelley has been with the company since his football career ended; today Kelley is director of personnel.

Mark Stier, another linebacker and the most valuable player on the 1968 Ohio State National Championship Team, is presently the general manager of the company's steel processing plant in Porter, Indiana. On the same team with Stier was Ron Maciejowski, a quarterback who is now a sales vice president.

Still another Buckeye star, All-Big-Ten defensive back Bruce Ruhl, today serves as the company's director of public relations. Bob Borel, vice president-engineering, was an Ohio State golfer, and Ed Ferkany, who played football at Bowling Green and later coached at Navy and Ohio State, is a group vice-president and company director.

With these athletes and several more, Worthington Industries has a team of executives who have firsthand knowledge of the application of teamwork on the playing field.

"While our intent is not to recruit athletes per se," Ike Kelley explains, "we do seek out individuals who are team oriented. If somebody has played team sports in the past, it's certainly an indicator that he or she is likely to function well in a team environment. During extensive interviews with a job applicant we'll ask specific questions that give us some clues on how he or she will function here at Worthington Industries."

Some of the company's ex-Ohio State football players have commented that John McConnell reminds them of their former coach, Woody Hayes. "Both of them are tough and committed," one employee expressed, "but unlike Coach Hayes, who would rant and rave and yell, Mr. McConnell is soft-spoken." When asked if they thought McConnell had what it takes to be a winning football coach, the consensus was affirmative.

Ike Kelley, the former athlete at Worthington with the longest professional career, has a favorite story about his boss that he thinks exemplifies outstanding team leadership. "Back in the early 1980s," Kelley tells, "some people in the benefits department came up with the idea of publishing a company cookbook with favorite recipes of Worthington employees. Late one Friday afternoon a little past five in the afternoon the group was working in the cafeteria where these books were being collated, and Mr. McConnell came through the room upon returning from a day-long business trip.

" 'What's everybody doing?' he inquired.

" 'We're putting together cookbooks,' somebody told him, 'and we're trying to get them finished in time to give them for Christmas presents.'

"With that, he took off his jacket and spent the next two hours helping out," Kelley continues. " 'It doesn't seem like we're going to get this done tonight,' Mr. McConnell said. 'How do you expect to finish it?'

" 'We'll be back tomorrow morning,' a woman answered.

"Early on Saturday morning he showed up and pitched in again. That is a wonderful lesson in employee relations. First, he demonstrated that no job is too menial. Secondly, and even more impressive, those people witnessed how the CEO of a major corporation thought enough about them to work with them to get the job done."

With a CEO like John McConnell at its helm, it's no wonder that Worthington Industries was chosen as one of the companies to work for in America in the 1985 bestselling book *The 100 Best Companies to Work for in America*, coauthored by Robert Levering, Milton Moskowitz, and Michael Katz. The company truly practices its golden rule: "We treat our customers, employees, investors, and suppliers as we would like to be treated."

An important message pertaining to citizenship is found on a pocket-sized plastic card titled *Worthington's Philosophy* that reads: "Worthington Industries practices good citizenship at all levels. We conduct our business in a professional and ethical manner when dealing with customers, neighbors, and the general public worldwide. We encourage all our people to actively participate in community affairs. We support worthwhile community causes."

Here too McConnell leads by example. He is a past chairman of the Columbus Area Chamber of Commerce, a trustee of Pilot Dogs, a director of Children's Hospital in Columbus, and a trustee of Ashland College. He has served as committee chairman of numerous special charitable projects such as the Columbus Zoo, the YMCA, Boy Scouts of America, the National Society to Prevent Blindness, the United Way, and many more.

Company employees are encouraged to be good corporate citizens, and they are. Worthington people serve on boards in those communities wherever the company actively conducts business in part because McConnell tells them: "I measure success by what you put back. It is not how much money you make; it is what you put back into society." He is fond of saying, "You can never pay back but you can always pay ahead." For John McConnell, these are not idle words.

Many years have passed since McConnell suited up to play

a game of football. Today his athletic activities are limited to an occasional round of golf and horseback riding whenever he visits his 2,500-acre ranch in Colorado. He has been a devout Pirates fan since his early boyhood growing up just forty miles west of Pittsburgh. In 1985 he became a part owner of the baseball team, which he calls "an investment from the heart. I wanted to make sure they didn't leave Pittsburgh—and for a while, it looked like that was about to happen."

Athletics have always been important to McConnell. When asked why he believes all young people should participate in sports, he concludes: "Athletics teach our youth to be competitive. And, let's face it, life itself is competitive."

10

■ RONALD W. REAGAN ■

Football Player, U.S. President

Few people have enjoyed as rich and full a life as Ronald Reagan. In addition to serving as this nation's fortieth President, he succeeded in an array of careers including radio sports announcer, actor, union leader, corporate spokesperson, and state governor. During his two terms as President beginning in 1981, Reagan dramatically renewed a spirit in America that had been waning for nearly two decades; he restored a sense of national pride. As the nation's chief executive officer he was admired for his high ideals and unflagging optimism; even his foes respected him for these virtues.

Reagan grew up in Dixon, Illinois (population 10,000), a rural community bearing a striking resemblance to small-town Americana depicted in a Norman Rockwell painting. On February 6, 1911, the day Reagan was born, his father, Jack, is reputed to have said, "He looks like a fat little Dutchman, but who knows—he might grow up to be President some day." For years the President-to-be preferred to be tagged "Dutch," thinking that "Ronald" did not sound particularly masculine. His only brother, Neil, who is two years older, was called "Moon."

Jack Reagan earned a modest living as a salesman. His

specialty was selling shoes, and although he was proficient at his trade, his on-again, off-again drinking problem created considerable havoc for his two sons and spouse. Nelle, a devoted wife and loving mother, was a strong woman whose life centered around her family and her deep belief in God.

Reagan entered Dixon High School in 1924. "I was thirteen," he comments, "and worshiped football more than anything else in the world. Being able to play for the school team was the most important thing in my life at that time. Our back door sat on an embankment that overlooked the high-school athletic field and the grandstand, so when I was a small boy I'd always watch the football practices and games from the hillside. I could hardly wait to grow up and represent Dixon High. When the field wasn't being used, my friends and I would have pickup games down there."

The fact that his older brother, Moon, was a star on the team made his desire even more intense. As a freshman Reagan was only 5'3" and weighed 108 pounds, so his size did not enhance his chances of making the football squad. In spite of exerting his best effort Reagan did not hear his name when the coach announced those boys who would become team members. "I climbed up the hill to my home with a feeling of rejection that really hurt," he recalls. "A whole year would pass by until I could try out again. It seemed like a lifetime."

Determined to add some bulk to his frail frame, the young boy worked the following summer doing manual labor with a pick and shovel for thirty-five cents an hour. In September he still wasn't chosen to play varsity football, but he did start as a tackle and later played guard on the school's entry in a conference established for players weighing 135 pounds or less. Reagan was elected captain of the squad. Although he enjoyed playing in the lightweight division, he looked forward to the days when he'd be playing with the bigger boys who were the "real" football team.

By his junior year he stood 5'10½" and weighed 160 pounds.

He made the varsity but spent the first half of the season as a bench warmer. Then, during a pregame pep talk in the locker room when the coach read off the starting lineup, to his surprise he heard, "Right guard . . . Reagan."

"I'll never forget that moment," he tells. "Once I got in I wasn't about to let the other guy get his position back. I started at right guard for the rest of the season and during my senior year."

During his sophomore year in high school Reagan took a lifesaving course at the local YMCA. The following summer he worked the first of seven seasons as a lifeguard at Dixon's Lowell Park, a three-hundred-acre forested sanctuary located on the Rock River and often referred to by the local residents as "the Hudson of the West." The seven-day-a-week job paid fifteen dollars, which later was increased to twenty dollars.

'I was the only lifeguard," Reagan recalls. "I started in the mornings and worked until sunset so working people could swim in the evenings. That meant there was no time for me to do anything but work. By the end of the summer, I was able to save every penny I made because there was no time to spend my earnings. One day a log washed up on the beach, and at the suggestion of my employer I started to cut notches in it whenever I made a rescue. My sole trophy from my lifeguard days was that log. At the end of seven summers it had seventy-seven notches."

In addition to football and lifeguarding, Reagan also took up acting. "By my senior year I began to lose my insecurities, the kinds that, as an adult, you realize every youth has, but as a young person, you think you're the only one who has them," he says with a smile. "I needed the reassurance and approval I received in school plays when an audience applauded. My success in football also built me up. Being the only one on the beach with *Lifeguard* written across my T-shirt plus saving so many people made a difference. I was also elected to my first office during my senior year when I served as the student body president. All of these were confidence builders."

When Reagan graduated from Dixon High School in 1928, less than 7 percent of the nation's graduates went to college. Both of his parents had received only a few years of grade-school education, and although his father did not discourage him from seeking a college degree, he made it clear that there were no family funds available—"If you want it, you'll have to earn the money to pay for it yourself," Jack Reagan told his two sons. Moon Reagan had graduated from high school two years previously and was employed at a local cement plant, making nearly as much as the working men in the town. Moon informed his younger brother that college was a waste of time.

"Dixon's star fullback, Garland Waggoner, had enrolled in Eureka College, a small liberal arts school owned by the Disciples of Christ located in Eureka, Illinois, about 110 miles southeast of Dixon," Reagan tells. "I literally hero-worshiped Waggoner and, because he went to Eureka and starred there too, I wanted to follow in his footsteps.

"As much as I'd like to say that my wanting to go to college was to receive a good education, at age seventeen my motivation was a result of wanting to play football for four more years. When my high-school sweetheart, Margaret Cleaver, enrolled at Eureka, that sealed it. I *had* to go there too. The combination of my savings from my pick-and-shovel job and my summer lifeguarding allowed me to bank away $400. But it wasn't enough to get me through four years of college where the tuition cost $180 a year, and the cost of room and board ran about the same. By qualifying for a Needy Student Scholarship that paid half my tuition and by waiting tables for my meals, I used my savings to pay the difference, which included $2.50 a week for my room, expenses for books, and so on."

The student body at Eureka was about 250, equally divided between men and women. "It was the same as growing up in a small town," Reagan recalls, "where everyone knew everyone else on a first-name basis. As governor of California I presided over one of the finest university systems in the country, and I've had the opportunity to visit many of the top universities in the world. Yet there's no doubt in my mind that if I had to do it all over again, I'd go to Eureka or another small college just like it. There's a tremendous advantage in going to a small school where you can get involved in many extracurricular activities. It's so natural in a small school because everybody is needed.

"There's something for everyone, whether it's being a member of the glee club, working on the school yearbook, participating in the student government—there's a job for everyone, and every student gets a chance to shine at something, which helps build his or her self-confidence. It gives you a chance to discover things about yourself that you might never learn if you were lost in the crowd of a big school. I have often wondered about how different my life would have been if I did not go to Eureka."

When Reagan arrived on the laidback campus in eastern Illinois, his six-foot frame, at 175 pounds, didn't have an inch of fat. The brash freshman had visions of starring on the small school's football team. He was ready and able but spent practically the entire season on the bench. He admits that this major setback "took some of the wind out of my sails."

In early 1929, prior to the stock-market crash, the farmers in the Midwest were already experiencing economic woes. Since much of Eureka's endowment depended upon local support, funds for Reagan's Needy Student Scholarship suddenly vanished. The following summer he took up his old lifeguarding job at Lowell Park and for the next three months debated on whether to return to Eureka the following year.

"I was disappointed that I didn't do well in football," he explains, "and I wasn't sure I'd be able to swing another year in college without the financial aid. In retrospect I suppose I wasn't much different from so many other college students who get second thoughts following their freshman year. When a rodman's job for a local surveyor became available, it looked very inviting to me.

"It rained the day that Margaret's parents were driving her back to school. Because I had nothing to do, I went along with them for the ride. Once back on campus I visited the TKE house and saw my friends, and I dropped in to say hello to Mac McKenzie, the football coach. Considering how I rarely got into any of our games the past season, I was under the impression that he didn't like me. But when I mentioned that I wasn't coming back, to my surprise he appeared to be disappointed. After I explained my financial situation, he said, 'Let me look into it for you, kid. Then check back with me later this afternoon.'

"About two hours later, I stopped by his office," Reagan remembers. "McKenzie said the college renewed the Needy Student Scholarship that covered half my tuition. 'They also agreed to defer the balance of your tuition until after you've graduated,' he said with a smile. The coach even arranged for me to get a dishwasher's job at the girls' dormitory—one of the most sought-after jobs on the campus for a guy. So there I was, back in college again.

"I called my mother to tell her about my plans to stay and asked her to ship my clothes to me. She informed me that Moon had had it with his limestone-shoveling job, and he decided to attend Eureka too. I went back to McKenzie and gave him a sales job about my big brother, and the coach arranged for Moon to receive a Needy Student Scholarship like mine. A few days later Moon was working in the TKE kitchen to earn his meals. As an upperclassman, it gave me immense pleasure having my older brother, the freshman, wait on me."

When football practice started, Reagan resumed his old position—warming the bench. "Evidently, McKenzie didn't like me as much as I assumed," the President says with a wry smile. "But I was determined to stay with it and practice my hardest, figuring I'd eventually catch his attention. Sooner or later I was bound to get my chance."

His chance came during a midseason scrimmage when the team was practicing a new play. "It was a wide sweep around my side of the line that required the right guard to take out the defensive back of the play," Reagan explains. " 'Okay, now, you play the defensive back,' McKenzie said, pointing a finger to an assistant coach, a former football star in his own right. 'And, you, Reagan, I want you to make sure you block him real good so he's out of the play.'

" 'You don't mean you want me to *really* block him?' I questioned.

" 'Yeah, come and try to block me,' the assistant coach butted in.

"So that's exactly what I did," Reagan continues. "Never before or since did I throw such a powerful block. The poor guy could hardly get up. I went back to the huddle and he went hobbling off the field toward the sideline. Well, that Saturday I was named for the starting lineup, and I attribute it to that block. Once I got in I played so hard, I made sure I was in for good. I was in every starting lineup for the remainder of my college football career.

"I played both offense and defense," the President boasts. "In fact one of the team managers was responsible for keeping track of the time each player was on the field. This way he could determine who earned a sweater. He told me that during my last two years I averaged all but three minutes of every game."

During the football season of Reagan's sophomore year—on October 29, 1929, to be exact—the stock market crashed, marking the beginning of the worst financial crisis in the nation's history. Severe economic times throughout the United States caused millions of Americans to lose their jobs.

"In the roaring twenties a lot of fellows like my brother

Moon graduated from high school and were able to find good jobs," he says, "so they didn't see any advantage in going to college. But when the Great Depression hit, suddenly jobs were no longer available, so these guys decided to go back to school. In fact I was the only player on the starting team who was directly out of high school; consequently most of my teammates were several years older than I.

"During a chalk talk one evening before a big game, Coach McKenzie asked us an unusual question: 'Do any of you ever pray before a game?' A long silence followed.

"I prayed before every kickoff but I kept quiet. In my prayer I asked the Lord to allow us to do our best, that nobody got hurt, and we'd do nothing to be ashamed of. The one thing I never prayed for was to win the game. I didn't think it was fair to ask the Lord to take sides.

" 'Well, any of you who prays?' the coach asked a second time. One by one each of the players on the team said that he did pray.

" 'What do you pray about?' McKenzie questioned.

"It was revealed that everyone had his own prayer, and each was along the same lines as mine. When the meeting ended, I was ashamed of myself for my hesitation about admitting I prayed until the other fellows spoke out. Looking back, I figured the older players would laugh at me so I didn't speak out. I learned a good lesson that day, and it was the last time in my life I was ever reluctant to let it be known that I prayed."

Few black athletes competed in organized sports at that time, and even fewer went to college. "Our team had two black players, and I was very proud about it," Reagan says. "One was the center, Burkie Burkhardt, who played next to me and was one of my closest friends.

"Once on a road trip we were scheduled to play a team in a town a few miles from Dixon but one without a hotel. The night before, our team's bus pulled into my hometown, and the coach informed me that I was no different from anybody else: 'You're not going home to be with your family, Reagan. You're staying at the hotel too.'

"I happened to know the hotel manager, so I accompanied McKenzie to introduce him. 'We got rooms for everyone,' he said and, to my horror, added, 'everyone, that is, except your two colored boys.'

"Remember now, this was many years before the civil rights movement, but just the same, I knew how wrong it was. I had been raised in a home where the biggest sin would have been to show religious or racial prejudice of any kind. 'You can't mean that,' I blurted out.

" 'I'm sorry, Dutch, but that's the way it is,' the manager said. 'Don't bother looking for another hotel, 'cause nobody else is gonna take 'em either.'

"McKenzie and I were incensed. We stormed through the lobby. 'We'll just have to sleep on the bus,' he mumbled as we made our exit. 'If the hotel won't let the two of them have a room, then none of us are going to have one.'

" 'If we do that, they're going to know it's because of them that the team can't stay,' " Reagan told his coach. " 'They're going to feel awful that the whole team has to suffer on their account. But I got a better idea.'

" 'Yeah, what's that?'

" 'Why don't we go out and tell everyone that there aren't enough rooms for all of us? And I'll take those two fellows with me to sleep at my home.'

"McKenzie, who was furious with the injustice, looked at me in surprise and said, 'You really want to do that?'

" 'Yes, I very much want to do that.'

"He put the three of us in a cab and we headed for my house," Reagan continues. "It was dark when we arrived at my house and my mother answered the door, and there I was, standing there with these two guys who were considerably bigger than I. I explained to her that there weren't enough

rooms at the hotel, so the coach sent the three of us to stay at
our house for the night. She threw the door open and said,
'Well, don't just stand there, come on in.' Although I anticipated that she would give us a warm greeting, it made me
swell with pride to know my parents practiced with such
sincerity what they had always preached to my brother and me.
They were absolutely color-blind when it came to racial matters."

The President recalls another incident that also pertains to
the prejudices in the 1930s: "We were playing a team located
a little further south than Eureka, and like other teams back
then, a lot of abusive language was directed toward our two
black players. One particular player didn't let up with his
flurry of insults aimed at Burkhardt. It wasn't just his vile
mouth; he was also a dirty player. In the huddle we'd say,
'Burkie, we're going to kill that guy.'

" 'This is my fight,' Burkhardt replied. 'I'll do it my way.'

"He was the kind of player who played hard football and did
everything only by the rules. The rules were different in those
days, and on defense a player could use the heel of his hand on
the headgear of an opponent, so that's what Burkhardt did. He
never said a word to the guy who was riding him. Instead
Burkhardt kept hitting him so hard that in the fourth quarter
the guy staggered off the field and a substitute replaced him.
At the end of the game, he wobbled to our side of the field, and
the guy was in tears. He walked over to Burkhardt and stuck
out his hand. 'You're the whitest man I ever played against,' he
said.

"I learned a great lesson about people that day. Burkhardt
had demonstrated that he was a man of character, and instead
of bringing himself down to the level of the other guy by also
resorting to foul play, he beat him by the book. In doing so he
won everyone's respect, including the bigot's."

Eureka's team didn't fare too well during Reagan's college
years. In fact he says that "a good season was when we won

half our games." The team's poor performance was blamed on playing in a conference known at the time as the Little 19, and Eureka was by far the littlest of the Little 19; the other colleges, such as Bradley University, Millikin University, and Knox College, were much larger.

"Once, after having lost a game to a school that was more than ten times our size," Reagan recounts, "two of my teammates and I approached McKenzie to complain about our schedule. 'Shouldn't we be playing some schools that are about the same size as us, coach,' I suggested, 'so we could win more games?'

"With that, McKenzie replied, 'Let me tell you fellows something. If you'd like, I'll make a schedule that's so easy you'll win every game. But are you sure that's what you want?' Then he proceeded to rattle off some small junior colleges. 'Are those the kinds of teams you'd prefer playing?'

"We didn't say anything," Reagan continues. "We were too embarrassed.

" 'For the rest of your lives you men are going to remember these years,' McKenzie said, 'and it won't be the wins and losses you'll remember. It will be the pride you had because you played schools that were a lot bigger than you, but just the same you gave them a good fight. You'll take pride in the fact that you represented a tiny school from some little town that nobody ever heard of, and you went up against teams from schools that were nationally known.'

"The coach was right on the money," Reagan smiles. "For years afterward I've told with immense pride about how I played opposite George Musso of Millikin, who must have weighed 275 pounds, and how he later played with the Chicago Bears for eight years."

Besides playing football at Eureka, Reagan was a member of the swimming team. In fact he was practically the entire swimming team. "To earn some extra money," he tells, "as a carryover from my lifeguarding days, I was put in charge of the school's swimming pool. In addition to keeping the place clean I was soon teaching children of the faculty how to swim. From that I started conducting lifeguard classes for college students. I also started coaching them with their swimming. Then I got the idea, 'Why don't we put together a swimming team?'

"The school was too small to hire a swimming coach, so the informal role of coach was bestowed on me, and later the fellows named me captain. Now bear in mind that there were only four of us on the team, so when we competed against other schools, we weren't able to enter every event. In my senior year we entered an all-conference swimming meet, and out of the nineteen teams that competed, we finished in fourth place. Not too bad for our four-man swimming team!"

A speed swimmer, Reagan swam the 50-, 100-, and 200-yard freestyle events and was a member of the freestyle relay and medley relay teams. "On the medley," he recalls, "I swam two legs of the relay—the freestyle *and* the backstroke. It was not as if I was so good at backstroke—only that nobody else on the team could swim it.

"In some of those sprints," the former President explains, "there were times about halfway through the race when the thought of quitting had entered my mind. After all, I was in several events, so sometimes I was near a point of exhaustion and was hurting all over. But *thinking* about quitting isn't quitting.

"No matter how much I ached, I would never give in to exhaustion. It was a matter of personal pride to hang in there, and of course I couldn't let down the team. Sometimes I've thought back about how I was behind in the last lap, and my arms were so tired I could barely lift them out of the water. But then I'd reach down deep inside me, and with a Herculean effort I'd pull ahead at the finish line. Believe me, there are times in a close election when it took the same come-from-behind spirit."

Between football and swimming, Reagan kept himself in excellent physical condition throughout his college years. He was a stickler when it came to obeying training rules, and only during the off-season did he on occasion smoke a pipe. "My father was a two- and three-pack-a-day smoker and my brother began smoking when he was fifteen," he remembers. "While I didn't like cigarettes, I sometimes puttered around with a pipe. Looking back, I acted under the influence of an ad in which a beautiful woman said, 'I love a man who smokes a pipe.' While I did put a pipe in my mouth, I never inhaled it. Back then we had no idea that smoking could be fatal. We only knew it shortened your wind."

Reagan has fond memories of his athletic participation in college. "Sports taught an important lesson about how you must never give up," he maintains. "Even when you're going down to defeat, and no matter how big the margin is that you're behind, you still must stay in there and do your best. This ingredient is something that stays with you for the rest of your life—I know it did in my case.

"There's also another lesson that a sport like football teaches in particular. In my day the main thing was to play your hardest, yet you had to win by playing fair and square. We were taught to play by the rules and *never* violate them. There was no tolerance for anyone who cheated. What's more, there was a sense of duty and obligation—we were representing our school. When we put on those football uniforms, we were committed to bringing honor to our alma mater. Sure we wanted to win, but there could be no victory without honor."

Reagan points out that athletes in his football days reacted much differently to making a big play. "When you made a great tackle, blocked a kick, recovered a fumble, or scored a touchdown, there was no spiking the ball, dancing in the end zone, or taunting the players on the opposing team," he states. "We were taught to lose with dignity and also to *win* with dignity. Frankly, I have never been able to get used to the way some of today's players carry on. In our day, by comparison, we showed a lot of humility following a big play. Rather than making a fuss about what you did, you'd get your reward in the huddle when one of your teammates slapped you on the backside and said, 'Hey, that was great.' It would make you feel ten feet tall.

"Coach McKenzie used to say to us, 'Don't make it look like such a big deal when you score a touchdown. Act as if you are used to it.' I suppose it's his advice that makes it difficult for me to get used to the way today's players jump all over each other when they make a big play."

In addition to participating in athletics, Reagan thrived on extracurricular activities while attending the small midwestern college. He enjoyed acting in student plays and in particular playing the part of Captain Stanhope in *Journey's End*. Although during his college days he never admitted his love for the stage, acting was his secret dream.

The year Reagan graduated college, 1932, was not a good time to enter the job market. And then to announce that he wanted to be a movie star would have been tantamount to saying he wanted to go to the moon. Hollywood and Broadway were in a different orbit from Dixon, Illinois. Reagan never dared mention to anyone that he had such hidden ambitions.

Chicago, however, was not too distant from Dixon, and it was the center of American radio broadcasting. In the 1930s radio was the big time. "Amos and Andy," Fanny Brice, and "Fibber McGee and Molly" were what television's "60 Minutes," Bill Cosby, and "The Tonight Show" are today. Furthermore, radio sports announcers were coming into their own.

As a student Reagan would frequently entertain his friends by giving a mock broadcast of a baseball or football game, using a broomstick as a make-believe microphone. He decided to head for Chicago to become a radio announcer.

"It didn't take long for me to learn that there were no openings in the radio industry for an inexperienced kid like me," Reagan acknowledges. "One kind woman who worked at

NBC radio, however, advised me to try to break into the business in 'the sticks,' and once I had experience working for a station in a small town, I could come back to Chicago and try again."

Down in the dumps, the young college graduate hitchhiked his way back to Dixon. A few days later his spirits were lifted when he heard about a new Montgomery Ward department store that was about to open and was looking for a young local athlete to operate its sporting goods department. "It paid $12.50 a week, and the prospect of getting it gave me a whole new lease on life," Reagan tells. "I applied for the job and told the interviewer, 'I'll be the best sporting goods manager Montgomery Ward ever had.'

"He seemed impressed, but evidently not enough. A former Dixon basketball player was hired as the new manager. I was discouraged and started to focus on the radio announcing dream again. When I told my father about what the woman in Chicago told me, he volunteered to loan me his thirdhand Oldsmobile to drive to the tri-cities area of Davenport, Moline, and Rock Island, about seventy-five miles southwest along the Mississippi River that formed the border between Illinois and Iowa. If nothing panned out in those towns, I would drive further west where there were still more small towns with still more radio stations."

Several days after his voyage began, after he had received rejections from a dozen or so radio stations, Reagan traveled to Davenport, Iowa, the hometown of WOC Radio. The call letters stood for World of Chiropractic; the thousand-watt station was owned by Colonel B. J. Palmer, who also owned the Palmer School of Chiropractic. "I told the program manager, Pete MacArthur, I was willing to take *any* job to get a start in radio," Reagan recalls, "and I told him about my dream of someday becoming a sports announcer.

" 'Do you know anything about football?' MacArthur asked.

" 'I played football for eight years,' I said.

" 'Could you tell me about a football game and make me *see* it as if I were home listening to the radio?' he asked.

" 'Yes . . . I'm sure I could,' I replied.

"With that he led me to the studio and said, 'When the red light goes on, I want you to describe an imaginary football game and make me see it.'

"Several games raced through my mind, but one that Eureka won in the final twenty seconds was the one I decided to broadcast. And just as I did with my friends when I broadcasted games with a broomstick for a microphone, I described how Eureka came from behind and beat Western State University 7-6. With the Eureka fans going wild, I signed off by saying, 'We return you now to our main studio . . .'

"MacArthur liked it. 'Be here Saturday,' he told me. 'You're broadcasting the Iowa-Minnesota homecoming game. You'll get five dollars and bus fare.' "

Reagan's debut was a success and he broadcasted Iowa's three remaining games of the season for ten dollars each. While his announcing was good, his employment coincided with the end of the football season, and thereafter he was again pounding the pavement seeking employment. He continued to job hunt during the cold winter of 1932-33, spending Christmas and New Year's Day out of work. It was a depressing time of his life.

In February, however, he received a call from MacArthur telling him, "A staff announcer quit, and you can have his job at $100 a month."

"I'll be there in the morning," Reagan responded.

Only weeks later Colonel Palmer purchased WHO in Des Moines and later received a permit for a 50,000-watt station. WOC was closed and its personnel were moved to Palmer's acquisition in Des Moines. At the time there were only fifteen 50,000-watt clear-channel stations in the country; overnight WHO became one of NBC's most powerful stations.

The next four years were wonderful times for the young

sports announcer. During this period Reagan covered football games, auto races, track tournaments, swimming meets, and baseball games—hundreds of baseball games. He announced for both the Chicago Cubs and the Chicago White Sox.

"For the majority of these games, I never even went into the stadium," he confesses. "I received the play-by-play description of the game by a telegrapher in the press box who tapped out a report in Morse code. I'd get only a brief description and it was up to me to elaborate the details. I did the same thing for football games. I recall one game between Iowa and Michigan in which the Wolverines' center was a guy named Gerald Ford."

Each winter the Chicago Cubs went to spring training camp on Catalina, an island off the coast of California. The White Sox traveled to Pasadena. In 1935 Reagan accompanied both teams. "I wanted to escape the cold Iowa winters," he explains, "so I offered to donate my yearly vacation in exchange for WHO's paying my expenses to the coast. My sales pitch was that I'd pick up a lot of good material about the players that I could use during the next season. The station bought it, and for several winters I enjoyed expense-paid work vacations in sunny southern California."

During the winter of 1937 the lonely young man from the midwest paid a visit to a friend, Joy Hodges, who had once worked for WHO in Des Moines. At the time Joy was working as a nightclub singer at the Biltmore Hotel. "During one of her breaks, she joined me for dinner," Reagan remembers. "Being caught up in the atmosphere of a nightclub, I confessed to Joy that I once had plans to be an actor. Then, somehow, she convinced me to meet with Bill Meiklejohn, an agent she knew, 'but don't wear those glasses,' she insisted.

"At ten o'clock the next morning I was face-to-face with a Hollywood agent, whom I could hardly see sans glasses. After a brief conversation, without saying a word he picked up the phone and dialed Max Arnow, a casting director at Warner

Brothers: 'Max, I have another Robert Taylor sitting in my office.'

" 'God only made one Robert Taylor,' I heard the voice on the other end of the phone reply. Just the same, Meiklejohn took me to meet Arnow. After being examined by Arnow as if I were a slab of beef, it was agreed that I should take a screen test."

After the screen test Reagan returned to Des Moines. Less than forty-eight hours later he received a telegram from Meiklejohn stating that Warner Brothers was offering a seven-year contract with a one-year option, starting at $200 a week. One month later Reagan packed his belongings in the new Nash convertible that he had purchased for $600 and headed to Hollywood.

"Here I was," Reagan recalls, "a twenty-six-year-old radio announcer from Iowa arriving at Warner Brothers and suddenly rubbing shoulders with stars like Errol Flynn, Pat O'Brien, and Olivia de Havilland. They were real actors, and it was five years since I appeared in a college play at Eureka. Did I ever feel out of place!"

Not long thereafter the new actor was appearing in the movies. He was cast as a radio announcer in *Love Is on the Air*, a frivolous B movie produced in three weeks. During his first eighteen months with the studio he appeared in thirteen pictures, none of which took more than a month to make. "Soon I began to get that same feeling I had as a freshman at Eureka when I sat on the bench. Being a B actor was no big deal. *I had to make the first string*," Reagan declares.

His big break came when Warner Brothers bought the rights to the life story of Knute Rockne, the famed Norwegian-born coach at Notre Dame credited with revolutionizing the game of football. Rockne was killed in an airplane crash in 1931. Upon hearing that the studio had tested ten actors for the part of George Gipp, Notre Dame's immortal Gipper, Reagan rushed to the producer's office and insisted on a screen test. Playing the

Gipper, his dream role, presented an unusual opportunity to combine his two loves, football and acting.

"You don't look like the greatest football player of our time," the producer commented.

"You mean Gipp has to weigh about 200 pounds?" Reagan asked. "Would it surprise you that I'm five pounds heavier than George Gipp was when he played for Notre Dame?"

Realizing that the producer was under the impression that football players were much larger—which they are in their uniforms—the hard-driving actor drove to his home and brought back an old photograph of himself dressed in his old football uniform. Upon his return to the studio he handed it to the producer and waited for a reaction. "Can I keep this for awhile?" the producer asked.

Later that day Reagan received a call telling him to report to the studio at eight o'clock in the morning to test for the role of George Gipp. The next day he was told the part was his. Pat O'Brien starred as Knute Rockne.

In one of the most famous deathbed scenes in the movies, Reagan delivered the following emotional line to his Coach Rockne, shortly before George Gipp dies: "Some day when things are tough and the breaks are going against the boys, ask them to go in there and *win one for the Gipper*. I don't know where I'll be, but I'll know about it and I'll be happy."

Ronald Reagan made the first team.

Not long after the release of *Knute Rockne—All American* Reagan was a matinee idol, appearing in films such as *King's Row*, *Desperate Journey*, *Stallion Road*, *The Last Outpost*, and *Cattle Queen of Montana*.

Shortly after his rise to stardom he became active in the Screen Actors Guild, the industry's major union. Founded in 1933, SAG today has a membership in excess of seventy-three thousand. Reagan served the first of six terms as the union's president beginning in 1948.

In his presidency of the union he met his wife-to-be, Nancy

Davis. In 1949 two actresses went by the name of Nancy Davis, one of whose name appeared on the membership rosters of several Communist front groups. Director Mervyn LeRoy called Reagan to clear the name of his studio's Nancy Davis and suggested he meet personally with the actress. "She's a worrier," the director said, "and she'll take it better from you than me. Why don't you take her out to dinner and talk to her?"

A few days later Ronald Reagan and Nancy Davis met, and it was the beginning of a friendship that eventually blossomed into romance. On March 4, 1952, they were married. Actor William Holden served as the best man and his wife, Ardis, was the matron of honor. While Hollywood has long been known for its high divorce rate, the Reagans' marriage is the proverbial match made in heaven. It is best described by the President in his 1990 autobiography, *Ronald Reagan: An American Life*, when he writes: "Coming home to her is like coming out of the cold into a warm, firelit room. I miss her if she just steps out of the room."

In 1954 Reagan became one of the most recognized personalities in television when he became the host of the *General Electric Theater*, a weekly Sunday favorite that always featured a different story and a different cast. On occasion he not only hosted the show but appeared in one of the many plays televised over the show's eight-year run. He also served as a company goodwill ambassador and traveled around the country to meet with employees at General Electric plants. His reception was so great that the company was soon sending him from city to city to address large audiences including United Way and Chamber of Commerce gatherings. It served as a good apprenticeship for his life as a politician.

After Lyndon Johnson's landslide victory over Barry Goldwater in 1964 the California Republican party first approached Reagan to run for the governorship. The party was in shambles, and Reagan was believed to be the Republican with the best chance of beating Governor Pat Brown, the liberal Democrat who beat Nixon for reelection in 1962. Ronald Reagan reluctantly agreed to run for the state's highest office.

After winning in the primary he became a definite underdog in the general election. The election's turning point came when the Democrats aired a commercial in which Pat Brown addressed a group of small children and posed the question: "I'm running against an actor, and you know who killed Abe Lincoln, don't you?"

In November 1966 Reagan won his first campaign for public office. He beat the incumbent governor by capturing 58 percent of the votes to his opponent's 42 percent. In January 1967 he was sworn in as the governor of the State of California. He served for two consecutive four-year terms.

In 1976 he made his first attempt for a national office and lost the Republican party's nomination for President to incumbent Gerald Ford at the Kansas City convention. It was a close race, with Ford ahead by a narrow 1,187-1,070 margin.

Reagan took the loss graciously. After the final ballot he and Nancy went down to the platform and congratulated the victor. Reagan asked the delegates to make the vote unanimous for the party's Presidential candidate and vowed to give Ford his full support.

He compares losing this primary race to losing a swimming race. "In either, when you lost, it's important to know that you did your best but it wasn't good enough so the other fellow won," he says matter-of-factly. "There's no shame in losing under those circumstances. You must be able to accept your loss and go on."

Jimmy Carter went on to beat Gerald Ford in the general election in 1976. Four years later Reagan defeated President Carter, and in January 1981 Ronald W. Reagan was sworn in as the nation's fortieth President.

During his eight years in the White House, Reagan was one of the most loved of all U.S. Presidents. He has since been recognized as the most able communicator ever to hold the nation's highest office. He explains: "I took an awful lot of abuse during my campaigns because I was a former actor, but my acting experiences have since paid off.

"As an actor you learn quickly that your success depends on how well you come across to your audience. To win them over it's essential for you to like them. They can sense your conviction. Well, many politicians don't like their audience because they feel threatened by them.

"There were also times as President when I wondered how I could have done the job if I had *not* been an actor. As an actor, I knew what it was like to read gossip and untrue stories about myself that appeared in the newspaper columns. I had first-hand experience with the newspapers panning a picture and/or my acting ability. Often a President receives the same kind of abuse."

Reagan points out that as a former football player he was also subject to the whims of the crowd and the Monday-morning quarterbacking of the press. He had his share of days in the arena when fickle fans cheered him and jeered him. Unquestionably his days on the gridiron served as an excellent preparation for his later careers in acting and politics.

In spite of being the oldest President to reside in the White House, Reagan was one of the most physically fit. In addition to keeping his movie-star good looks, he has maintained his athletic physique by doing calisthenics each morning. "The good health habits that I picked up in athletics," he stresses, "are something that became ingrained in me and have ever since been a vital part of my life."

"Participation in sports provides many benefits," President Reagan concludes. "There's much more to it than what happens on the playing field." While it's a long way from the gridiron to the White House, certainly some of the character building of a great man like Ronald Reagan is attributable to his days as an athlete.

11

▪ ROGER STAUBACH ▪

Football Player, Business Executive

Roger Staubach is an All-American, Heisman Trophy winner, and resident in the Pro Football Hall of Fame—a legendary quarterback in the history of NFL football. Yet he is quick to say that he faced many players in collegiate and professional competition who were bigger, faster, and stronger. Several were blessed with quicker throwing arms. Now a successful business executive and civic leader, Staubach acknowledges that those he squares off against in the fiercely competitive world of real estate often have advantages over him and his company.

What then accounts for his record as a winner in each step of his remarkable four-stage career?

"Nobody works harder than I do," he declares simply and directly.

"I have always felt that combining your work with your talent will gain results," he continues. "That's true in athletics and in business—in all walks of life. There are no short trips to success. You just have to pay the price, and that takes time, effort, and hard work. I have seen a lot of talented people who haven't accomplished much."

When complimented on his own record of accomplishments,

Staubach will say, "As an athlete, I mentally and physically gave everything I could. By doing so at various levels of my career, I was passing by people who might have been smarter than I was or more talented. The difference was I was utilizing what I had to the fullest of my capabilities." His creed holds that "it takes a lot of unspectacular preparation to achieve spectacular results."

Others speak with admiration of his perseverance and consistency. Those who know him best say, "Roger never gives up." Tight end Billy DuPree, Staubach's teammate on the Dallas Cowboys, declared: "The one thing that will always stand out in my mind about Roger is that he never knew when it was over. At the end of a game, even if we're down by 20 points, he'll be standing there by himself trying to figure out a way we can win it."

And win he has, beginning early in a star-studded career. As a sixth grader, he was the catcher on a baseball team that won thirty-nine straight games, including the Ohio state championship. He experienced only one losing football season throughout a playing career that included four years at Purcell High School in Cincinnati, a year at New Mexico Military Institute, four years at the Naval Academy, and eleven campaigns with the Cowboys.

The teams he led as a professional won three out of every four regular season games (85-29) and never lost more than two games in a row. While Staubach was at the helm the Cowboys went to four Super Bowls, two of which they won, and were in ten National Football League playoffs. In 1985, his first year of eligibility, Staubach was elected to the Pro Football Hall of Fame.

But no accolade reveals more about the superstar than a tribute from the normally taciturn Tom Landry, the Cowboy's coach, who said on the occasion of Staubach's retirement: "We'll miss Roger tremendously. But I'm not sure the National Football League and the sport won't miss him as much or more. His was the type of image you wanted in the game for young people. You can't afford to lose that type of person."

Both winning and losing in sports—particularly football—have been key factors in most of Staubach's life and have contributed to making him "that type of person."

Looking back from today's vantage point on his years growing up in a suburb of Cincinnati, Staubach realizes that as a boy he thought his family was wealthy. Now he more accurately characterizes his home as "lower middle income."

It is easy to see why he felt he was growing up rich; he was enveloped in an environment of warmth and devotion from his parents, both of whom doted on him. "My Dad struggled, but we had a nice two-bedroom home," Staubach remembers. "My mother went back to work at General Motors when I was nine years old. I was given everything I wanted, as far as I knew to want. My parents sure couldn't have bought a second home in Aspen to ski, but they saw to it that I had what I needed, including a lot of love and support."

Little in his family's history indicated that he would inherit exceptional athletic ability. His father had played a limited amount of semi-pro baseball and football but was never a standout. In his book *Time Enough to Win*, Staubach observed, "Yet in a physical sense I was fortunate to be born of Robert and Elizabeth Staubach. Both were strong, tall and sturdy. Dad stood a fraction over six feet tall and weighed about 195 pounds. Mother was around 5'7", maybe 140 pounds. It was because of them I grew to 6'3" and carried 200 pounds as a professional athlete." Nevertheless, as Staubach is quick to point out, "being blessed from birth with physical equipment is no advantage unless you are competitive."

He has always been intensely competitive and self-assured. Those instincts just seem to have been there, although he reasons that these winning characteristics probably came from his mother, who always wanted to be the best at whatever she was doing. "My father was an easygoing man, the kind of guy you wanted as a friend. He'd give you the shirt off his back—nothing seemed to bother him. My mother was more ambitious.

"I had this competitive instinct in me to win. I am sure a lot of it boils down to the fact that I had two people who cared about me—supported me win or lose—and I cared about them. But most of all, I wanted them to be proud of me. That made me work real hard.

"I also have had a lot of confidence all of my life," he says. "It's a state of mind. I really believe I can make things happen when everything is on the line."

He recalls that even as a youngster playing sandlot baseball he wanted the ball to be hit to his position for every out. "My father kidded me a bit about wanting to be at bat when the bases were loaded, because he said when he was a youngster he always hoped someone else would be there. He didn't want the ball hit to him, either."

Beginning as early as his days at St. John's Catholic grade school for boys in Deer Park, a suburb of Cincinnati, Staubach showed promise of the superior athlete he would become one day. His inherent abilities and instincts to run with the ball made him a natural selection as a halfback and fullback.

The emerging athlete weighed 125 pounds when he finished junior high school in 1956. Amazingly, he put on an additional 30 pounds by the time he reported for his freshman year at Purcell High School. An all-boys Catholic school where about 100 of the total 1,200 students came out for the football squad, Purcell was a hotbed for sports.

When Staubach entered high school he encountered an overabundance of candidates for backfield positions. He had demonstrated he could catch the ball and run with it and automatically gravitated to an end position, where he had a fine year. But Purcell's head coach, the late Jim McCarthy, saw something in Staubach beyond a young man with exceptional catching and running abilities. He recognized Staubach's potential as an athlete and leader; he saw a quarterback.

Considering what the future held for him, it is ironic that Staubach was not entirely happy about moving to this new position his sophomore year. Nor was he, in his own words, "an instant success." The competition from older, bigger boys was tough; second-year squadmen hardly ever saw action on the varsity. Despite his best efforts, Staubach got to play in only two games during the entire season. Unfortunately, that was long enough to suffer a broken hand.

Staubach's junior year as the second-string quarterback and starting defensive halfback wasn't anything to write home about either. Not until his senior year did he hold down the regular position as the team's number-one quarterback.

He was by his own admission a "wild and inefficient passer"; the record shows he completed less than one-half of his passes. Still he was good enough at throwing the ball to pose an impressive option that set up his rather considerable talents as a scrambling runner.

Staubach's record his senior year, when Purcell won the city co-championship, leaves little doubt concerning his primary skill or his preference. He ran for over 500 yards (more than he gained passing), although the team did not have a single play for the quarterback to run with the ball.

During his high school years Staubach lettered in football, baseball, and basketball. He had been elected president of his senior class as well as the student council. But it was time to move on to the next phase.

Staubach had known for a long time that he wanted to go to college. For the first time in his life, however, he was truly confused and upset. Considering his family's finances, a scholarship was an absolute must if he were to get a college education.

He was driven by an ambition to play big-time college football. At the same time, he felt he should stay near home in view of the fact that his father was critically ill. While some forty scholarships had been offered to the young man who stood 6'1" and weighed 180 pounds, only two were possibilities in the Cincinnati area—Xavier University and the University of Cincinnati. Both were fine institutions, but neither met the criteria for a major football program.

After considering Ohio State, hoping in vain to hear from Notre Dame, and even signing a tender with Purdue, Staubach chose the Naval Academy. To this day he can't fully explain the selection because there was no particular military influence in his background. He only can say he was attracted by the total environment of academics and athletics. "I realized," he explains, "that my study habits were not the greatest. I needed the discipline I knew I would get in the classroom at Annapolis."

But the road from Purcell High School to the Naval Academy was not a direct and easy one. When Staubach took the College Board examinations he scored high in math, but his English results were too low to pass muster at Annapolis. With his eye firmly on the goal of going to the Naval Academy he took a preparatory detour on a football scholarship through New Mexico Military Institute, which turned out to be a fortuitous trip.

Despite being "as homesick as a dog" and worrying about his father, he had a splendid year in Roswell. He developed his skills as a passer and gained recognition as an All-American junior-college quarterback for the 1960 season. His coach, Bob Shaw, took a strong arm and made it into a passing arm. He also taught the young man the strategy of winning football. Moreover, Staubach learned a great deal about studying while in junior college.

His second try with the College Board tests was successful. But ironically he flunked another test, an eye examination that revealed he was color-blind. This physical impairment would have disqualified him for the navy, but due to a red-tape

snafu the problem wasn't reported until he was already enrolled at the Academy. By then it was too late to rule him out;
Staubach attributes this lucky turn of events to the hand of
fate, a principle for which he has considerable respect.

Staubach entered the Naval Academy in the fall of 1961. He
had grown two inches taller and ten pounds heavier during his
year in New Mexico.

Plebes at Annapolis, no matter how promising, rarely leave
many marks behind them. Such was the case with Freshman
Staubach, although he did earn a position on the junior-
varsity football, basketball, and baseball teams.

He didn't play much football at the beginning of his second
year, but the pace began to quicken for him and the team as
the season progressed. The Naval Academy almost upset
Southern Cal as that West Coast powerhouse marched to a
national championship. Also that year Staubach first experienced the excitement and satisfaction of playing Navy's arch-
rival in the annual Army-Navy game in Philadelphia.

Navy's coach, Wayne Hardin, had publicly pledged, "We're
gonna run up the score on Army," despite the fact that West
Point was an odds-on favorite. Hardin's prediction, headlined
in the newspapers, came true the next day. Navy beat Army
32-14 in front of one hundred thousand fans, including such
notables as the President of the United States, an abundance
of admirals and generals, and numerous business tycoons and
movie stars. Staubach was the star of the day, throwing for two
touchdowns and running for two more.

Staubach performed admirably in the classroom at the
Academy and spectacularly in sports. In the beginning, however, the strict regimentation and discipline of the navy were
another matter. Then, as now, he is a man driven to lead and
was always more comfortable when in charge. It was not easy
for him to take orders every step of the way. Fortunately, most
of the demerits he received were for minor infractions of the

rules such as neglecting to shine his shoes. By the second semester of his first year, he had adjusted to military life and the demerits had begun to slack off.

By all counts, 1963 was his best year at Annapolis. The football team won nine out of ten games; he was awarded the Heisman Trophy and was selected for *The Sporting News*'s All-America team.

His record at the Academy was outstanding. In athletics, he had lettered in three sports: football, basketball, and baseball. He was awarded the Thompson Trophy (best all-around athlete) for three consecutive years, the only man to be so honored.

But Staubach's prime time as a college player passed. He suffered injuries that sidelined him for much of the next season. Navy had a losing year, the worst aspect of which was an 11-8 defeat at the hands of Army.

Staubach sees the whole of his career at the Naval Academy as a very positive experience. He credits those years for his learning leadership, responsibility, and organization, some of the most important skills that were to make him a success in professional football and in business.

In the summer of 1965, after his graduation from the Academy, Staubach received proposals from both the Dallas Cowboys, who had selected him as a "future choice" in the tenth round of the 1964 NFL draft, and the Kansas City Chiefs. Both teams were interested in his potential as a pro despite the fact that he had to take time out to fulfill a four-year active-duty service obligation to the navy.

By today's standards, the offers from the Chiefs and the Cowboys appear prehistoric. The offer from Dallas looked like the better of the two; it provided him with a $10,000 signing bonus, $500 per month while he was on active duty with the navy, and $25,000 per playing season for three years. Staubach eagerly signed a contract. This was less than other notable quarterbacks of the time—Bob Griese, Archie Manning, and

Ken Stabler—were receiving. "I could have haggled with management or held out or raised a stink, but that's just not me," Staubach said later. He would get a raise each year so that his annual pay for each of his last two seasons would be $230,000.

"Those were important proposals from the Chiefs and the Cowboys," he says, "but not the most important one I was involved in during 1965. That's when I proposed to Marianne. Thankfully, she wasn't a holdout, so we were married in September."

It was time for Staubach to complete his required four years of active-duty military service. He served one year as a supply officer in Vietnam, then three years at Pensacola Naval Air Station. Although his service obligations claimed his priority attention, football was never far from his mind. The war zone offered few opportunities to hone his talents as a quarterback, but upon returning to Pensacola he played with the base team, the Goshawks, which allowed him to get back in the groove.

It was 1969. The time was approaching when his tour of duty with the navy would end and he would have to make a major career decision. Should he stay hitched to the navy, where he was virtually assured of a successful career, or should he abandon that known territory for the challenge of professional football?

He told the Cowboys to save a locker for him. He was on his way to rookie camp.

Staubach did not share with anyone how important that trial period would be for him. He believed he could make the grade with the pros, but there was no denying how difficult it would be to overcome his three-year hiatus from football. If he didn't earn a position with the Cowboys, he planned to carry on his career in the navy. Typical of the man, he mounted an all-out campaign of hard work to get ready.

Two months before he was to attend his rookie camp with

the Cowboys, a severe pain developed in Staubach's throwing shoulder as a result of his intense practice sessions. If he threw passes one day he would have to lay off for a week or two. Repeated trips to an orthopedic surgeon, who prescribed anti-inflammatory medicine and physical therapy, didn't seem to help.

"I was in a sweat," Staubach recalls. Finally a second doctor administered a shot of cortisone that found the spot. Soon the shoulder improved; a career-threatening crisis had been averted.

His performance at the rookie camp proved to everyone's satisfaction that he could play in the big league. He was ready to enter another phase of his career. There is a tendency to think of Staubach's tenure with Dallas as one long parade of successes, but he had some tough hurdles to overcome.

The Cowboys were loaded with talent at the quarterback position. "Dandy Don" Meredith, the starting quarterback, was already a legend at age thirty and seemed to have a long way to go. He had just led the team to a record 12–2 season, the best in the history of the franchise. Next in line behind Meredith was Craig Morton, an All-American from Stanford with whom Staubach played in the 1965 College All-Star game. Morton had three seasons of experience under his belt and as an understudy to Meredith he looked like the shoo-in replacement should anything happen to the popular starter.

Still more job competition appeared in the person of Jerry Rhome, number-three quarterback, a veteran of five professional seasons. Then came Staubach, a rookie in the NFL at the not-so-tender age of twenty-seven who was trying to make a name for himself in major-league football after his downtime in the navy.

Fate stepped in when Rhome left the team. The bombshell came five days before the squad was to report for training camp; Meredith stunned the sports world by retiring at age thirty-one. Craig Morton took over as field general and Staubach found himself in the number-two spot, competing for the top job.

The next few seasons were trying for Staubach. He went through a period of warming the bench—hard duty for an aggressive competitor who had become accustomed to being in the middle of the action. At one time Coach Landry went to a strategy of alternating quarterbacks, partly because Landry had misgivings about Staubach's style of play, which favored running over passing.

Staubach talked a lot about being traded after many ups and downs competing against Morton and trying to win Landry's complete approval. Finally the number-one position belonged to him midway through the 1971 season. He now says Morton was plagued by injuries and some bad luck and also wasn't willing to adapt his life-style to make room for the dedication and hard work required of him as leader of the Cowboys.

The Cowboys' record under Staubach's leadership proves he was the right man in the right spot at the right time. Under his leadership the Dallas Cowboys earned the reputation as a "never-say-die" team. They came back from the graveyard to claim twenty-three victories, fourteen of them won in the last two minutes of regular play or in overtime.

Pro football devotees still talk about the Cowboy's epic come-from-behind victory over their arch-rivals, the Washington Redskins, on December 16, 1979. With just under four minutes left to play, the Cowboys trailed 34-21. Ignited by Staubach, the Cowboys scored two touchdowns in the final 2:20, one a three-play drive that covered 59 yards and was climaxed by a 26-yard touchdown pass from Staubach to Ron Springs. The second touchdown came as the result of a seven-play campaign that rampaged over 75 yards. Staubach heaved the winning pass, an eight-yarder to Tony Hill, with just 39 seconds left to play.

When the smoke cleared away that cold winter's afternoon,

Staubach had completed 24 of 42 passes for 336 yards, his second-best passing day as a professional. Staubach described the game, played in Texas Stadium, as "the most thrilling sixty minutes I ever spent on a football field." Others observing the game said they even saw the stoic Tom Landry surrender to a rare moment of emotion by leaping in the air, shouting, and clicking his heels together.

"Staubach was super," Landry declared. "What can you say about a guy who has done it so many times?"

In 1979 at age thirty-seven, with thirty years in organized football—eleven of those seasons with the Cowboys—Staubach came reluctantly to the conclusion that it was time to hang up his cleats. He found himself fighting against the routine of the game. Much of the challenge was gone since there was no competition for the starting quarterback position. He had a growing dislike for leaving his family every summer for six weeks at training camp.

Worst of all, he was injury-plagued; doctors were tactfully advising him to quit while he was physically ahead. He had suffered at least twenty concussions on the football field dating back to his playing days at Purcell High School. In fact a particularly bad season of concussions caused him to resolve the question of retiring from professional football.

One of the worst injuries occurred in a game against Pittsburgh in 1978. By accident the giant defensive end L. C. Greenwood crashed his helmet into Staubach's headgear just over the earhole as the quarterback stumbled forward on a broken pass play. He was down for the fifth concussion of the season and the sixth in a calendar year, but following this one his left arm and hand as well as his face were numb. The feeling returned, but later that season he was knocked unconscious for thirty minutes, after which he was vomiting.

The neurologists who examined him determined that the reflexes in his left foot were slightly less responsive than those of the right. That could mean some scar tissue had formed on the brain, or it could show a condition that had existed all his life. It was no time to gamble with his future health; he announced his retirement from football.

Staubach had recognized from day one that his career as a professional athlete would have to come to an end some day, so from the early days of his career in Dallas he started preparing to do something else when he reached that juncture.

In 1970, his second year with the Cowboys, he had become a part-time broker with a Dallas real estate agency, the Henry S. Miller Company. Three years before he left football he joined Robert Holloway, Jr., to set up the Holloway-Staubach Corporation. The company built several office buildings; Holloway saw to the construction, and Staubach found the tenants.

For a while he made the most of his reputation by doing television commercials and providing sports commentaries for CBS-TV, but in 1982 the former quarterback left behind even this involvement with sports to concentrate his full attention on the business of real estate. He bought out his partner and steered the company away from commercial development toward a new objective, that of becoming a national leader in representing corporate clients who seek to lease or buy space.

Like a winning quarterback who knows how to read and react to the defense, Staubach is credited by industry experts such as the publication *Business Facilities* with "having picked up early on some of the fundamental changes occurring in real estate in general and corporate real estate in particular." He in effect introduced a new order by representing the interests of the client seeking to find space as opposed to the client attempting to sell space.

The Staubach Company, as the corporation was renamed, has grown spectacularly in recent years in spite of a disastrous real estate market. For four straight years (1984-88) the firm was named by *Inc.* magazine as one of the country's fastest growing companies. It employs 125 men and women. Revenues went from $4.5 million in 1986 to $20 million in 1990. During the same period the value of transactions increased mightily from $181 million to over $445 million.

Offices are located in Atlanta, Georgia; Washington, D.C.; Boca Raton, Florida; Nashville, Tennessee; Los Angeles, Irvine, and Palo Alto, California; Detroit, Michigan; Cincinnati, Ohio; and Houston, Texas. Clients include such companies as AT&T, GTE, Mobile Oil, and MCI.

Much of what Staubach has to say about building the business and his role of leadership can be transferred easily to athletics. Any endeavor is a team effort. The challenge, he notes, is to get the team to work together smoothly. "This is a business which attracts people with powerful personalities and egos," he notes. "And we're mixing two very different types of business personalities—the sales personality from SMU is on the same team as the financial type from Harvard."

Staubach's character also comes through when he speaks of using the power of money and business. "People who handle power properly, with humility and sensitivity, are the ones who will be successful," he insists. "People who handle power poorly, who are callous, will not succeed."

Looking at Staubach's life an observer is tempted to conclude that his has been an easy ride: an athletic career few can rival, a beautiful family with loving relationships, success in business, bona fide celebrity status, personal serenity and confidence, and a promising future. The introspective superstar quickly acknowledges he has been blessed in many ways but goes on to say all hasn't been a bed of roses.

"I know a lot of young people have that view that I—and others like me—have had it easy, but that is a mistake. Nothing worthwhile comes easy. Nothing has been handed to me," he asserts. "I am like everyone else. If I want to achieve my ambitions I have to pay a price, and I have paid a very big price to be where I am as far as time and energy and effort are concerned."

The Staubachs have known the pain of deep personal tragedies along the way. He and Marianne, blessed with five healthy children, experienced the agony of losing one child, a daughter stillborn, less than a year after his father died from diabetes and complicating factors. Not two years later his mother succumbed to a long and agonizing struggle with cancer.

Staubach has known defeat in sports as well. Early on he learned a lesson from losing that he still vividly recalls even as he sits in his handsome glass-walled chief executive's office at The Staubach Company, just off the LBJ Freeway in Dallas. "It was my senior year at Purcell High School," he relates. "Although I preferred football and baseball, I was a decent basketball player. Anyway, it was one of those times I craved. We went into overtime. With five seconds to go, we were one point behind; the game was on the line. I drew a foul for a one-and-one free throw.

"I missed the first free throw, so I didn't even tie the game," he confesses. "We lost. I just ran to the locker room. I didn't even take a shower—I just grabbed my clothes, raced downstairs, jumped in my car, and got out of there. Some of the guys weren't even in the locker room yet.

"I didn't want to sulk or complain. I just wanted to get away from everyone and think about it. I was beside myself. I swore that I would consistently make my best effort to see that that never happened again."

Staubach says he has relived that night many times as he moved on through his career, because "I know I still can miss the one-and-one. But as long as you are giving the best that you can you'll make a lot of one-and-ones, too."

Clearly one of life's winners, Staubach still feels he is richer in all regards because of the lessons he has learned from adversities, not the least of which came during his tour of duty in Vietnam.

Staubach was not exposed on the front lines of battle, since he was assigned to a responsible support duty with the supply

corps some distance away. "Although there wasn't any immediate danger for us, one of the everyday hazards of that existence was the periodic mortar attacks," he says.

"Somebody would scream 'mortar attack' and we would all
dive for cover. The first couple of these attacks really shook me
up. I'd lay there wondering if this was the end of my world. It
was pandemonium. But by and by the shelling would stop and
life would get back to normal. We came to look at those
mortars coming in on us as just another occasional fact of
military life."

He believes that life is a series of such events that can occur
without warning and totally disrupt the flow of everyday
existence. The key is not to stop them; that can't be done. The
point is to treat them as challenges—to ultimately learn and
grow from them: "The true test of courage comes from the
daily mortar attacks. When everything is going well it's easy
to handle life. But what counts is how we handle it when
things get tough and the pressure is on."

He goes on to say that none of his attainments have been
the result of a solo act. "I have been blessed with tremendous
support. I have a great wife, Marianne [whom he met in the
fourth grade]. We have always been faithful to each other. We
have five great kids—Stephanie, Amy, Michelle, Jennifer, and
Jeff. I've had outstanding coaches and team players. We've got
an excellent group of people in The Staubach Company. We
have had some tremendous losses in our business and some big
gains, but we've always stuck together."

Through the bad times as well as the good Staubach has
been buttressed by his tenacity. He believes that when you get
knocked down what happens next is up to you. You can either
stay down or you can pick yourself up. That's true in athletics,
in business, and in life generally.

"You are going to have disappointments," he says. "There
will always be times when things aren't going the way you
would like. When you are behind, down, and out, you think

everything is over, but you have to persevere and fight
through those problems.

"Life is all about the ability to deal with the tough times,"
he continues. "I get down. I get discouraged. I get frus-
trated—all of these things, because I am as emotional as the
next guy, but I won't ever give up. If you have enough perseverance, it is amazing what you can accomplish."

Another key factor in Staubach's accomplishments is a deep
and abiding religious faith that came early in his life. He
credits the Catholic church, along with his parents, for the
consistent system of values he lives by: "I think a religious
faith, if it is strong, is with you all of the time. That's good,
because each of us is tested every day."

While Staubach is not overzealous with others in trying to
promote his faith, he does not hesitate to publicly share his
beliefs. When he does elaborate on his convictions, it is easy
to perceive the sustaining role religion has played in his life.

"I think God knows how life is going to go," he has said.
"We are predestined from the standpoint of His knowing. But
we have a free will to determine our own fate."

He cites a Biblical verse that declares, "Knock at the door
and it shall be opened; seek and ye shall find." Some people,
in his opinion, take that advice literally, believing all they have
to do is pray, then sit back while their prayers are being
answered.

"I believe that along with prayer a lot of effort must go into
a decision. My view is that if a lot of hard work and effort are
put into anything, good things will happen," Staubach explains. "Sometimes you don't even realize they're good. They
may look bad. But this approach is the best of other alterna-
tives."

He has learned a lot about other people as well as himself in
surviving the mortar attacks in athletics, in military service,
and in business. "People set patterns, especially when times
are tough. Some you can depend on, others you can't. You

really don't know a lot about people and their values until they are under pressure. Those people who stick with you and get the job done when the heat is on are the ones you can always count on.

"That's true in athletics, and it's true in business. Some athletes are not going to play as well when they are under the mortar attacks; they can't handle it. In business those who can't take the heat are likely to break the value system. They won't be honest with themselves, with you, or the organization. You can't rely on them."

Staubach frequently emphasizes the need for each individual to establish a set of priorities for his or her life and to live with those values. Surprisingly, this man who is such a competitor and such a winner makes the point that while winning is important, it is not the sole objective of high school and collegiate sports.

"I grew up with a pretty decent perspective because my Mom and Dad loved me and fully supported me whether I won or lost a game," he reiterates. "When we lost that basketball game because I missed the foul shot the world didn't come to an end, although I had a hard time getting over it. But I wasn't going to get drunk or use drugs or do something stupid because we lost a game."

Still Staubach believes that one ought to hurt when he or she loses a game or a business deal, although not to the point of becoming dysfunctional. "As you mature through the process of life you've got to have a very strong distaste for losing, but at the same time you can't let it destroy your next chance to win."

Staubach readily admits that as a professional when he lost a game he didn't feel like loving the winners and running over and shaking hands with them. "These were guys who had just beaten us. I didn't want to go into the locker room like it was just another day at the office. I wanted to hurt enough because of the loss that I would not let it happen again."

That kind of pain is essential to his game plan because in his view "if you don't hurt, you are not going to be as competitive as you have to be to win consistently. What you don't want to do is feel so guilty [about losing] that your personality changes and you can't function."

Mondays after losing were never good days for Staubach and those around him, he admits. While he didn't take his disappointment out on his wife and children, he did sulk. "I kept it inside, but I tell you I wouldn't allow my sulking to go past Monday. By Tuesday I started getting ready for the next game because I knew if I didn't I would have a real problem."

He sees business in the same perspective. "You've got to give your best until you get to that moment when the decision is made. If the client doesn't select your company, it is good to feel a little pain, but then you need to get over it. Do better next time," he says.

He campaigns for these values in the many speeches he makes to high school and college students, particularly athletes. "At the professional level of athletics, winning is always the top priority: it's my job to go out there Sunday, give it everything I have got, and win. If I don't win, I don't get paid—I'm out.

"If you are going into a game in high school or college your priority at that point is to win. But your life and your livelihood don't depend on it. It is not your business as it would be if you were a professional player. Your business is to get an education to get ready for the rest of your life. At the high school and college levels, the number-one priority has to be education and being a good human being. Then athletics falls in there, hopefully in sync with the rest of life."

Today Roger Staubach appears to be a happy man, content with his personal beliefs and exhilarated by the challenges of his social concerns and business opportunities. Of course, while he knows retirement from football was the best decision he could have made, he still misses the game.

"I miss the competition more than I thought I would, but I have never second-guessed the decision. I don't think I'll ever have that same feeling again of victory, of beating the other guys," he says.

"Competition is actually tougher in business than in athletics, but it is also different. In business it is an ongoing competition. In football it is better defined. When the game is over you can sit back and count the result, although you still have to win the next one. Business just keeps going; there is no halftime.

"But there are times when it is similar," he acknowledges. "When we win a big transaction, it's like winning a big game. We feel good about it and go around high-fiving each other."

Where will Staubach turn in the future to satisfy his competitive drive and to fulfill his sense of public responsibility? Many speculate that he will venture into politics.

"Politics is not something I am preparing for right now. It's subject to timing, how our business grows, a lot of factors. But it is not out of the question down the road," he says. "There is a lot of work to be done. I'm in the middle of all of that, so the next five—or maybe twenty years—could be consumed by business. But then again," he considers, "politics would be the most dramatic swing as far as change in my life."

Whether or not politics as a full-time profession is in Roger Staubach's future, he is deeply involved in a number of public issues. His primary concerns involve youth and education. His schedule of speeches to youth groups, civic gatherings, and business conferences is demanding year round. He was one of the original organizers and now helps coordinate the Pro Football Legends Bowl, an annual flag-football game which features a number of all-time greats from the professional ranks and benefits the Juvenile Diabetes Foundation. Other organizations that benefit from Staubach's work include the Special Olympics, the Leukemia Society, the American Cancer Society, the Fellowship of Christian Athletes, the Salvation

Army, the Boys and Girls Clubs of America, Easter Seals, and the Ronald McDonald House.

His long-time assistant, Roz Cole, sums up this private aspect of Staubach's life. "I have worked with Roger for almost twenty years and I am still touched by the number of people he helps financially and through encouragement and contact. Yet it is done very privately. He is very much influenced and affected by other people's tragedies and mishaps. He actively steps in to make a change. His priorities have never changed, although his status has grown."

Whatever direction his life takes, there is one safe bet. This man who has provided so many thrills and so much inspiration for so many people by his performance on and off the playing field will be engaged in services for his fellow man. By dint of hard work, perseverance, religious faith, and sheer decency, Roger Staubach is one of life's true winners.

12

■ RANDY VATAHA ■

Football Player, Entertainment
and Sports Agent

After Randy Vataha was named to the 1967 All-Orange County team in his senior year of high school, he had visions of being offered a full athletic scholarship by a major college. And why not? He was Rancho Alamitos's star player and the pride of his hometown, Garden Grove, California. The small quarterback had just led the Vaqueros to an 8-0-1 record, putting them in a first-place tie for the Crestview league championship. As an all-county player Vataha even got a chance to show his stuff in the big Southern California All-Star Game. Vataha was mostly a running quarterback and only threw the ball sixty-six times the entire season, completing thirty-three passes for 491 yards. His completed-passing percentage was decent, but passing an average of only nine times a game was by no means what you'd call a major aerial attack. High-school coach John Callard believed only three things could happen when his small-statured quarterback put the ball in the air—and two of them were bad.

That winter Vataha was looking forward to meeting a host of football recruiters so he could select which college to attend in the autumn. There were several big-time schools on his list, but in his own mind he would seriously consider only Notre

Dame and Southern California. He was willing, however, to be open-minded; he would listen to all offers before he'd make a final decision. "Just line them all up outside the door, coach," he told Callard, "and I'll meet 'em, one by one."

Not a single recruiter came to visit Rancho Alamitos High School that winter or spring. Disillusioned, the heartbroken athlete asked his coach, "What happened? Why didn't anyone come to see me?"

Callard put his arm around the saddened boy and said, "Well, Randy, to be perfectly honest with you, they're probably not interested in a 5'9" quarterback who weighs 155 pounds and can't pass."

The young athlete was devastated. But scholarship or no scholarship, Vataha was determined that he would be in college that autumn. His father, who left high school at sixteen, had lied about his age to join the army during World War II and afterward had been employed as a truck driver. "My father deeply regretted not going to college," Vataha recalls, "even though when I was a small boy he did attend night school and earned his high-school diploma. Although he never pushed me, it was always clear how much my going to college would mean to him. So a long time ago I made up my mind I'd go."

A standout baseball and basketball player in high school, Vataha had a basketball scholarship offer from Fresno State and was invited to try out with the New York Yankees. "Baseball was probably my best sport, but I wasn't interested in either offer," he comments. "My only interest at the end of my high-school career was to play major college football."

Vataha had been a high honor-roll student, and his grades were good enough for him to be accepted by most schools. He selected nearby Golden West, a small two-year community college. "I made this choice for two reasons," he explains. "First, all state-owned junior colleges in California were free to every resident with a high-school diploma, so the only thing I had to pay was the cost of my books. Second, I planned to play on Golden West's team and hopefully do well enough to earn a full athletic scholarship for my last two years at a major football college." It was a simple enough plan; the ambitious quarterback would grow a couple more inches, put on some extra beef, and transfer to a football powerhouse in 1969.

Golden West coach Ray Shackleford recognized a lot of potential in his new player—but not as a quarterback. "He could have done well anywhere," Shackleford tells, "but the best move for him was to flanker, where his speed could be utilized.

"When we recruited him, we told him all those neat things about a quarterback who would be running the ball himself twenty or thirty times a game. Now all of a sudden we tell him that he should move to flanker, and if he has a great season he'll touch it sixty times all year," Shackleford recalls. "He's gone from handling the ball sixty times a game to about six, and that's no easy matter for a kid to accept. But it was the best move for him. He wasn't really negative, but it wasn't something to dream about."

Vataha accepted his role as a receiver, although in the beginning he confesses that it took some time to make the adjustment. "Like a starting pitcher," he explains, "the quarterback is the pivotal person on the team who brings the other players into the game. Sports like basketball, soccer, and hockey are different because the ball and puck are continually moving so the players must go to the ball. But the pitcher and quarterback are involved in every play. As a receiver it was frustrating because the ball wasn't thrown to me every time our team ran an offensive play."

Although Vataha admits that he was not exceptionally fast in comparison to star players at major colleges, he was considered a speedster in the community-college league. Consequently he was a starter on Golden West's specialty team on the kickoffs and was the team's second-string flanker. Still, he broke into the junior-college ranks in a big way.

In his first game against Grossmont Community College, he returned the opening kickoff 94 yards for a touchdown. "It was the very first time I touched the ball as a college player," he smiles, "and it did wonders for my confidence." In the same game he scored on another 49-yard run. With the exception of the opening game, he started for the rest of his football career at Golden West.

In 1968, his sophomore year, Vataha had a sensational year—good enough to be named to several small colleges' All-American teams. His performance at Golden West also attracted three major schools—Utah, Oklahoma, and Stanford—that offered him athletic scholarships. "I quickly narrowed it down to Oklahoma and Stanford," he comments. "Oklahoma had an exceptional football tradition, plus they had just produced an All-American receiver, Eddie Hinton, who went on to star for the Baltimore Colts.

"I figured I could fill Hinton's spot on the team. Then too I wanted to play for a major school, and what a football tradition the Sooners had! While Stanford was no football powerhouse, they had an assistant coach, Dick Vermeil, who was cultivating his star quarterback, Jim Plunkett. So one of the major factors was: 'Do I go with tradition or the quarterback?' Well, when you're a wide receiver you must weigh heavily who's going to be throwing the ball.

"It was a tough decision," Vataha continues, "particularly because Oklahoma was so much better at recruiting than Stanford. My wife, Debbie, was my girlfriend at the time, and the final night before I made my decision both she and my parents were convinced I'd be going to Oklahoma. The next morning when I got up, I announced to them that I was going to Stanford.

"My final decision was based on changing my focus from football to scholastics and realizing that I'd have to do something besides play football when I graduated. At the time I didn't have the slightest notion that I'd someday play in the NFL."

After he graduated from Golden West with a 3.8 grade-point average, Vataha was given a full academic and full athletic scholarship to attend Stanford, where he majored in political science.

"It's odd that nobody wanted him because he was 5'9" and weighed only 155 pounds as a high school senior," his former coach, John Callard, remarks. "But then at 5'9" and weighing 160 pounds the major colleges came calling on him. He only needed to gain five pounds?"

In the first game of spring practice Vataha was Stanford's second-string flanker. "The backup quarterback and I had a good game," he recalls. "In the second game we clicked again, and then I had a chance to play with Plunkett and I had an even better game." By the time the 1969 season was underway Vataha was the first-string wide receiver and well on his way to becoming Plunkett's favorite target.

"A good part of the relationship between the quarterback and receiver is that the quarterback really has to develop confidence—number one, that you'll be where he thinks you'll be; number two, that you can get open; and number three, that you'll catch the ball.

"There's a chemistry that must develop between the two players," he goes on. "If every pass pattern was simply for the quarterback to draw back three steps, and everybody did exactly what he was supposed to do, it would be pretty simple. But college football has become fairly sophisticated, and the defensive units have a variety of coverages. However, Plunkett was not only a great passer but he was also terrific at dropping back and could run exceptionally well out of the pocket. We were fraternity brothers and good friends, so we worked hard together during the season and were very close throughout the whole year. After a while it got to the point where I could think where Jim would want me to go. If I came out of my break and the ball wasn't in the air, then I would know where to go next."

Vataha was a much smaller target than many other receivers who towered over him by several inches and weighed considerably more. At an obvious disadvantage in a sport where the worth of an athlete is measured in large part by his size, Vataha compensated by being a smart football player. As an ex-quarterback he was able to think like a quarterback—he truly understood the offense and knew how to read the defense. And most importantly, he was an intelligent thinker.

"I worked very hard at not only keeping myself in excellent physical condition," he explains, "but at analyzing the game. As a wide receiver I realized two things. First, nothing matters unless I caught the ball. I could run the greatest pattern—be wide open, but unless I caught the ball, all the other stuff was for naught, so I spent a large amount of time working on my concentration.

"I also devoted a lot of my time to developing a technique whereby I could get my head turned around even before my shoulders turned so I could always get the longest time to look at the ball. I was determined to give myself the maximum opportunity to be proficient at catching the ball."

This, Vataha believes, is the main reason he and Plunkett had such a good rapport. "I never had any doubt in my mind that he could reach me any place on the field. And he never had any doubt in his mind that if he got the ball there, I would catch it. It's very negative when a quarterback has the thought run across his mind that his receiver might drop a good pass.

"Second, I made it my business to be a good student of pass defenses," he continues. "I spent a lot more time studying films of our opponents' defenses, and once I determined how to read them it was just a matter of being in the right place at the right time. There's no sense, for instance, to put a move on a guy who's in a zone defense, and he's not going to be where I was going to be when I received the ball. What I'd figure out is who's the defensive player that will be where I'd end up, and I'd adjust according to him.

"As an example, if I was going to run a pattern that called for me to cut across the middle and I recognized that the secondary was playing a zone coverage, I would know that the cornerback who lined up across from me would not follow me across the middle. I'd have to anticipate whether to go deep around the linebacker, or would the free safety or the strong safety be in that zone? Once I'd determine who would be covering me at the point I should be catching the ball, I would concentrate on him. I don't understand it when I see a receiver putting moves on somebody in a zone defense who's not even going to cover him when he completes his pattern.

"When you think about the game of football, there are twenty-four starters on a team—that is, eleven on offense and eleven on defense, plus a kicker and punter, and then some seven or eight more players on the special teams," Vataha explains. "It's very difficult for the coaches to get that many guys to do everything right, so they try to keep everything rather simple. In spite of their big, thick playbooks, most of the plays are not so complicated. This means as a receiver there were a lot of things I was able to learn by studying the films and really analyzing them. As a little player who wasn't as gifted as some of the bigger, faster athletes, this was my edge. Without it I don't think I could have played the game in major college football.

"Another thing," he adds: "a receiver must never second-guess himself. I've observed many players who'd drop a pass and then put added pressure on themselves by worrying that they'll drop two passes in a row. I've never allowed myself to fall into that trap. Instead, when I'd drop one, I'd say to myself, 'Randy, you've caught this thing a thousand times, and with all the work you've put into practice this week there's not a chance in the world that you'll drop two consecutive passes.'

But the player who is worried about dropping the next one is likely to."

The Plunkett-Vataha team was a winning combination. The Indians, from a school not known for its football supremacy, went 7-2-1 during the 1969 season. Vataha caught thirty-five of Plunkett's tosses for 691 yards; his 19.7-yard average still ranks second in the school's single-season records. The following season he caught forty-eight passes and had a 63-yard punt return for a touchdown against Air Force. His two-year punt return average of 14.7 yards still stands as a school record.

Vataha's 96-yard touchdown pass from Plunkett in the 1970 game against Washington State is also in the Stanford record book. That same year the team had a 9-3 season, enough to win the Pac-8 and a berth in the Rose Bowl. A victory on New Year's Day would be the university's first Rose Bowl conquest since 1952.

To win, they'd have to beat Ohio State, a Buckeye team of seniors that had been national champs as sophomores and lost only one game as juniors. The Ohio seniors came undefeated to Pasadena for their final game together as the nation's top-ranked team. They were an awesome foe, with highly heralded athletes such as Jack Tatum, John Brockington, and Rex Kern, each of whom had been named to several All-American teams. Los Angeles columnist Jim Murray wrote that the computer hadn't yet been designed that could compute the odds against Stanford.

Playing in the Rose Bowl, the nation's granddaddy of all bowls, before a record crowd of 103,839, was a dream come true for the Stanford wide receiver. "As a Southern Californian, all my relatives and friends were there," Vataha tells. "This was the big game that I grew up with. I attended every Rose Parade since I was a little boy. Most importantly at the time I thought it was my last football game."

Plunkett was clearly the game's star, hitting twenty of thirty passes for 265 yards. However, it was Vataha, his favorite target, who caught six of those passes for 51 yards. Late in the final quarter Ohio State was behind by a score of 20-17 but threatened to score when Stanford intercepted a Buckeye pass at Ohio State's 25-yard line.

The Indians moved the ball down the field, and on a 21-yard pass Vataha sealed a victory with a brilliant touchdown catch that left the great defender Jack Tatum on his knees. The final score was 27-17, marking one of the biggest upsets ever in the history of college football. The game's final touchdown was scored by the local boy from Garden Grove—the kid who everyone thought was too small to get a scholarship offer coming out of high school.

Stanford's coach, John Ralston, recalls what Vataha told him about his final touchdown catch: " 'When Jim let go of the ball, I knew we had won the game,' and that was so typical of him. He was an outstanding player, a great receiver. If he touched the ball, he could catch it."

The passing artistry Plunkett displayed during the Rose Bowl was viewed by millions of TV watchers. "After the Rose Bowl game was over everybody was all over Plunkett, talking to him, taking pictures, measuring him," Vataha recalls. "Nobody even talked to me." As a result of his New Year's Day performance Plunkett cemented his place as the number-one pick in the NFL draft to go along with the honor of winning the 1970 Heisman Trophy. As far as Vataha was concerned, he had played his last football game. The political-science major planned to attend law school in the autumn.

The night of the NFL draft he went home to Garden Grove for a long weekend where he made a speech to a group of youngsters at a local high school. In the middle of his speech a woman grabbed him by the arm to tell him what she believed was important news. "Whatever it is, can it wait until I'm finished with my talk?" he asked politely.

"I just heard on the radio coming here that you were drafted," the woman said.

"You're kidding!" he exclaimed. "That's unbelievable. Which team?"

"The Rams."

Having grown up in the Los Angeles area, Vataha was elated. "Did you happen to catch the round?" he asked.

An embarrassed expression appeared on her face. He asked the question again. "It was the seventeenth," she mumbled.

Driving home from his speech Vataha thought to himself: "Well, the seventeenth round is not the greatest endorsement, but at least I was drafted. I am sure that somewhere in the Rams organization there is somebody who is a great football scout—someone who recognized that, in spite of my lack of size and speed, I was an exceptional athlete."

The next morning when Vataha got out of bed he rushed to the front door to read about the draft in the *Los Angeles Times*. "To my amazement, there was an article about me on the front page," he recalls. " 'Why is it about me?' I wondered to myself. After all, the Rams drafted Jack Youngblood as their first pick, not me!

"The article elaborated about a Rams tradition whereby the newest secretary in the office got to make the seventeenth-round choice. 'So much for my theory about some brilliant football scout who selected me,' I thought to myself."

Rumor has it that Dick Vermeil, who had served as an assistant coach at Stanford and was named assistant coach for the Rams after the Rose Bowl, was the person to whom credit goes for actually selecting the small wide receiver. Although Vataha received a bonus of $1,500 for signing with the team, his was a short-lived career with the Rams. He was released by the team before the regular season got underway.

To Vataha's good fortune, the following week the Rams played the New England Patriots, a team that went 2-12 during the previous season. The Patriots had Jim Plunkett as their quarterback. Vermeil was Plunkett's quarterback coach for two years at Stanford and the two men were good friends.

"Do you know that we cut Randy last week?" Vermeil asked his former player.

"Yeah, I saw that," Plunkett replied. "I've only been in the pros for a few weeks, but, you know, I think Randy could do us some good. He's better than anybody we've got now."

Following their conversation Vermeil and Plunkett met with Upton Bell, the Patriots' general manager. A few days later Vataha was invited to try out for the team.

Plunkett picked up his former roommate at Logan Airport. "Jim was staying at Bob Woolf's home," Vataha recounts. "Mr. Woolf was a sports attorney who was representing Jim in Boston. He insisted that I too should stay at his house until it was determined if I would receive a contract. This led to Bob Woolf becoming my attorney and close friend."

Vataha does not think he would have ever played professional football if not for his good friend, Jim Plunkett. "I honestly believe the Patriots kept me because the coaches felt Jim had a high level of comfort with me. They knew that I could get open and catch the ball, and they didn't have anyone who was a star at the position. So they kept me around to help make Jim feel better."

Vataha suited up for the final exhibition. While he didn't start in the season opener against the Oakland Raiders, he did get to play his first professional football game. The Patriots were behind in the third quarter when he was put in. After catching a 40-yard pass he played the rest of the game.

"It was a pattern that I had run a hundred times at Stanford, and we beat the Raiders, who were the heavy favorites. Jim had confidence to go to me," Vataha explains. "A lot of rookie quarterbacks might question their receivers. Most rookie quarterbacks on a team don't have somebody they've worked with for two years."

The former Stanford wide receiver played on the Patriots' starting team for the rest of the season. Once again he became Plunkett's favorite target. Vataha recalls a game late in the season against the defending Super Bowl champion Baltimore Colts, quarterbacked by the legendary Johnny Unitas: "It was late in the fourth quarter and it was third-and-8 on our own 12-yard line. Plunkett looked at me in the huddle, winked, and called a bomb. The logical thing when you're two points ahead was to do something about ten yards down. We connected for 88 yards and put the game out of reach." The touchdown pass stood as a team record for fifteen years.

Vataha's first year as a pro was impressive. He caught fifty-one passes for 872 yards and scored nine touchdowns, good enough to rank third best in the NFL for the year. Plunkett received the honor of being named the NFL's rookie of the year.

The Patriots finished the 1971 season with a 6–8 record. It was not a winning season but the New England fans expressed renewed interest in the team. Vataha's paycheck for his first year as a pro was for fifteen thousand dollars.

It didn't take long before the "Stanford connection" became two of the most popular players in New England sports. On one occasion more than 61,000 spectators at Schaefer Stadium sang "Happy Birthday" to the twosome—their birthdays are only one day apart (Plunkett is older by 366 days). Well liked and respected by his teammates, Vataha became New England's player representative in 1974 after NFL players staged an aborted strike.

The next summer the Patriots held a protest, skipping a preseason game against the New York Jets. This time New England struck alone, marking the first time an NFL game was canceled because of a labor action. In 1976, because of his leadership role, Vataha was elected to the players' executive committee, which negotiates the collective bargaining agreement with team owners. The committee consisted of only four representatives who were nominated to serve by the twenty-eight player reps, each representing his own respective team.

In the last 1976 preseason game the small wide receiver suffered his first serious football injury—a fractured cheekbone that required plastic surgery. He regained his starting position for the second half of the season and played very well, helping the Patriots finish the regular season with a five-game winning streak. They ended with an 11-3 record, the team's best ever, and also participated in their first playoff since 1963. The game was a heartbreaking loss to the Raiders in Oakland that went down to the wire and ended with a score of 24-21.

A controversial call by the referee might have been the deciding factor when the Patriots' Ray Hamilton leaped in the air on a fourth-down play and tipped a Ken Stabler pass that was thrown out of bounds. The referee called a roughing-the-passer violation and the Raiders got a first down to keep possession of the ball. "Calls go both ways," Vataha sighs. "It was a tough call, but you learn to live with it. You look back and say the Raiders weren't even challenged after that. They went on to win the Super Bowl, and it could have been us."

In Vataha's sixth year with the Patriots he caught 178 passes with an average of 17.2 yards. In spite of an impressive record, he was released by the Patriots when the 1976 season ended. Rumor had it that his cut was a result of his involvement as a player representative.

The Green Bay Packers consequently acquired him, but it was difficult for him to leave the Boston area where he and his young family had lived since his college graduation. In particular Vataha didn't want to leave a new business he had launched the previous year in Boston, a company that owned and operated several successful racquetball and fitness clubs.

His football career came first, however, and by the start of the 1977 season he was dressed in full uniform as Green Bay's starting wide receiver.

He was having a fine year up through the halfway point of the season, when he suffered another injury. This time he broke four ribs and was sidelined for the remainder of the year. Although he received his biggest paycheck that year—a sum of $82,000—his earnings from his business were even better.

America's physical fitness craze was in full swing, and the time was right to devote his energies to Playoff Fitness Clubs. "In December I called Bart Starr, the Packers' head coach, a month before the draft, to let him know I wouldn't be coming back even though my contract was good for two more years," Vataha recalls. "I wanted to give him some lead time before the draft so he could plan accordingly, and he was very appreciative that I let him know upfront."

Before long there were ten Playoff Clubs located throughout the six New England states, making it by far the area's most successful physical fitness organization. It was a big business and employed more than four hundred people. In time Vataha's reputation as a successful athlete-turned-businessman began to spread. This fame prompted David Dixon, a man from New Orleans who founded World Champion Tennis, to contact him; Dixon was now interested in starting a new football league that would play in the springtime.

Dixon is credited with getting the New Orleans Superdome built, and his track record with professional tennis was equally impressive. In 1981 he met with Vataha to discuss his latest innovation, the U.S. Football League. "Dixon asked me if I was interested in the Boston franchise, and in turn I brought in a local businessman, George Matthews, as my partner," Vataha remembers. "We attended the first USFL meeting ever held and were impressed enough to go back for subsequent meetings. We helped put the league together and became the owners of the newly formed Boston Breakers."

Vataha sold his physical fitness centers and reinvested the lion's share of his profits in his newly acquired football team, giving him a 50 percent interest. Originally the team's home games were to be played in Harvard's stadium, which seats 42,000, but at the last moment the deal fell through. As a last-ditch effort the Breakers had no other choice but to move to Boston University's stadium. It was a 19,000-seat stadium, however, and Vataha calculated the organization's break-even point was 27,000 fans per game.

Although the budget did not project a profit until 1985, the lack of an adequate stadium presented a significant handicap. In the spring of 1983, the Breakers' inaugural season, the team finished 11-7 for second place in the Eastern Division. Midway through the season they were playing before sellout crowds. Even with an ABC television contract to broadcast each of its Sunday afternoon games, the team operated in the red.

"When it became absolutely certain that we could not obtain a satisfactory stadium," Vataha tells, "we decided to move the franchise to another city. One weekend I visited New Orleans to meet with Cliff Wallace, the president of the Superdome. Over the weekend we worked out a stadium lease for the Super Bowl. That Sunday night I called my wife and told her to send my clothes and prepare to relocate to New Orleans with the kids when school was out.

"A couple months later I met with a group of local businesspeople who wanted to purchase the team. They bought it for $8 million, with $2.5 million down and the balance over three years. The down payment enabled us to meet all of our financial obligations and retrieve the bulk of our investment. Unfortunately, with the league going under two years later, we never received the full $8 million."

Vataha chalked up his losses as a great learning experience. "I ran an organization that had an annual budget of $9 million and employed 124 people. After the sale I agreed to remain as president for one year. During that period Donald Trump and another group came into the league and began buying existing franchises. They wanted to play in the fall and go head-on against the NFL. I opposed their idea and strongly supported sticking to springtime football. It would be economic suicide to do otherwise. After the 1984 season the team was moved to Portland Oregon, to pave the way for the league's move to the fall season in 1986, and I returned to Boston. They played for a single year and the league went under."

Once relocated to Boston Vataha joined Korn/Ferry International, a leading worldwide executive search firm. "At the time the company had about 135 partners worldwide," Vataha explains. "There were two in Boston, and they were interested in a third. They thought I'd fit in because I had so many contacts across the country. Then too Korn/Ferry was looking for entrepreneurial types—people who don't sit around an office waiting for the telephone to ring but instead go out and make things happen. As I learned in football, I had to be aggressive in the business world too. I liked the idea of working for a large organization, which I had never done before. And for a change I wanted to get into something that wasn't related to sports."

Two years later, in 1986, Vataha contacted his old acquaintance Bob Woolf, who had provided him with room and board when he tried out for the Patriots. Woolf is the founder and CEO of Bob Woolf Associates, Inc., one of the nation's leading agencies representing entertainers and professional athletes. Woolf also served as Vataha's attorney during his NFL career.

"I wanted to see if there was something Korn/Ferry could do for his agency," the ex-football player explains. "When I approached a prospect such as Woolf I didn't say, 'Let's see if we can find you some executives.' On the contrary, I asked to take a close look at his or her business, and only then would I be in a position to offer some guidance. 'Perhaps another pair of eyes is what you need,' I'd say.

"Two months later and after many extensive visits to Woolf's office, I presented my recommendations. In brief I said the firm should hire a chief operating officer who would be in charge of the day-to-day operations," Vataha explains. "An unnecessary burden would be taken off Bob, and, in turn, he would be free to do the things he was so good at doing. Woolf is an attorney who had been representing athletes and entertainers for nearly twenty-five years; his reputation is impeccable, and he's considered among the very best in the field.

"My proposal also outlined how the agency could expand on a much larger scale by putting on some other key people who would be brought in on a timely basis, dependent upon maintaining a certain level of growth."

Woolf studied Vataha's proposal in detail and responded: "Randy, you've played, and you've owned a team. You've negotiated hundreds of contracts from the ownership side. You were even nominated to serve as president of the players' union. You know both ends and the middle, which is the whole collective-bargaining side of the process. The only thing you haven't done is negotiate from this side of the table. You ought to be doing what *I'm* doing."

Vataha joined Bob Woolf Associates in mid-1986. "I would never have considered this business with anybody else," he comments. "Bob's and my philosophy are the same. We take a reasonable, rational approach. Our idea is to create a situation that benefits everybody."

The move was the perfect fit for the former football star. During his first year as the firm's chief operating officer (his official title is Managing Senior Partner), Vataha spent much of his time learning the business. In the beginning, like he had done with so many game films, Vataha meticulously studied the firm's twenty-five-year-old history. Equally important, he observed the operations of competing agencies.

He then established a long-term plan that included setting certain benchmarks for the firm to reach within specific time frames, whereupon specialists in areas such as finance and marketing would be recruited. Since he joined the firm, all of Vataha's goals have been reached, and many have been exceeded. Accordingly, the agency has enjoyed unprecedented prosperity.

"It's important to understand," Vataha emphasizes, "that Bob Woolf was incredibly successful before I came aboard. He was not only the rainmaker [an individual who brings a lot of clients to the firm] but the agency's operational head. Since I joined the firm we have totally reorganized to free Bob so he can spend a major portion of his time with clients and doing negotiations. In turn we've put experts in the other areas of the business who are equally proficient at what they do.

"Today Bob Woolf Associates, Inc., employs thirty-five people. Among them are top-notch individuals who specialize in marketing, endorsements, financial planning, wills, trusts, corporate structures, and investments for its clients. Bob and I are the main negotiators. The firm works on a team concept whereby each specialist works in his or her area of expertise directly with the client. This is much different from other agencies."

Vataha elaborates: "Typically our competitors are structured to assign one agent to handle a specific client. That particular agent is the only person of his or her firm who has direct contact with the client. While part of that agent's job is to become the client's best friend, I think our system serves the client better. It's not that we don't become close friends too, because we do. But most importantly the client has direct contact with each of our specialists, and this communication, I believe, is to his or her definite best interest. Additionally, our specialists discuss the client's needs and problems as a collective group, thereby coordinating a team effort to serve him or her."

The agency is indeed a team of specialists—so much so, in fact, that it employs a service manager with the sole responsibility of handling logistics for clients. "This person handles travel accommodations, including hotel and airline bookings," Vataha continues. "There is a group of specialists in the marketing division that handles endorsements; one of them is in charge of arranging free services and products for the firm's clients. These freebies range from golf clubs to automobiles to travel accommodations. There's another person who serves as a booking agent for handling speaking engagements while somebody else books appearances as a public service for gratis."

The team concept works well at Bob Woolf Associates. As a result, the agency provides a wide range of services for its clients, a system that Vataha believes is superior to its competitors'. "An agency consisting of a handful of people can't do what we can," Vataha explains.

"What makes it all work is that it's a coordinated effort of many people working together in the same direction. If each of our specialists operated independently within his or her sphere of expertise, everyone would be pulling in a different direction and the mass confusion would overwhelm the client.

"The same thing is applicable to a football team. Every player has to do his job, but he must do it in conjunction with the other ten members of the team, so he learns to work with others and depend on them to do their jobs. No matter how well a defensive back covers his man, for example, if the safety doesn't cover his man, the other team will throw a touchdown pass and win.

"In my present work I must also depend on the performance of others—I can't do their jobs for them—I must trust the people hired to play on our starting lineup to do their work satisfactorily," Vataha declares. "There's a valuable lesson here to be said about the art of delegation. A lot of executives possess a fear that nothing will succeed unless they do it themselves." As in football, no single person can attain the team's goal by himself or herself.

Vataha has one underlying goal for the firm's clients: to plan a financial program that guarantees security after one's entertainment or sports career has ended.

"There's absolutely no reason why a young athlete, for example, who signs a five-year contract paying an annual salary of one million dollars shouldn't be able to be financially set for life," he insists. "In order to accomplish this, however, we inform a client how he or she must establish a comfortable life-style that under the worst-case scenario would be adequate to continue without ever again having to earn any more money.

"A million-dollar-a-year salary nets $700,000 after taxes," he explains, "so if we can convince the client to live on $150,000 for the next five years, then $550,000 with interest with be worth over three million dollars when his contract expires. The three million dollars can then be invested at 7 percent tax-free income, enough to produce $210,000 a year. But if somebody says, 'I want a life-style that requires $300,000,' and is only willing to put away $400,000 after taxes, he's not going to have enough to provide even half of what it takes to maintain the appetite to which he is accustomed.

"Of course, a retired athlete is still a young person, so there's no reason why he or she shouldn't be capable of earning some money outside of sports," Vataha maintains. "As I said, I present a worst-case scenario which is the most conservative approach. There have been so many horror stories of professional athletes who made big money and afterward ended up broke, so that's something we don't want to ever happen to one of our clients.

"It sometimes takes a lot of convincing to educate a young person to cut back on today's life-style and put away the bulk of his earnings," Vataha adds, "but this is part of our service."

Not every person adheres to his or her financial consultants' advice, however. Vataha tells about one client who spent $265,000 in a six-week period: "He didn't buy a single asset. The guy just blew the money having a good time. We told him that we'd continue to work with him on his contract but it would be silly for us to handle his finances. At the rate he was going, there wasn't going to be anything left to handle."

Bob Woolf Associates is one of the most respected agencies in the industry. The firm has been in business for nearly thirty years without having a lawsuit brought against it. In a business in which clients frequently voice complaints against their agents, this is indeed a fine testimony for the agency's integrity.

Although Bob Woolf Associates represents hundreds of outstanding performers and professional athletes, it does not sign contracts with its clients. "We do business on a handshake," Vataha explains. "Two weeks later, if a client doesn't like the way we do things, he can find somebody else. We rarely lose a client, however, because I believe we do a great job for them.

"On the other hand, there are agents who sign a new contract with an athlete and lock him into his next two contracts. Afterward they stop returning his calls. When the guy calls to complain, he's told, 'That's tough, but I've got you under contract so there's nothing you can do about it.' "

Vataha's company maintains very casual business relationships with some very high-profile clients. The agency's long list of celebrities includes athletes such as Larry Bird, Doug Flutie, Dexter Manley, Don Majkowski, and Anthony Carter. Show business clients are equally impressive and include Larry King, Gene Shalit, and the New Kids on the Block. A high percentage of Bob Woolf Associates' clients are millionaires.

Although there is a lot of excitement and glamour in Vataha's life at the agency, not every business venture revolves around entertainers and sports figures. Recently Vataha has been working on a project as the head of a group within the agency that's putting three major Russian art exhibits on tour across the United States in 1992.

The first exhibit is from the Kremlin Museum and consists of valuable art objects collected by Catherine the Great as well as Russian czars. The second exhibit is a priceless art collection on loan from the famed Pushkin Museum that includes masterpieces of Van Gogh, Monet, and Renoir. The third exhibit will present a collection of famous jewels from the Russian Diamond Depository, including a crown containing 5,000 diamonds (minimum size is one carat) and a rose in a vase constructed with 15,000 diamonds.

Vataha has been jetting back and forth between Boston and Moscow to meet with Soviet dignitaries to make sure that plans for the tour will go without a hitch. He points out that putting together a deal like this one can be a complex and extremely time-consuming undertaking. "It takes months and even years of planning," he explains, "and it isn't unusual to invest considerable time and money only to have a deal fall through. The same applies to signing up clients. Frequently we're competing with two or three other agencies—so while we get our share, we don't get everybody.

"When I lose a deal, I want to know why," he continues. "Like I did during my football days when I'd review the game films, I analyze what went wrong in my presentation and what I must do to succeed the next time out. Similarly, just like I'd study the films on Monday morning to see what caused us to lose Sunday's game and then begin my preparation for next Sunday's game, I never dwell on my failures as a businessperson.

"What's fascinating about sports," he adds, "is how it's an acceleration of life. In business several years can pass from the start of a venture before its bottom line can be determined— the Russian art exhibit is a good example. But in athletics, you play on Saturday or Sunday afternoons. You win or lose.

You celebrate that night with your win, or you're down in the dumps with your loss.

"On Monday you look at the films and analyze what went right or wrong. On Tuesday you rest for a day, and on Wednesday you have to put last week's game out of your mind and start over again. The athlete can work hard and, with determination, realize immediate results.

"What's more, athletics teaches another valuable lesson for life after sports," he concludes. "There are many disappointments that happen along the way, but you can't allow them to defeat you. For instance, I could have thrown in the towel when I didn't get a football scholarship upon graduating from high school. Nobody would have blamed me if I said, 'What the heck, it's not my fault. I'm too small to play for a major football power.'

"I could have said the same thing when I got cut by the Rams and every team I ever played on when I sat on the bench in the beginning of the first season—I didn't start in high school, in junior college, at Stanford, or for the Patriots, so there were lots of opportunities for me to quit."

Vataha draws on another example to illustrate the rewards of maintaining an optimistic perspective. Among the athletes Bob Woolf Associates represents is Jeff Hornacek, the starting guard with the Phoenix Suns. "Jeff didn't get a basketball scholarship so he was a walk-on at Iowa State," Vataha says. "At 6'3", nobody took him seriously as a professional either, but he managed to get a tryout and went late in the second round of the NBA draft. Second-draft choices are rare in the NBA, but Jeff got his chance to play and now he's a star. We redid his contract and he's making nearly two million dollars a year. Not bad for somebody they said couldn't make it.

"In business, as every successful businessman knows, most deals don't happen—they fall by the wayside. But you can't allow yourself to become discouraged and quit," Vataha continues. "There are so many people who never attempt anything because they're afraid of failure. A lot of kids, for example, don't have confidence in themselves so they cop a plea, 'I probably couldn't do it anyway.' Consequently they never try, or if they do, they make a feeble, half-hearted attempt.

"I try to encourage everyone to do whatever it takes, no matter how much work is required to maximize their chances of success. By consistently putting forth this kind of effort you can never really fail. Sometimes success is postponed, but eventually you will prevail.

"Of course, true success comes from within and is the aggregate of one's accomplishments. Some of the greatest ball players of all time never reach a World Series or Super Bowl, which I am sure was one of their major goals. However, their hard work and perseverance paid off during their careers in so many other ways you could never consider them failures. Time and time again they had proven themselves to be winners."

As Randy Vataha has proved, he too is a winner on and off the field.

13

▪ WILLYE B. WHITE ▪

Track Star, Public Servant

Willye B. White, a legend in her own time, says that if she ever
writes the story of her life she will title it *I Lost by Inches, but
I Won by a Mile*.

After growing up in the cotton fields of Mississippi and
overcoming adversities at almost every step of her life, she
appeared in five consecutive Olympic Games, more than any
other woman in the history of track and field competition. *The
New York Times* declared, "Women's track and field began with
Willye White." Known as the "Grand Old Lady of Track," she
won medals and honors galore during a career that spanned
twenty-six years, but her life's goal eluded her again and
again, each time by inches or split seconds.

"At one time I thought the greatest accomplishment in my
life would be to win a gold medal. I can tell you tragedies that
I don't understand. I went to five Olympics. I was one of the
top jumpers in the world—made it to the finals in every
Olympics in which I participated, but I came out tenth, eleventh, or twelfth, except when I won two silver medals," she
says.

Willye B. White became a world-class winner on and off the
field in a universe light years away from her birthplace. She

was born on the first day of 1940 in a sharecropper's shanty in the middle of a cotton field near Greenwood, Mississippi, where the Yazoo and Tallahatchie rivers meet.

"They said my father took one look at me, a baby with a wisp of reddish hair, green eyes, and skin so pale they said you could see my veins, and declared, 'She is not my child,' " White recalls. "Three days later my grandfather came across the Tallahatchie River and carried me and my mother about fifteen miles away to where my grandparents, Louis and Luella Brown, lived on another plantation.

"My mother stayed about a month until I was weaned from breast feeding, then she left, too.

"I bore no animosity toward my father," White says now. "It was just ignorance. Before he died, he realized that I was his child." White's mother died when the girl was barely twelve years of age, her father five years later.

White now refers with deep affection to the grandparents whom she recognizes as her parents. "Although my grandparents couldn't read or write, they were people of wisdom, especially my grandfather. It was from them that I learned to work hard for what I wanted. They also taught me to believe in myself and to be honest in everything I did. They made me believe that if I worked hard enough and gave 100 percent, I could accomplish anything I set out to do.

"We were not in poverty," she recalls. "My grandfather would go to the restaurants in town and pick up the leftover garbage to feed his brother-in-law's hogs for a share of the meat at slaughter time. He had another brother-in-law who raised cows. My grandmother had a garden and she raised chickens, so we got the basic meats and vegetables. We were poor as far as money was concerned, but we had what the earth could give us."

She remembers that her grandfather, a very strict disciplinarian who showed little emotion, taught her the lessons of life by hard examples. The principal work available for young black girls in those days was cleaning the homes of the whites and babysitting their children, relatively easy chores compared to the alternative of laboring in the fields. "My grandfather would never let me do the housework," she explains. "He would make me go to the cotton fields.

"That was the absolute pits. I was afraid of snakes and I have never liked bugs. There was nothing in the fields but dust, hot sun, rattlesnakes, and water moccasins. We'd start chopping cotton at daybreak with a long hoe called the 'ignorant stick' and keep at it for twelve hours. We got paid $2.50 a day. Lord, it was hot, and those rows were long; it seems now like it took a week to finish one of them."

All the while the young girl's grandfather was drilling in her mind a basic message: if you don't get an education, you will spend the rest of your life in this cotton field.

Willye B. White had to make a journey outside the cotton fields that was every bit as tough to handle as the rows she hoed. "I was reared by grandparents, both of whom were illiterate, so I didn't learn the basic education of how to read and write when I should have. Because I didn't have anyone at home to take me through my lessons and explain things, I would have to ask questions in school."

White recalls that the teacher came to think of her as a slow learner. "But I wasn't a slow learner. No one had ever taught me how to do my ABCs, how to write, how to do my math, so I had to dig down deep into myself and say everyday, 'I can do it, I can do it.' "

Looking back on those days, White says she realizes now that she was an outcast. "Even the blacks were prejudiced against me because I was so light-complexioned. Parents would not let their kids play with me," she remembers. "In the South there was a color system among blacks, as well as whites. If you are what they call a 'high yellow' with pretty hair you are accepted by other blacks. I didn't pass that test; I am not 'high yellow' and my eyes are different; my hair is, too. I wore it with a thousand braids, which was not fashionable in those days. On top of all of that, I was a tomboy. They gave me the nickname 'Red.'

"In school, whenever there was a play or a dance, the instructors would choose the black girls with wavy black hair, starched dresses, and patent leather shoes. It did not matter that I could sing and dance better. Because of all of this, I never felt I could be just as good as—I had to be better than."

Her grandfather was helping the only way he knew how by constantly reminding her that she could be anything in the world she wanted if she was willing to pay the price. By the time she turned ten years of age White discovered there was one way she could get recognition; she had special athletic abilities. "I started running and jumping. All of a sudden I found this is something special I have that no one can take away from me. I can be the best in the world at this," she declared.

White was later to say, "Sports began as an escape. Running was survival—it was a means to an end. It was a way out of the cotton fields of Mississippi. It gave me everything, an education, academically and of the world."

The young girl began running in a serious way when her cousin invited her to try out for the high school track team. By dint of raw natural ability this child from elementary school won a place on the varsity track team at Stone Street High School.

Paul Thomas, the football coach at Stone Street High, insists that he would never forget the first time he saw Willye White. "We were having practice and a player—one of my fastest halfbacks—was fooling around on the sideline throwing rocks at this little girl. When he hit her, she went after him. He started running, and durn if she didn't catch him. Barefooted! I knew right then she was something special."

Thomas freely admitted that he had little knowledge about

coaching track. About all he knew was what he read in books, but he could recognize talent.

"I was a regular ten-year-old, just a little girl about five feet tall. I doubt I weighed 100 pounds soaking wet with rocks in my pockets," White recalls. "Every day the teacher would let me out of class and I would walk over to the high school to practice with the big kids.

"Now I had something that was mine. It was not judgmental. I found out that if I beat you across the finish line, I won. I liked that! I did everything. I ran. I hurdled. I long-jumped."

Coach Thomas always tried to get the best equipment for White. On one occasion, after a great deal of effort, he secured a pair of kangaroo-leather track shoes for her. "We were at Alcorn College for a meet when she told me she didn't like the shoes. She said they felt funny and that she wanted to run barefooted. I let her, and she won easily," the coach recalls.

Willye B. White soon emerged as a budding star among high school athletes in Mississippi. From age twelve until she graduated from high school in 1959 she almost single-handedly won the state championship each year. By the time she was sixteen years old her reputation had attracted a great deal of interest on the part of the coaching staff at Tennessee State University at Nashville, which sponsored one of two summer programs in the nation for promising young black women athletes.

As a high school freshman in 1956 White was invited by track coach Ed Temple to spend the summer at Tennessee State. She remembers her extreme elation because she didn't have to go to the cotton fields: "I knew that if I trained hard and earned my spot at Tennessee State I could leave home every May and not return until the fall.

"We were the Tiger Belles. It was sort of like a farm team," White explains. "You run for them. They take you to various cities for competition in AAU meets and similar events. That was the first time I had had any real coaching."

White performed so well that she was selected for the 1956 U.S. Olympic team that would compete in Melbourne, Australia; Wilma Rudolph was among her teammates. She returned home in September—the first black from the state to earn a place on the U.S. Olympic track team—to prepare for the trip in October to training camp and on to Melbourne in November.

The trip from high school in rural Mississippi to a college campus to the Olympic Games in Australia in a few short months was mind-boggling, to say the least, White recalls. The community of Greenwood had a "Willye White Day." The townspeople gave her spending money for the trip; merchants provided clothes and other essentials. "I got to choose my underwear and my stockings, my shoes and my suits from stores in town that I would have been afraid to go into before. My aunts, who sewed, made sure I had other things I needed to dress properly.

"Our teachers in home economics had taught us etiquette. I had learned how to conduct myself," White says. Still, while she was prepared in many basic ways for what she would encounter, the new environment came as a shock.

"When I got to the Olympic Games, I discovered there were two worlds: Mississippi and the rest of the universe. Where I had grown up everything was totally segregated," she explains. "But then all of a sudden there I was in a community where blacks and whites ate together, danced together, socialized together. We were friends on an equal footing. I realized that the world is bigger than Mississippi and my own experience."

She found another challenging world in the level of competition she would be facing. "I never had a long-jump coach, up until then or in the twenty-seven years I competed in that event. I realized I had a lot more to learn and my education had to be fast," she relates.

She went to the track every morning to watch the other athletes from countries around the world go through their paces. "I would watch them for hours. Then I would think about what I had seen and go out and try over and over to do what they had done. I didn't really know what I was doing. All I knew was that these girls had been coached; they were good, but they were not going to beat me because I hadn't tried."

She surprised the world with an outstanding performance in the actual competition. Her best long jump, measured at 19'11¾", won a silver medal. An older woman from Poland, Elzbietha Krzesiniska, who was making her second appearance at the Olympic Games, took the gold medal with a jump of 20'2".

Willye White and her world would never be the same again. She came back to Mississippi before Christmas a different person. Not yet seventeen years of age, she had won the distinction of being the second-best athlete in the world in her event, the first black from her state to compete in the Olympics, and the first Mississippian to win an Olympic medal.

Those were uneasy and confusing times for the young woman. She had traveled abroad and acquired a degree of worldliness, yet she was still a teenager. She came back to live in a world strictly segregated by race after the heady experience of equality. Those who had shunned her now wanted to associate with the celebrity she had become.

To no one's surprise she continued to dominate the women's high school track events in Mississippi. "We won the state championships every year, and I continued to go to Tennessee State in the summers," she explains. "This allowed me to become a member of two international teams while I was still in high school, which meant I spent my summers in Europe. You talk about growing up fast!"

Along the way, she became a drum majorette with the high school band. "I didn't do much twirling, though; I just did a lot of strutting," she admits.

In fact the accelerated pace of her athletic abilities and her education in the real world were to become a source of problems for White. She had a full athletic scholarship to Tennessee State—room, board, books, and tuition—waiting for her the day she graduated from high school. Unfortunately, she lasted only six months at that institution before a conflict with her coach and teammates resulted in her leaving school.

"They wanted me to be the typical nineteen-year-old girl they thought I should be, but my experiences made me older than nineteen. I had already been where they wanted me to be. We didn't understand each other. I knew what I had to do to survive," she explains with a strong undercurrent of regret.

White faced a critical career choice. "All of my life I had wanted a college education, and I wanted to be a registered nurse," she says. "I felt so lucky that Tennessee State provided me with the opportunity in athletics, plus the fact that the school offered a program in nursing tied into Maharry Hospital in Nashville. In total, it was a four-year degreed course. Well they discontinued the program at Maharry soon after I got to Tennessee State. Then came the problems that caused me to leave the college.

"Here I was at loose ends. I wanted to be a nurse and I wanted to continue my career in track by going to the 1960 Olympics."

At this point the powerful force of Chicago mayor Richard J. Daley entered the picture. "I had heard about the Mayor Daley Youth Foundation; it was a key factor in sports locally and internationally," she explains. "They would sponsor athletes, help them get jobs, and find places for them to live so they could train and compete in the Olympics and other such events."

White called Joe Robichaux, track coach for the foundation. "I told him I wanted to do two things: continue my education to become a nurse and make it to the 1960 Olympics. I wanted to come to Chicago. Could he help me get a job and find a place to stay? He said, 'Take the next bus.' He and his wife took me in until I could get on my own."

White began a rigorous triple life training for the Olympics, working as a nurse's aide, and trying to get into nursing school. "I got a job at Provident Hospital, Chicago's public hospital for blacks, and I took the examination—eight hours long—to get into training at Cook County Hospital. I passed the exam, but I was not accepted because, as they informed me, they took only one black per year and that person had to be number one in his or her high school graduating class. I was not number one or two, or even tenth, so I could not get in. That was the first shock of my life north of the Mason-Dixon line."

Meanwhile the determined young woman was faring better in athletics. She earned a position on the 1960 U.S. Olympic team for the games in Rome. She finished twelfth in the broad jump.

Back in Chicago she took the examination to enter nursing school again, this time at Michael Reese Hospital. The answer was the same as at Cook County Hospital.

She was to take the same examination a total of four times. The last time the admissions director at Provident Hospital denied her entrance, saying that after being on two U.S. Olympic teams she was "too worldly"; she would be a bad influence on the other students.

"There I was twenty-three years old," White says. "They said maybe I should go into another field. Anyway, they asked, why would I want to give up this lucrative job of running and jumping in meets around the world? In their minds they visualized all of this money I was making. I was practically on welfare."

In September 1963 she capitalized on her brief education at Tennessee State and her experience as a nurse's aide to breeze through the practical nursing program offered by the Chicago Board of Education. She was hired to work as a practical nurse in obstetrics at Cook County Hospital.

"One night, after I had been there about three months, I was working on the midnight shift—I had been on it about a month at that point. I was so tired and sleepy I decided I would skip my break for a meal and take a nap," she relates. "I just fell into one of the beds. The head nurse came by and ordered me to get up and go out of the hospital if I wanted to take a nap because I was not allowed to sleep on my breaks.

"I said to myself, 'You know, if I have to live like this at twenty-three, what am I going to do when I am older with responsibilities?' Well, I was young, single, and free, and I was suffering, or at least I thought I was. I decided I was going to do more with my life. I wrote out my resignation that night."

Under the auspices of the U.S. Olympic Committee, White journeyed to São Paulo, Brazil, where she stayed for two months while participating in the Pan-American Games. She brought home two gold medals for her performance in the long jump and the 4 × 100-meter relay.

Back in Chicago she took a position with a private doctor and began to prepare for the 1964 Olympics in Tokyo. There she was to win her second silver medal, this one as a member of the 400-meter relay team. In that same year, in another competition, she broke Wilma Rudolph's indoor 60-yard dash record of 6.8 seconds with a 6.7.

When she returned home, she accepted a starting position in health education with the Chicago Health Department. It was her opportunity to fulfill a promise she had made to Mayor Daley when she moved to the city. "When I joined the Health Department Mayor Daley told me the City of Chicago would give me all the support I needed to reach my goals. He said I could go to school, compete in athletics, and work. All he asked of me was once I stopped competing I would give back to the city what the city had given to me by supporting the children of Chicago. That's why I have stayed in various positions with the city through these years. I am paying a debt to those who allowed me to have my career in athletics plus an education."

Over the years White worked her way up from her starting position to the top post as Director of Health Education. The responsibilities along the way have remained basically the same: educating the people of Chicago on the prevention of illnesses. "We concentrate on the young children and young adults—teenage pregnancy, drug awareness, child abuse, AIDS, and personal hygiene," she explains. Her job provided her with a steady income so that she was able to pursue a double career with a sense of security.

The 1968 Olympics in Mexico City proved to be an unsettling and disappointing time for White. This was the year of the black boycott, the black leather gloves and the raised fist, the bare feet.

The controversy cast a pall over the Olympic Games.

White was to suffer personally in other ways too. A heat lamp fell over on her while she was lying on a rubdown table, causing a severe burn on her leg. "Someone had broken the lamp and then propped it back in place," she recounts. "It fell across my leg. A few seconds passed before I realized the red hot coils were burning me. When I knocked the lamp off my leg it fell on the floor and burned a hole in the wood.

"They iced my leg, then drained the blisters. They couldn't give me anything to ease the pain because drugs would have shown up in the urinalysis. In order to compete I had to be free of drugs, so I just had to bear the pain."

White qualified with a jump of 20 feet, but she finished in eleventh place. She came back to Chicago determined to complete her education and try at least one more time to win the gold. But she was still pursuing her other dream: "I never gave up on my goal of earning a college degree, so I kept taking courses in chemistry and biology and such subjects at

Kennedy-King College, Roosevelt University, Loop Junior College, and most of all at Chicago State University." In 1976, at the age of thirty-six, she finally succeeded in earning a B.A. degree in Public Health Care Administration from Chicago State University.

Looking back, White recognizes that the star-crossed Olympic Games of 1972 in Munich signaled a turning point in her personal life and in the way the world viewed the Olympics in general. Those games are remembered by the world primarily for the horrifying spectacle of Palestinian terrorists holding hostage a group of Israeli Olympians and ultimately killing twelve of them.

White, there for her fifth Olympic competition, finished in twelfth place and came home from Munich troubled and disillusioned.

For the first time she seriously began to question her desire to compete in the Olympic Games. The games, once a peaceful international community of rivalry between competitors who respected each other on the basis of abilities and spirit, had begun to be a hotbed of politics and strife, and White was beginning to experience nagging self-doubts. Would she have the heart and the stamina to try again for that elusive gold medal? Did she really want to?

Deep in her heart, White knew the answer had to be yes. She had not yet abandoned the search for the Olympic gold.

Soon she returned to competition and the arduous task of preparing for her sixth attempt to qualify for a place on the U.S. Olympic team. She recalls it as one of the more difficult times in her life.

"Practice had been the first love of my life," she says. "Then I began to recognize that I got more enjoyment out of not going to practice than from going.

"A lot of things happened in my life in 1975—it was a turning point for me. I really took a good look at where I had been and where I was going. My grandfather—my *father—*

became very ill. I was traveling back and forth to Mississippi to be with him until he died late that summer. To make everything worse, I pulled a hamstring muscle, and it turned out to be very serious. I began to find things to do with my life other than running and jumping and psyching myself up for competition."

The injury continued to hamper her from August of 1975 until the eve of the Olympic trials in July of the next year. "Now I am thirty-six years old," White recalls. "I don't think I had more than one hundred days of training without injuries in those eleven months. But I couldn't quit. I had made up my mind I would go to the Olympics one more time, win or lose."

A week prior to the Olympic tryouts in Eugene, Oregon, White went to the National Outdoor Track and Field Championships in Los Angeles. On her second jump she met the standard to qualify for the Olympic trials. But instead of stopping there, she came back to take a third jump. She tore the hamstring muscle again.

"It takes a year for that kind of thing to heal under normal circumstances at my age then," she explains. "I could hardly walk, and running was terribly painful, but I went out to Eugene for the trials. I was determined that I would go as far as I could because I knew I would not be back again. I was at the end of my athletic career. . . . I tried to make it to Montreal in 1976 against all odds because I wanted to win the gold medal, to be the best.

"I made it to the finals. Every jump felt like there was someone inside my muscles tearing them apart. I can still remember every pain that shot through my body. I promised God that if I could just get off that runway, He would never catch me there again. Then it was over. I had placed fifth. The woman ahead of me in fourth place was ruled out, so I was moved up a notch. Had I gotten third, I would have been on the Olympic team. I missed by one-half inch."

The buoyant black woman says that she was "bitter for

months, even years," after what she saw as a failure in her life.

Inspired by a testament to faith she read in an in-flight magazine, she came to realize that she "had the greatest medal of all." She often quotes that verse, which is by a writer whose name she can't recall, in her speeches to diverse groups around the country:

For I asked God for strength that I might achieve,
Instead I was made weak that I might learn humbly to
    obey.
I asked for help that I might do greater things,
Instead I was given infirmity that I might do better
    things.
I asked for riches that I might be happy.
I was given poverty that I might be wise.
I asked for power that I might have the praises of men.
I was given weakness that I might feel the need of God.
I asked for all things that I might enjoy life.
I was given life that I might enjoy all things.
I got nothing that I asked for, but everything I had hoped
    for.
Almost despite myself, my unspoken prayers were an-
    swered,
Because I am among all athletes who have been most
    richly blessed,

You see, I lost by inches, but I won by a mile.

The game was over for Willye B. White. But what a game it had been. In addition to the Olympics, White was a member of thirty-nine international teams and competed in 150 nations. She brought home trophies from four Pan-American Games; won seventeen national indoor and outdoor track titles, including ten in AAU outdoor long-jump competitions (nine consecutive) and five indoor; and held the American record for the long jump for sixteen years.

White received other honors as well, including memberships in the Tennessee Hall of Fame, the Women's Sports Foundation International Hall of Fame, the Chicago Sports Hall of Fame, and the Black Athlete Hall of Fame. Aside from her medals from Olympic competition, the two honors that mean the most to her are the Fair Play Award, presented in March 1966 by the International Committee for the Pierre de Coubertin Fair Play Trophy, and her election to the Mississippi Hall of Fame.

White says it "really was quite simple, the way the Fair Play Award came about." She was facing Mary Rand, an Olympic long jump gold-medal winner from England, in a competition at Madison Square Garden in 1966. Rand was considered White's most dangerous opponent.

"Mary wasn't familiar with the jump boards on the indoor track in New York," White says. "Consequently she missed one of the qualifying jumps, so I had won. But I didn't feel that was fair, so I went to the judges and explained what had happened.

"The judges gave her another chance; she qualified and went on to beat me. She won the national championship and I spent three weeks in Paris for the Fair Play Award ceremonies at UNESCO headquarters."

However, White thinks that the most thrilling and satisfying honor of her athletic career came in 1983, when she was inducted into the Mississippi Hall of Fame. "When I was elected to that high honor, the governor of Mississippi, William Winter, called personally to invite me to be a guest in his home, the governor's mansion in Jackson," White relates.

"You have to realize what it meant to have been born and reared a black in the Mississippi Delta, to not even be able to walk in some areas at one time without fear, and then to have the governor himself issue a personal invitation to be a guest in his home. That is some accomplishment."

Summing up her life—past, present, and future—for a young friend who was writing a term paper titled simply *Willye B. White* she said, "Athletics were my flight to freedom— freedom from ignorance and prejudice, freedom from segregation. Athletics have meant everything to me—socially, spiritually, morally, and academically. Had I not been in athletics my life would have been totally different, in a negative way. Through athletics I found myself."

In addition to her duties with the City of Chicago, White maintains a schedule of speeches and public appearances around the country to share the values she has learned from her life of challenge, defeats, and victories.

Of competition she says, "When I was competing—and I still have the same approach—I would walk up to the starting line and say to my opponents, 'You get nothing free from me today. You'll have to work hard for it. To beat me you will have to set a world record.'

"When I won in competition I wanted to beat my opponents when they were at their best. I got no satisfaction from beating someone who was working under a handicap. If you and your opponents are not evenly matched, playing under the same set of rules, how can you tell if you are as good or better than the others?"

On preparation and hard work, she comments, "There is no road to victory that does not mean hard work. I used to go to track practice at five o'clock in the morning. I would pretend every day that I was at the Olympic Games getting ready for competition. If my event was the 100 meters and I had to run 11.1 or 11.2, I would keep running until I achieved that goal. If I didn't have enough time before going to work in the morning, I would go back at lunchtime to practice the long jump. I knew the distance I had to jump and I would keep at it until I did it. I figured that if I could meet that objective in practice I would do even better in the actual meet when the adrenaline was flowing.

"Every day, every track meet was a special event that was getting me closer to where I wanted to go," she says about the need to set goals. "Nothing is forever. You have to keep planning for the next step. A dream without a plan is only a wish, and wishes don't get you far in this world.

"I've seen a lot of great athletes come crashing down because they didn't realize that some day it would end. You must plan for the time when it is over. A lot of people have difficulties after sports. When they stop competing they have to live with unfulfilled dreams. That can be tough if there are no new goals.

"I believe in the philosophy that the tragedy of life doesn't lie in not reaching your goal. The tragedy is in not having a goal to reach. Now is the time to recognize where you are and what you want to do with your life," White advises, adding, "Ignore those who tell you that you can't reach your goals.

"Before you can win, you have to overcome the fear of failure. You can only do that by believing in yourself. If you have never made a mistake, you probably never tried very much. Show me an athlete who has never lost a race and I will show you an athlete who will never become a true champion.

"Mistakes are a natural part of life," she philosophizes. "Failure is an attitude. You have as much right to make a mistake as you do to succeed. When you do fail, there is only one thing to do: kiss it off as a part of living and growing. Pick yourself up and try again. Find out why you lost and correct it in the practice arena.

"Don't hang around with losers. Motivate yourself by associating with strivers. You are likely to perform at the level of those around you."

Today Willye B. White is prepared to make the most of the rest of her life. After twenty-six years in health education, she moved to a new position with the City of Chicago: Director of

Recreation Services for the Park District. She says the job is a dream come true. She will "sell" the value of sports and recreation.

"My goal now is to bring our children back to the parks, to help them realize the importance of participating in athletics—to help them develop their skills.

"I have more appreciation of life than I have ever had. That's because I know I have been blessed, but I don't have fifty more years to live—to do what I was put here to do," she declares soberly. "The play is no longer in rehearsal. I am onstage and this is the real thing.

"If I am granted good health, I can reach my goals. I can find happiness because I will not allow myself to be unhappy."

One has the feeling that Willye B. White can indeed mold life to her liking. After all, she created her own name. "I decided to spell Willye with a Y so people wouldn't confuse me with being a boy," she explains with a mischievous smile. "They gave me B as a middle initial. It doesn't stand for anything. My parents were so poor they couldn't afford to give me a full middle name.

"Actually I decided later," she says, "that the B in my name stands for B.I.T.C.H.: *b*eautiful, *i*ntelligent, *t*rustworthy, *c*onfident, and *h*onest."